◇

Guide to Ezra Pound's
*Selected Cantos*

◇

# Guide to Ezra Pound's
## *Selected Cantos*

◇

## George Kearns

◇

Rutgers University Press
New Brunswick
New Jersey

LIBRARY OF CONGRESS CATALOGING IN PUBLICATION DATA

Kearns, George.
    Guide to Ezra Pound's Selected cantos.

    Bibliography: p.
    Includes index.
        1. Pound, Ezra Loomis, 1885–1972. Cantos.
I. Pound, Ezra Loomis, 1885–1972. Cantos. Selections. II. Title.
PS3531.0'82C294        811'.52        80–10306
ISBN 0–8135–0886–X cloth
ISBN 0–8135–0887–8 paperback

◇

# Contents

◇

◊

# Acknowledgments

◊

I MUST FIRST OF ALL EXPRESS my gratitude to D. S. Carne-Ross, who read with imaginative attention an early version of this work. His long familiarity with the *Cantos* and, above all, his fine sense of proportion have been invaluable. Emily Dalgarno, who patiently read the same undisciplined manuscript, has long been a conscience in matters of scholarship and style.

Hugh Kenner is cited often in the following pages, but there is no way his influence can adequately be acknowledged other than to say that the book should bear a note, "Kenner, passim." Nor does my documentation suggest how often I have turned to Donald Gallup's meticulous and elegantly conceived bibliography. With the exception of Donald Davie, who is so stimulating and quotable, other critics who have taken part in the cooperative effort of reading the *Cantos* have not received sufficient mention in a manuscript that has had some trouble finding a publishable size. (I would like particularly to mention M. L. Rosenthal.) Their works, all of which have instructed me, are listed in the bibliography. I trust they will recognize, too, a Poundian difficulty in remembering where one learned what first.

Denis Donoghue has been generous with his time and encouragement. I appreciate, too, the encouragement I received at Boston University from Helen Vendler, Harriet Lane, Morton Berman, and William Vance. At Rutgers I have been fortunate to have so many colleagues whose knowledge of Pound has provided stimulating conversation: Wendy Flory, Steven Helmling, Andrew Welsh, James J. Wilhelm, and the translator of the *Cantos* into Spanish, José Vásquez Amaral. Other friends who have contributed to this work, some in ways they are not aware of, are Thomas R. Edwards, Paul Fussell, Daniel F. Howard, C. F.

Main, Richard Poirier, Barry Qualls, and my patient editor, Joseph Esposito. To my sister, Maureen Howard, and to Floyd Barbour and Robert Sealy, I owe special kinds of thanks.

My serious interest in Pound began with one of those speculative asides with which Lionel Trilling made his classroom such an interesting place to be; I regret that I can thank him only in memoriam. The same is true for Ezra and Dorothy Pound, who were so kind to a young soldier in Washington many years ago. My students at Rutgers have supplied me with friendship, encouragement, and many of the questions this work attempts to answer.

◊

# Texts

◊

THE NEW DIRECTIONS EDITION of *Selected Cantos* includes some passages Ezra Pound did not select for the Faber and Faber edition. There are, as well, occasional variants between the two texts, as there are among all editions of the *Cantos*. Page numbers in this *Guide* refer first to the New Directions *Selected Cantos* and in parentheses to the Faber edition. The Faber text does not include the following passages:

1. Canto 52: New Directions has added the 78 concluding lines of the canto.

2. Canto 83: New Directions has added the first 107 lines of the canto.

3. Canto 99: To the one-page excerpt in the Faber edition New Directions has added the six remaining pages of the canto.

4. Cantos 115 and 116: These passages from *Drafts and Fragments* are not included in the Faber *Selected Cantos*.

◇

# Key to the Complete *Cantos*

◇

READERS WITH A COMPLETE EDITION of the *Cantos* will have little difficulty using this *Guide* for those cantos that are complete (1, 4, 9, 13, 14, 16, 31, 44, 45, 53, 81, 84, 95, *from* 115, and 116). For those cantos that are excerpted, the following list shows where selections begin and end. (Faber editions published prior to 1976, however, have a different pagination.)

*from* Canto 38: from "A factory" to "that the mind of man was bewildered" (190)

*from* Canto 42: from "FIXED in the soul, nell' anima," (209) to end of canto

*from* Canto 43: from "to the end" (216) to "consumed 1 hour and 17 minutes" (217)

*from* Canto 52: from "Know then" (258) to end of canto

*from* Canto 62: from "Talleyrand . . . Mr A. not caught asleep by *his* cabinet" (349) to end of canto

*from* Canto 83: from beginning of the canto to "between dark cloud and the mountain" (531)

*from* Canto 85: from beginning of the canto to "and jump to the winning side" (544)

*from* Canto 88: from "Père Henri Jacques still" (582) to "page 446 / column two" (583)

*from* Canto 99: from "And if your kids don't study" (705) to end of canto

*from* Canto 105: from "You cannot leave these things out" (750) to end of canto

*from* Canto 108: from "ELIZABETH" (768) to end of canto

*from* Canto 109: from "Wing like feldspar" (773) to end of canto

◊

# Introduction

◊

MY INTENTION IN THIS GUIDE is to provide a reasonably thorough introduction to the *Cantos* by commenting in detail on those passages Pound has chosen for *Selected Cantos*. Taking Pound's selection as text (for I cannot hope to give a thorough commentary on more than a selection), I supply a brief essay on each canto, discussing it as a whole and placing it within the larger scheme of the poem. This is followed by a page-by-page annotation of the canto. In addition, there are introductions to each of the independently published sections of the poem, beginning with *A Draft of XXX Cantos* (1930), briefly reviewing Pound's career to the time of publication, and allowing some discussion of questions not directly raised by the passages in *Selected Cantos*. The notes and bibliography at the end of the volume provide a reading list on specialized topics as well as on Pound and the *Cantos* in general.

A remarkable shelf of criticism and scholarship has emerged about what Pound first described as a long poem, later as an epic. Indeed, in the presence of necessarily massive scholarship, reading the *Cantos* may have become more formidable as it has become more possible. Even for readers who have no intention of becoming Poundians, a basic understanding of the poem requires a major investment of time. It is only a slight overstatement to say that, if one wants to read even a single canto, one must assemble information from a great many sources. After the difficulty of reading a single page, there remains the problem of seeing how one page, or one canto, goes with the next.

This guide may not be the introduction for Pound's ideal reader. It is open to the objection that it makes a superficial reading too easy and circumvents the very involvement with the poem's composition and sources that is part of Pound's aesthetic-didactic purpose. On balance, the approach seems practical—at least it has proved so for my students and for readers who have asked for copies of my notes. A great deal of the *Cantos,* much more than readers think at first, may be understood simply by paying attention to what is on the page and by listening closely to its voices; yet the fact remains that most of us are discouraged by so many references we do not recognize and by so many languages we do not read. So this guide is a moderately thorough introduction at the end of which readers may stop but beyond which I hope they will continue with the assurance that there remain great areas and depths in the *Cantos* that this guide does not map out.

Inevitably, my judgments pervade the commentary and, to some extent, even the annotation. Broadly speaking, they lead to a conclusion quite other than Geoffrey Hartman's in *Beyond Formalism,* that the *Cantos,* "which ransack the high culture of both West and East, remain a nostalgic montage without unity, a picaresque of styles." My purpose, however, is less to insist on my own reading than to supply sufficient information for the reader to make an independent judgment.

"Knowledge is NOT culture," Pound remarks. "The domain of culture begins when one HAS forgotten-what-book." So, too, a guide such as this is not the poem, and the experience of reading the *Cantos* may begin when one has forgotten the notes. As an antidote to the "slow" reading in the following pages, I quote at length from Donald Davie on how to read the *Cantos.* He urges us to listen for

> the large-scale rhythms that ride through the *Cantos* in our experience of them when we read many at a time, and fast. And this is just the sort of reading we ought to give them—not just to begin with, either. This, indeed, is what irritates so many readers and fascinates an elect few—that the *Cantos,* erudite as they are, consistently frustrate the sort of reading that is synonymous with "study," reading such as goes on in the seminar room or the discussion group. It is hopeless to go at them cannily, not moving on to line three until one is sure of line two. They must be taken in big gulps or not at all. Does this mean reading without comprehension? Yes, if by comprehension we mean a set of propo-

sitions that can be laid end to end. We are in the position of not
knowing "whether we have had any ideas or not." Just so. Which
is not to deny that some teasing out of quite short excerpts, even
some hunting up of sources and allusions, is profitable at some stage.
For the *Cantos* are a poem to be lived with, over years. Yet after
many years, each new reading—if it is a reading of many pages at
a time, as it should be—is a new bewilderment. So it should be,
for it was meant to be. After all, some kinds of bewilderment are
fruitful. To one such kind we give the name "awe"—not awe at
the poet's accomplishment, his energy, or his erudition but awe at
the energies, some human and some nonhuman, which interact,
climb, spiral, reverse themselves, and disperse, in the forming and
re-forming spectacles which the poet's art presents to us or reminds
us of.

It was, after all, my own pleasurable bewilderment, and the sheer
movement of language in the poem, that kept me coming back to
it long before I had an idea what any of it "meant." Well, we must
read both fast and slow, as Davie does so well.

## Selected Cantos

For two reasons, I choose *Selected Cantos* as an introduction to
the complete poem. First, the volume has the authority of being
Pound's own redaction, made in 1965 and published by Faber in
London in 1967 and by New Directions in New York in 1970. I
have followed the American edition, in which the publisher has
added a few passages not chosen by Pound and two selections from
the 1969 *Drafts and Fragments*. Page numbers refer to the New
Directions text, followed in brackets by the page numbers in the
Faber text. A second reason for using *Selected Cantos* is that it is
inexpensive and widely distributed.

In a long career, Pound never made things easy for himself or
for his readers, and at the end of that career he still refused to do
so in *Selected Cantos*. This careful choice from the "rag-bag," from
a lifetime's "catch" (as he calls it in the brief foreword, almost the
last words he wrote for publication), provides a better introduction to the *Cantos* than any selection I might have made for the
occasion. That is, I suspect that my own choices, although many

would have been the same, might have emphasized passages more accessible, more conventionally poetic, and in the Pisan cantos, more autobiographical; but at this point it becomes only a game to speculate on what I would have chosen. Certainly the beautifully Ovidian Canto 2; the first half, probably the whole, of Canto 30; those two marvelous lyrics, Cantos 47 and 49; the first of the Pisan cantos, 74; and the two final fragments. I would almost certainly not have used the passages from Cantos 38, 42, 44, 53, 88, 99, 105, and 108. In short, I might have avoided the direct confrontation we have in *Selected Cantos* with the poem's economics, its (at times) bizarre scholarship, and its failures. We have, as the publisher's note to the Faber edition says, "those complete Cantos (and short passages from a few others) that he himself considers to provide the best introduction to the whole work for those coming to it for the first time." *Whole*, not only in including selections from each of the separately published installments of the *Cantos*, but in providing samples of all the principal poetic modes and historical, religious, and didactic concerns of the poem.

I have often gone beyond the demands of immediate explication to suggest how Pound's mind works (for he expects us to follow the working of his mind) and the extent of research and attention he asks of the reader. One source of Pound's obscurity is his peculiar didacticism, differentiating the *Cantos* from most modern literature and much earlier literature, inviting us to leave the poem, as it were, and to turn to such works as the Confucian Classics, the Adams-Jefferson correspondence, or Sir Edward Coke's *Institutes*. In most cases my enthusiasm for these works equals Pound's, but my brief descriptions of them are nothing more than an attempt to provide some sense, some of the flavor, of the books behind the *Cantos*.

## The Ideogrammic Method

IT MAY BE HELPFUL to look at the "ideogrammic method" that underlies the poem and then to glance at Pound's own comments on his overall scheme and analogues. These comments, however, date from more than a decade after he began writing the poem and, in the form in which we find them, are not a precise indication of what he had in mind during early stages of composition and revision. Ronald Bush argues, I think convincingly, that the ideogram, as Pound later came to think of it, was not a major structural principle in the poem until some time in the 1920s. We are concerned here with the poem as we now have it; the reader interested in its development through the publication of *A Draft of XVI Cantos* (1925) should see Bush's excellent study, somewhat larger in scope than its title suggests, *The Genesis of Ezra Pound's Cantos*.

What Pound calls his ideogrammic method was crystallized by his encounter in 1913 with Ernest Fenollosa's "The Chinese Written Character as a Medium for Poetry," but it derived naturally from a paratactic cast of mind that can be seen in his earlier writings. The *Cantos* presents juxtaposed images and allusions without providing narrative or syntactic connections for its "phalanx of particulars" (C.74). Names, facts, languages, voices, images, fragments of literature and document are carefully assembled, but it is often up to the reader to discover the principles by which they are assembled and why one thing stands next to, or near, another.

The Poundian ideogram resists the Western logic of the "schoolmen" who, as Fenollosa puts it, "despised the 'thing' as a mere 'particular,' or pawn" useful only in arriving at "abstractions, concepts drawn out of things by a sifting process." (Pound's famous demonstration of the ideogram is in the early pages of his *ABC of Reading*.) Extrapolating from Fenollosa's vibrant understanding of the Chinese character and of the Chinese poem, in which a line is formed from characters juxtaposed without a syntactic map of prepositions, tenses, or declensions, Pound adapted his natural way of thought to arrive at the ideogrammic method.

When Pound looked at one of his favorite Chinese ideograms

明月

he read the component on the left as "sun," the component on the right as "moon" (sun character with rays descending). Juxtaposed as *ming*[2] they defined for him, though not in the manner of Western definition, "the total light process, the radiation, reception and reflection of light; hence the intelligence. Bright, brightness, shining." To what extent the Chinese reader still sees or is aware of the radicals for sun and moon in *ming*[2] is hard to say, and most Chinese characters do not work on exactly this principle; but to the willful or wishful eyes of Pound and Fenollosa, the ideogram retains—persistently transmits—the energy, the process, the verbness of sun-and-moon in a way that no abstraction, no phonetic transcription of sounds that stand for something (say, "clarity") can.

The *Cantos* may be said to consist of innumerable smaller ideograms, which in turn form the larger ideograms of single cantos and groups of cantos, which gathered as the *Cantos,* embracing thousands of correspondences and contrasts, form a single poem. Large or small, a Poundian ideogram brings a number of concrete "things" or "facts" into a new whole that is beyond paraphrase; but to understand "things" or "facts" in this sense, we must extend them to include tones of voice and what people have felt or imagined, as well as objects and events that actually happened.

I have used the word *ideogram* seldom in the following pages because, although the method is central, the word itself becomes a distraction, suggesting some more rigidly or mechanically applied theory than the poem in fact demonstrates. The method is really a mode or tendency, not a dogma, and Pound will, from page to page, write as he chooses. More important than the theory of the ideogram is its immediate usefulness for a poem that, by its very ambition—to encompass history, to tell "the tale of the tribe"—might easily be attracted to generalization. The "particulars" offer resistance. The *Cantos,* as a didactic poem, certainly aims at presenting "truths"; but the degree to which Pound knows them, or to which they carry conviction, will only be demonstrated through the thousand particulars, distinct yet forming a tradition.

Finally, we should see that the Pound-Fenollosa concept of the ideogram is not of something static. In the Chinese character and poem, Fenollosa said, we see "entangled lines of forces as they pulse through things. Thought deals with no bloodless concepts but watches *things move* under its microscope." As such, the ideogrammic method both corresponds to and produces the vision of history in the *Cantos*. Pound uses "ideogram" often in his prose, uses it in different ways, but a sensible definition in *Guide to Kulchur* tells us more about its function in the poem than do many technical discussions:

> The ideogrammic method consists of presenting one facet and then another until at some point one gets off the dead and desensitized surface of the reader's mind, onto a part that will register.

The first lines of Canto 4 present a good example of the ideogrammic method in operation:

Palace in smoky light,
Troy but a heap of smouldering boundary stones,
ANAXIFORMINGES! Aurunculeia!
Hear me. Cadmus of Golden Prows!

The lines are an ideogram in which overt and hidden themes provide material that is elaborated in unexpected ways throughout the canto. Four "things" that seem to have little to do with each other are assembled within a declamatory epic voice. The canto then adds to this invocation additional things: Ovidian myths, a poem by Cavalcanti, a painting by Stefano da Verona, the poems and lives of troubadours (not their "real" lives, but what someone decided to record about them), a reference to a classic Japanese play, and more. Placed together, interwoven and repeated, they form a virtuoso exercise in unity-in-diversity that is about those particulars quite as much as it is about any generalizations we may draw from them. We may say that Canto 4 provides examples of constructive and destructive passion; of certain varieties of religious experience; of relationships among art, civilization, and the psychology of love; but as ideogram, the canto's present-tense juxtaposition of gestures and voices makes such formulations or propositions seem lifeless and unfocused.

## *Analogues*

POUND SUPPLIED two brief sketches of the poem's structure and analogues. They are useful if we remember that their tripartite elements are not distributed in the poem with the medieval "tidiness" Pound thought available to the age of Dante but not to the twentieth century. He wrote to his father in 1927:

> Afraid the whole damn poem is rather obscure, especially in fragments. Have I ever given you outline of main scheme : : : or whatever it is?
>
> 1. Rather like, or unlike subject and response and counter subject in fugue.
>
> A.A.  Live man goes down into world of Dead.
> C.B.  The "repeat in history."
> B.C.  The "magic moment" or moment of metamorphosis, bust through from quotidian into "divine or permanent world." Gods, etc.

In 1944 he told his readers:

> For forty years I have schooled myself, not to write an economic history of the U.S. or any other country, but to write an epic poem which begins 'In the Dark Forest' crosses the Purgatory of human error, and ends in the light, and 'fra i maestri di color che sanno' [among the masters of those who know].

These two sketches, taken together, provide a rough outline of the themes and movement of the poem. Of course, the generalizations of any such plan or summary are precisely what the ideogrammic method resists.

1. Pound/Odysseus/twentieth-century man, finding himself in the confusion of the modern world (like Dante in the Dark Forest), begins a journey by descending to the world of the dead, the past, to gain experience and to find his bearings.

2. Time or history is a purgatory of human error; but we may discover within it certain beliefs and actions revealed and repeated beneath surface differences of language and culture. The poem/ journey through the dark seas of history will present these "durable" (as opposed to "eternal" or "permanent") states of mind. Purgatory, a place of suffering, is also a place of hope. The poem discovers in history not only the workings of avarice and destructive passions but a series of great creative efforts: Malatesta's Tempio, the growth of common law, the Constitution of the United States, the science of an Agassiz.

3. The purgatory of time and history is occasionally broken by "magic moments," visions of the light, divine energies, paradisal states of mind. Although this vision cannot be sustained, our knowledge of it (largely through the testimony of art and the records of "masters of those who know") is essential to what should be our first concern: an improved civic order. There is a strong, and genuine, religious element in the *Cantos,* which, if somewhat forced in earlier sections, becomes more deeply felt in the later cantos. But from the start, the magic moments and "Gods, etc." are more than a literary conceit.

In his two short outlines, Pound has assembled the three major analogues for the *Cantos,* each containing correspondences with the others: Homer for the Odyssean voyage toward the restoration of civic order; Dante for the pilgrim's ascent through infernal and purgatorial regions toward Paradise; and Ovid for transformations, one energy passing through gods and men, everything connected with everything else, many stories woven into a single tale.

◇

# A Draft of XXX Cantos (1930)

◇

"FOR FORTY YEARS I have schooled myself . . . to write an epic poem." Shut off from English-speaking readers, writing in Italy, in Italian, in 1944, Pound traced the impulse for the poem that became the *Cantos* to his days as an undergraduate at Hamilton College. Between that distant beginning, about 1904, and June 1917, when readers of the Chicago outpost of modernism, *Poetry,* first heard that Pound was writing "A Poem of Some Length," his travels had taken him to the University of Pennsylvania (M.A., 1906), where he continued the studies that became *The Spirit of Romance* (1910); to a brief career as a professor of Romance languages at Wabash College in Indiana; to Venice, where in 1908 he paid for the publication of *A Lume Spento* ("A collection of stale creampuffs," he thought it in his old age); and a few months later, to London, where he remained until 1920.

Pound's career in London, even before the publication of the 1917 "Three Cantos," contains enough energy and achievement to make more than one reputation and is itself the subject of several books. The years 1908–1917 were a remarkable period for the flamboyant young American who established himself as a poet, translator, editor, critic, journalist, and propagandist. He paid homage to older writers—James, Hardy, Yeats—and gave vigorous support to men and women of his own generation: Eliot, Joyce, Wyndham Lewis, Frost, H. D., Williams. The word *modern* was assuming a belligerent quality it had not had before; and an English avant-garde—Pound (with Lewis) as close to its center as anyone, gathering courage from the French tradition of art-as-scandal—set out to shock the public-at-large and to create a new public for the art its members were producing, or admired. So successful were they in producing that public, that their most concerted effort to shock, the *Blast* manifesto of 1914, of which Pound was a signer, now seems almost charming, more a classic of English humor than a cry to revolution.

# BLAST First (from politeness) ENGLAND

## CURSE ITS CLIMATE FOR ITS SINS AND INFECTIONS

### DISMAL SYMBOL, SET round our bodies,
of effeminate lout within.

### VICTORIAN VAMPIRE, the LONDON cloud sucks
the TOWN'S heart.

. . . . . . . . . . . . . .

# CURSE

**the flabby sky that can manufacture no snow, but can only drop the sea on us in a drizzle like a poem by Mr. Robert Bridges.**

The English weather that is blasted becomes a symbol for everything Pound and his fellow Vorticists despised in art: anything soft, blurred, indistinct, familiar, compromised. The vocabulary of praise tends toward "hard," "intense," "concentration," "primary form," and above all, "energy." Inventing an ancestry for Vorticism (the ancestors being Pater, Whistler, Picasso, Kandinsky, and himself), Pound thought his contribution to the movement a definition of the image: "that which presents an intellectual and emotional complex in an instant of time." "The image is not an idea. It is a radiant node or cluster; it is what I can, and must perforce, call a VORTEX, from which, and through which, and into which, ideas are constantly rushing." Energized by Vorticism, and perhaps especially by an art that puzzled and fascinated him (i.e., Lewis's drawings for *Timon of Athens*), he began work on the "Three Cantos" in September 1915. His critical vocabulary of this period runs to formulations such as "units of design," "radicals in design," "pattern-units," and "forms in combination." The aesthetic problem he was privately working out, during the first years of composition and revision of the *Cantos,* was how to retain the concentration of the image and the energy of the vortex in "a poem of some length."

Twenty years after the *Blast* manifesto, Pound was certain that there had been, in those years in London, a "revolution in the arts" and that "all our work was the work of outlaws." Yet, as the revolution proceeded, Pound was as busy studying, absorbing, and reevaluating the past as he was in shaping the future. He was learning to speak through, indeed inhabit, his many masks or *Personae* (as he came to call his collected shorter poems); to extend his mastery of rhythm and voice; and to free himself, and poetry in English, from cadences and diction that had become so habitual that one who wanted a poetry "austere, direct, free from emotional slither" could no longer think in them. He discovered his freedom by breaking vigorously with the immediate past and embracing a much larger, redefined "tradition" (here Eliot and Pound worked closely together), one "not limited by the conventional taste of four or five centuries and one continent." Rejecting or ignoring most of English and American literature (though with praise for Shakespeare, Chaucer, and a few others), Pound discovered more useful models in Dante, Cavalcanti, the troubadours, selected Greek and Roman classics, and, through Fenollosa's notes, Chinese poetry.

His work as a poet during the London years now seems less directed at producing poems, although he produced many fine ones, than, as Thomas H. Jackson says, at attempting "to articulate for himself what poetry is all about" and then "working out a language with which to express these discoveries and convictions." What "obfuscated" him, he thought in retrospect, was "the crust of dead English, the sediment present in my own available vocabulary." The results of his reeducation—a flexible, precise, and vastly enlarged "language to think in"—are apparent throughout the *Cantos*. What happened to Pound as poet in the decade following *A Lume Spento* may be seen simply and dramatically in two "slides," as he would call them. The first, from *A Lume Spento*, presents a Dantesque moment in English still under the spell of Rossetti; the second is a short passage from his *Homage to Sextus Propertius* of 1919:

### Comraderie

*"E tuttoque io fosse a la compagnia di*
*molti, quanto alla vista."*

> Sometimes I feel thy cheek against my face
> Close-pressing, soft as is the South's first breath
> That all the subtle earth-things summoneth
> To spring in wood-land and in meadow space.

> Yea, sometimes in a bustling man-filled place
> Me seemeth some-wise thy hair wandereth
> Across my eyes, as mist that halloweth
> The air a while and giveth all things grace.

> Or on still evenings when the rain falls close
> There comes a tremor in the drops, and fast
> My pulses run, knowing thy thought hath passed
> That beareth thee as doth the wind a rose.

### from *Homage to Sextus Propertius*

> We were coming near to the house,
> and they gave another yank to my cloak,
> And it was morning, and I wanted to see if she was
> alone, and resting,
> And Cynthia was alone in her bed.
> I was stupified.
> I had never seen her looking so beautiful.

Finding the language represented by that passage from *Propertius* was Pound's most important achievement during his London years. After the disciplines of Imagism and the *Cathay* translations (1915), he was able to speak, as he turned to the composition of cantos, whatever language he chose, with the assurance that it was his choice rather than any "crust of dead language" within which he was imprisoned. Ronald Bush suggests, however, that it was not until after Pound had seen the *Waste Land* manuscripts that he allowed the language of the *Cantos,* a work intended to follow in the highest tradition of the long poem, to range beyond a certain decorum or "epic gravitas." The poem as finally written allows the widest possible range of language, in which image is speech and speech, image. The voices and dialects of the *Cantos* take on many colors—Elizabethan, Chinese, that of the reporter of documents and overheard remarks, Old Ez as Stage Yankee—but the voice we first hear in Canto 1 telling Divus to lie quiet is the basic voice of the poem, speaking in twentieth-century American. We should be aware of it and of its range. It can be noble:

> the man who at certain points
> > made us
> at certain points
> > saved us
>
> > > > > > > (C.62)

fussy, trying to get it right:

> That was Padre José Elizondo
> > in 1906 and in 1917
> or about 1917
>
> > > > > > > (C.81)

lyrical:

> out of all this beauty something must come
>
> > > > > > > (C.84)

humorously nagging:

> I shall have to learn a little greek to keep up with this
> > but so will you, drratt you
>
> > > > > > > (C.105)

elegiac:

> A blown husk that is finished
> > but the light sings eternal
>
> > > > > > > (C.115)

displaying prophetlike anger:

> And those who had lied for hire;
> the perverts, the perverters of language,
> the perverts who have set money-lust
> Before the pleasures of the senses
>
> (C.14)

In the years following the publication of the (to be drastically revised) "Three Cantos" of 1917, versions of cantos appeared at intervals in small magazines and in Pound's collections of verse. In 1925 *A Draft of XVI Cantos* was published at Paris in a deluxe edition of less than a hundred copies. By that time Pound had said his formal farewell to London and to aestheticism in *Mauberley* (1920) and, after three years in Paris, had settled in Rapallo, where he remained except for brief excursions, until in 1945 he returned to the United States at the expense of the American government.

In 1928 another limited edition, *A Draft of the Cantos: 17–27,* appeared in London. Then in 1930, the Hours Press published, at Paris, slightly over two hundred copies of *A Draft of XXX Cantos.* It was not until 1933 that a commercial edition of the poem became available.

The beautifully cadenced passage based on the story of Ignez da Castro (C.30) presents a suspended image of the mixture of beauty and horror, constructive and destructive states of mind, which *A Draft of XXX Cantos* encounters as it "crosses the Purgatory of human error":

> Time is the evil. Evil.
>                     A day, and a day
> Walked the young Pedro baffled,
>                     a day and a day
> After Ignez was murdered.
> Came the Lords in Lisboa
>                     a day, and a day
> In homage. Seated there
>                     dead eyes,
> Dead hair under the crown,
> The King still young there beside her.

The first sixteen cantos move from Homer, through the Renaissance, to modern London and Paris, and end with echoes of war and revolution. Canto 17 begins with an Ovidian vision, and Canto 27 concludes with an overlayering of Ovid's story of Cadmus and the Russian Revolution. The last three cantos of the volume return to troubadour tales and to Renaissance history.

Pound was aware of the problems he was creating by his allusive method and by "radicals in design" presented without consistent narrative or chronology. In 1937 he wrote to a friend:

> Part of the job is *finally* to get all the necessary notes into the text itself. Not only are the LI Cantos a part of the poem, but by labeling most of 'em draft, I retain the right to include *necessary* explanations in LI-C or in revision.

A defensive note is heard in another letter of 1939:

> I believe that when finished, *all* foreign words in the Cantos, Gk., etc., will be underlinings, not necessary to the sense, in one way. I mean a complete sense will exist without them; it will be there in the American text, but the Greek, ideograms, etc., will indicate a *duration* from whence or since when. If you can find any *briefer* means of getting this repeat or resonance, tell papa, and I will try to employ it. . . . There is *no intentional* obscurity. There is condensation to maximum attainable. . . . As to the *form* of *the Cantos:* all I can say is: *wait* till it's there. I mean wait till I get 'em written and then if it don't show, I will start exegesis.

He expresses, in the same letter, annoyance at "Yeats' bloody paragraph" (which attempted an elaborate explanation of the scheme of the poem) as a smoke screen that prevents people from reading the cantos "for what is *on the page.*" Late in life, asked by Donald Hall, "Now that you come near the end, have you made any plans for revising the *Cantos,* after you've finished?" Pound answered:

> I don't know. There's need of elaboration, of clarification, but I don't know that a comprehensive revision is in order. There is no doubt that the writing is too obscure as it stands, but I hope

that the order of ascension in the Paradiso will be towards limpidity.

But time ran out on possibilities for clarification, exegesis, or revision. The title *A Draft of XXX Cantos* remains; the "draft" is the final version.


◊   ◊


# CANTO 1

CANTO 1 CONTAINS the longest stretch of straight narrative in the poem, Homer's story of Odysseus's visit to the underworld to consult with the prophet Tiresias. Yet, before we reach the end, it becomes clear that we are to expect neither continuous narrative nor an orderly presentation of history. "And then Anticlea came," the story goes, but abruptly a new voice is heard speaking to another ghost, Divus, who appears to have published something in 1538, "out of Homer." Then a suggestion of the *Odyssey* returns briefly: Odysseus has left the underworld and is sailing "outward and away." Finally, there is a mixture of Latin and English, a cryptic reference to a Cretan, and an impassioned address to a formidable Aphrodite, who appears in ambiguous chiaroscuro of "dark eyelids" and gleaming copper and gold. The canto ends on a suspended note, the rising inflection of "So that:"

Canto 1 is a prelude to the long poem that follows, introducing the reader to themes and methods that can be only partly understood at this point: an epic voyage beset by dangers; the future approached through the past; religious awe inspired by blood rites and a pagan goddess; unexplained shifts of voice, language, and perspective. In fact, later cantos will never explain who Divus and the Cretan are nor translate these Latin phrases. The promise of "So that:" will never be fulfilled in any of the ways for which poetry written earlier than this canto can prepare us. When we turn to Canto 2, we find nothing that looks like a continuation:

Hang it all, Robert Browning,
    there can be but the one "Sordello."
But Sordello, and my Sordello?
Lo Sordels si fo di Montovana.

The part of Homer's story that immediately precedes the voyage to
the underworld will not be told until Canto 47, when Hermes
brings Odysseus the magic herb that protects him from Circe's
charms. Before that, the poem will have visited, without chronology, many times and places, including Renaissance Italy, the China
of Confucius, an already-betrayed America of Adams and Jefferson,
and the battlefields of modern Europe. "So that:" is neither the
"and then" of a tale, nor the "therefore" of syllogism. Yet in its
own way it manages to be both of these, announcing that the
voyage will be the poem that follows, a sailing after "knowledge to
be verified by experience."

The poem begins as a translation of Divus's Latin version of
Book 11 of the *Odyssey,* metamorphosing a dead past and dead
languages into living present. Pound thought Book 11, which he
called the "Book of the Dead," to be the oldest part of the oldest
work of Western literature. It "shouts aloud," he wrote, though
scholars do not agree with him, "that it is *older* than the rest," for
the *Odyssey* itself, which incorporates this primitive matter, was
already a reflection of "a very human and high state of culture."
The canto looks beyond that Homeric culture into a darker past,
as if the modern mind, before it can escape the labyrinthine con-
fusions of its age, must establish contact with forgotten beginnings.

In the course of the poem, Pound will return to other beginnings,
among them, the first civilization in China, Magna Carta, the
Italian Renaissance, the American Revolution. Although our age
may be, for Pound, an age of usury, producing "the sticky, mo-
lasses-covered filth of current print," the poem never expresses a
romantic yearning to live in some more colorful or more harmonious past. It always reminds us that it belongs to the twentieth century, and it discovers in the past only isolated moments of
civilization and cleaner values, willed by individuals who belong
to an ongoing "conspiracy of intelligence." The ritual of Canto 1

prefigures the poet's bringing blood to innumerable ghosts so that they may return to teach us whatever we are willing to learn.

There is in the *Cantos* a yearning, not for the past, but for a new sensibility, a sense of culture that the poet hopes to see manifested in a better civilization. His impatience sometimes leads him into dogmatisms such as Major Douglas's economic solution to the infamy about us (C.38). But beneath these dogmatic certainties, most of which are stimulating, some of which (the antisemitic touches in particular) are intolerable, the poem enacts a finer, more tragic sense of history. As early as 1912, Pound set forth in *Patria Mia* what can be read as an early program for the *Cantos:*

> One wants to find out what sort of things endure, and what sort of things are transient; what sort of things recur; what propagandas profit a man or his race; to learn upon what the forces, constructive and dispersive, of social order, move; to learn what rules and axioms hold firm, and what sort fade, and what sort are durable but permutable. . . . All the fine dreams of empire, of a universal empire, Rome, the imperium restored, and so on, came to little. The dream, nevertheless, had its value, it set a model for emulation, a model of orderly procedure. . . . Yet it came to no sort of civic reality.

Canto 1, by returning to the *Odyssey,* a poem standing at the beginning of a tradition and displaying "intelligence above brute force," begins the long meditation on these questions and an attempt to discover the possibilities of the dream. Odysseus is a figure of the poet, as well as of the reader who will accompany him, because he has seen the cities of many men and has learned their ways of thinking; and he is *polumetis,* a many-minded man, versatile, sharp, a survivor, with a mind (Pound said) that approaches the godlike: "And as Zeus said: 'A chap with a mind like THAT! the fellow is one of us. One of US.'"

That, too, in an idiom quite other than the language of Canto 1, is a translation from Homer, by a poet who had struggled in the years around 1915 to forge for modern poetry a language without archaisms, "departing in no way from speech, save by heightened intensity (i.e. simplicity) . . . no book words . . . no inversions.

. . ." Yet that same poet now begins his *Cantos* with inversions
("Then prayed I many a prayer"), poeticisms (*cam'st*), and obsolete diction (*dreory, bever, swart,* for *bloody, drink, black*).

The *Cantos,* for all Pound's notorious use of other tongues, is a
poem in English, and the language of Canto 1 pays homage to another beginning, the earliest English poetry, represented by the
Anglo-Saxon *Seafarer.* The choice is not arbitrary, for the bardic
world of the *Seafarer* roughly corresponds to Homer's Greece, and
its subject is similar to that of Books 10 and 11 of the *Odyssey:*
setting out on a dangerous voyage, abandonment of comfort, loss
of companions. Moreover, Pound had translated it in 1911, suggesting—and often reproducing exactly—the Anglo-Saxon kennings
and four-beat alliterative line. It is the language and rhythm of
Pound's own *Seafarer* translation (though less clogged by alliteration, less pedantic than that of 1911) through which Homer and
his Renaissance translators, Divus and the Cretan, who used the
language of Virgil, now speak.

There is one more voice to be heard, the most important for
seeing in Canto 1 the beginning of a modern poem rather than a
virtuoso antiquarian exercise. Among the many voices of the
*Cantos,* this is the one to which the poem always returns, the
voice aware of all others, that of the twentieth-century poet who is
making this poem. It enters for only two lines:

Lie quiet Divus. I mean, that is Andreas Divus,
In officini Wecheli, 1538, out of Homer.

The abrupt appearance of this voice is clearly heard in Pound's
recorded reading of the canto. He begins with a firm bardic
chant, as much song as speech, giving quantities to the verse. That
voice carries mourning: "Heavy with weeping . . . Souls stained
with recent tears . . . Pitiful spirit." Then fierceness, as Odysseus
places duty before pity, denying the "impetuous impotent dead,"
and even his own mother, "whom I beat off." (*Whom I beat off!*
Rouse gives only "I would not let her come near"; Rieu, "I would
not let her approach.") Elegiac tenderness for Elpenor, awe for
Tiresias, then a suggestion of tenderness again, as Anticlea is at
last allowed to come closer. With that, the bardic chant breaks off

(and Homer's scene between mother and son avoided) for the conversational modern voice: "Lie quiet Divus." After two lines the heroic song resumes, then swiftly rises to a new pitch of awed chant (so intent on its vision it seems unaware it is switching between Latin and English) as Aphrodite rises from spiteful Neptune's sea. Many voices, but the voice that quiets Divus is, to adopt a term of Pound's, the great bass beneath them all. We will hear it, with a considerable range of its own, throughout the poem.

Once we are aware of all the voices in the canto—Homer, Virgil, Divus, the Cretan, the Anglo-Saxon bard, Pound—we see more clearly in the structure of the canto one of Pound's essential methods, "cultural overlayering." The scheme below may appear elaborate for what looks like one of the more direct of the cantos, but it is the unmistakable effects, not the scheme, that matter: a descent to the world of the dead, a primitive rite, a Greek tale told with a mixture of Greek and Latin names, the Anglo-Saxon coloration of diction and rhythm, a modern interjection. The aim of such overlayering is to create a new whole; yet each of its ingredients retains something of its own identity, its own language and flavor. We may draw up a table of the traditions enclosed:

| Canto 1 | 1917–1925 |
| --- | --- |
| Pound's translation of the *Seafarer* and his efforts to reform his own poetic practice and that of modern English verse | 1911–ca. 1916 |
| Divus's Latin *Odyssey* and the Cretan's Latin version of the *Homeric Hymns* | 1538 |
| The *Seafarer* | Ninth century? |
| Virgil's *Aeneid*, an earlier imitation of and homage to the *Odyssey*, with particular reference to the Golden Bough and Aeneas's descent to the underworld | First century B.C. |
| The *Homeric Hymns* to Aphrodite | Ca. seventh century B.C. |
| The *Odyssey* | Ca. eighth century B.C. |
| The matter of *Odyssey* 11, "the Book of the Dead" | Prehistory |

There are three questions we should consider briefly before we pass beyond the canto's final *So that:*

1. What does Pound/Odysseus learn from the encounter with Tiresias? The blind prophet seems puzzled and slightly scornful as he asks why the voyager (in whom he does not recognize a modern poet) has returned to the "joyless" kingdom "a second time." The poem/voyage, he predicts, will take place with difficulty, over a dark sea ruled by a spiteful god, and the "return," the Homeric *nostos* or homecoming will take place.

But how might this poet/voyager, in 1917, expect to "lose all companions"? As he begins his poem, he knows that much of it— the economics, the religion, the politics—will move, for all its "modernism," against accepted opinions of his time. Surely he knows that the long, scholarly, obscure epic he envisions will find at best a small audience and may have trouble finding a publisher. Yet Pound could not have foreseen another way in which Tiresias's prophecy would come true: that his life and opinions (which were to be coextensive with the poem) would bring him to a prison camp at Pisa in 1945 and then, for thirteen years (one-quarter of his working life, as Hugh Kenner points out), to an insane asylum in Washington, D.C. In retrospect the brave "So that:" at the canto's end is somewhat ominous.

2. "Odysseus shalt return"—but to what? For Homer's hero the destination is clear: Ithaca, where he is reunited with his family and restores order to his kingdom. In Pound's plotless epic, where the poet is Odysseus only by loose analogy and at selected moments, the *nostos* is harder to define. Forrest Read, discussing the importance of the *Odyssey* to Pound's final conception of the poem, says that

> the *Cantos* was not to be a poem written from within modern civil-ization, but a poem about a break with modern civilization and a search for a new basis. This "break" is reflected in his personal life, in *Mauberley.* . . . it became for him a theory of history, of which the *nostos* is a symbol.

"Quite simply: I want a new civilization," Pound wrote in 1928. "It must be *as good* as the best that has been. It can't possibly be the *same,* so why worry, novelty is enforced. . . ." *Nostos* without nostalgia. Pound begins the poem with a clear sense of direction, but where specifically it will lead him, he can not know until he moves, canto by canto, to its end, a lifetime away.

3. Why, as the canto turns in the last five lines from narrative to lyric, the obscure tangle of allusions and Latin phrases that, even when translated, are not entirely clear? Perhaps at this point the poem must be obscure. We are not accustomed to gods appearing, really appearing, in our time. Later, we will see them more closely, and get used to their presence. Pound is trying to recover the elements of a lost language, one in which it is natural for the affairs of men to be fused with the affairs of gods. Hence, when the gods arrive, they often appear with fragments of the languages in which they lived.

Aphrodite appears, rising from the sea, her birthplace, adorned with signs of civilization, worked copper and gold, and associated with Cyprus, where her shrines are enclosed within walled places (*munimenta*). Ambiguous, silent, mirthful, but with "dark eyelids," she carries the golden bough said to belong to Hermes Argicida, one of whose functions is that of guide to the underworld. Here we have a flash, a vision of the *nostos* we can not understand until later. Hidden in these lines are themes the long poem will elaborate: the recovery of a lost past; the arduous journey toward rebuilding civilization; the vision of divine energy and beauty. The god/goddess as monster-slayer, then, provides the hero with the indispensable aid he will require (as the heroes of all epics require it). Hermes will be useful: In addition to being a guide to the underworld, he is associated with music and with eloquence, and he is a cunning thief (almost everything in the *Cantos,* as in most long poems, is borrowed or "stolen"). But without Beauty, represented by Aphrodite, the whole enterprise would be pointless.

◊   ◊   ◊

### Page 3 (*13*)

Circe's this craft / After a year on Circe's island, Odysseus seeks the goddess's help in returning to Ithaca. She tells him he must first travel to Hades, the house of Pluto and Persephone (Proserpine), in order to consult with Tiresias. Through her craft, or witchcraft, she provides favorable winds.

Kimmerian / The voyage brings Odysseus to the western edge of the ocean stream and to the land of the Kimmerians, where the sun never shines.

Perimedes and Eurylochus / Members of Odysseus's crew.

### Page 4 (*13–14*)

Tiresias / The blind prophet of Thebes who figures often in the mythical history of Greece. Alone among the flitting souls in Hades, he is one (C.47) "Who even dead, yet hath his mind entire!"

Erebus / A place of darkness, through which souls pass into Hades.

Proserpine / Pluto and Persephone, gods both of death and of fertility and renewal, suggest some of the religious mystery in the *Cantos*. Persephone will appear as a presiding goddess throughout the poem.

Elpenor / A member of Odysseus's crew, who died on Circe's island. When he returns to the island, Odysseus performs the burial rites Elpenor's shade here begs of him.

Avernus / The infernal regions.

### Page 5 (*14–15*)

Anticlea / Odysseus's mother, who had died during his long absence from Ithaca.

Neptune / Earlier in the voyage, Odysseus blinded Poseidon-Neptune's son, the Cyclops. The god's final spiteful act is recounted at the end of Canto 95, when he wrecks Odysseus's raft.

Andreas Divus / In a bookstall on a Paris quai, the young Pound discovered the 1538 Latin translation of the *Odyssey* by Divus, a minor figure of the early sixteenth-century Italian Renaissance who made close translations of Homer's epics, apparently for the use of students. See "Early Translators of Homer" (*Literary Essays*), where Pound gives the Latin passage on which Canto 1 is directly based.

In officina Wecheli / Divus's translation was published in Paris "at the printing shop of Christian Wecheli."

the Cretan / The copy of Divus's *Odyssey* also contained a Latin translation of the *Homeric Hymns* (once attributed to Homer, they postdate him by a century or more) by Georgius Dartona, who called himself Cretensis, the Cretan.

Venerandam . . . Cypri munimenta sortita est . . . orichalchi / Turning from the *Odyssey*, Pound quotes from Dartona's version of the "Second Hymn to Aphrodite." Freely translated: "She is to be worshipped . . . the high places [walls, fortifications] of Cyprus are her appointed realm . . . of copper [referring to her earrings]." Aphrodite-Venus, like Persephone, will appear throughout the *Cantos*.

golden bough / Aeneas had to pluck a golden bough before he could descend to Avernus. There is surely a nod toward Frazer's *Golden Bough*, as well.

Argicida / An epithet for Hermes-Mercury as "the slayer of Argus," from the "First Homeric Hymn to Aphrodite."

◇  ◇

# CANTO 4

THE CANTO BEGINS and ends amid the fallen stones of civilizations: Troy and its successor, Rome. From the image of the smoldering boundary stones (Odysseus has just departed after having sacked Troy's holy citadel), the canto moves through a series of vivid scenes at which we have the illusion of being present, until, in the last lines, we suddenly find ourselves removed watchers in an age that no longer supports such passionate, if sometimes destructive, encounters with gods. The dots after "And we sit here . . ." suggest not only an ellipsis of centuries but an emotional ellipsis as well. We are tourists, latecomers to the civilization that was once alive in the arena. The mood is somewhat like Gibbon's at the moment when he conceived the idea of writing the *Decline and Fall*:

> It was at Rome, on the 15th of October, 1764, as I sat musing amidst the ruins of the Capitol, while the barefoot friars were singing vespers in the Temple of Jupiter.

The opening lines may be considered as an ideogram:

*Destruction of a City* (Troy)
*Anaxiforminges* (Poetry/Music)    *Aurunculeia* (Fertility/Love)
*Foundation of a City* (Thebes)

The invocation draws on powers needed if a destroyed civilization is to be rebuilt or a new civilization is to be imagined. Poetry is not to stand alone, divorced from social purpose; the lords of the lyre (*Anaxiforminges*) must be accompanied by an awareness of sex and love, as idealized in Catullus's marriage hymn for Aurunculeia, and by the civilizing instinct of a Cadmus. Aurunculeia's wedding, celebrated by poetry, music, and dance, is not a romantic, private union but has a clear civic function. Catullus says that, if the invoked god refuses to bless the marriage (as he refused to bless that of Tereus and Procne), then:

No house without thee [Hymen] can give children, no parent
rest on his offspring; but all is well if thou art willing. What god
dare match himself with this god?

A land that should want thy sanctities would not be able to produce guardians for its borders—but could, if thou wert willing.
What god dare match himself with this god?

Pound implies in this opening ideogram, each element supporting
the others, a refusal to accept a fragmented sensibility in which
art, private emotions, and government are kept separate from each
other. The poem will move "toward the gt/ healing" (C.91).

Following the invocation, we find ourselves present at a dawn
ritual, nature alive with demigods. After the formidable and
distancing bardic cries, the verse seems to take it for granted (as
the pronoun glides by on an unstressed syllable) that this is "our"
waking, that the gods are there to be seen. This dance is no romantic "as if," but actual:

<blockquote>
pale ankles moving.<br>
Beat, beat, whirr, thud, in the soft turf
</blockquote>

Since the revival of the gods in the Renaissance, there has been
no poet who brings us so intimately into their presence.

In "Psychology and Troubadours" (1912), we can see Pound's
sense of the continuity of myth, why it is natural for him to bring
together, in Canto 4, Greek myths, Provençal troubadours, Guido
Cavalcanti, and a twentieth-century half-pagan procession in honor
of Mary:

> If a certain number of people in Provence developed thir own
> unofficial mysticism, basing it for the most part on their own ex-
> perience, if the servants of Amor saw visions quite as well as the
> servants of the Roman ecclesiastical hierarchy, if they were, more-
> over, troubled with no "dark night of the soul," and the kindred
> incommodities of ascetic yoga, this may well have caused some
> scandal and jealousy to the orthodox. . . . The rise of Mariolatry,
> its pagan lineage, the romance of it, find modes of expression which
> verge over-easily into the speech and casuistry of Our Lady of
> Cyprus, as we may see in Arnaut, as we see so splendidly in
> Guido's "Una figura della donna mia." And there is the consum-
> mation of it all in Dante's glorification of Beatrice. . . .

I believe in a sort of permanent basis in humanity, that is to say, I believe that Greek myth arose when someone having passed through delightful psychic experience tried to communicate it to others and found it necessary to screen himself from persecution. Speaking aesthetically, the myths are explications of mood: you may stop there, or you may probe deeper. Certain it is that these myths are only intelligible in a vivid and glittering sense to those people to whom they occur. I know, I mean, one man who understands Persephone and Demeter, and one who understands the Laurel, and another who has, I should say, met Artemis. These things are for them *real*.

The degree to which myth is real, he continues, depends on the degree to which the mind is "close on the vital universe."

By the time he had completed Canto 4, Pound's sense of myth and religion had deepened (see the important essays "Religio," 1919, and "Axiomata," 1921), and if the dawn scene is a "delightful private experience," it soon leads to darker encounters with divine energies. The scene ends with the crowing of the cock, and we are confronted with an old man speaking in a low drone. Is it Tereus bemoaning the death of Itys? The couch, its wood metamorphosed into "claw-foot and lion head," brings us indoors, out of the green cool light in which gods and men were momentarily in harmony with nature.

The two passages that follow, Itys/Cabestan and Actaeon/Vidal, form a remarkable balance, variations on a theme. Glamorous surfaces mask tales of passion as each story from Ovid turns before our eyes into a troubadour legend and then turns back again. It is impossible to see the exact points where the metamorphoses take place. The "she" in the first tale may be either Procne, about to be transformed into a bird, or Soremonda, the troubadour's lady, about to leap to her death. The cry of the swallows is both Procne's and that of the birds who have come in with the wind from Rhodez to witness the death of the Provençal lady. For a moment Soremonda pauses—just long enough for us to observe the wind catching her sleeve—and her plunge is suggested only by the excited cry of the swallows, " 'Tis.    'Tis," caught in a rhythm

that swings effortlessly back into the name of Itys, as the pun
(*It is!*) answers Soremonda's question, "It is . . . ?"

"Then Actaeon: Vidal." The Greek youth and the old troubadour stare at each other across two points, less a punctuation mark
than a sign of relationship, a slight gap for a spark to leap, like
the colon in the first version of "In a Station of the Metro":

> The apparition        of these faces        in the crowd        :
> Petals        on a wet, black        bough.

The syntax reaches across the colon fusing the names Actaeon/
Vidal, and the insistent phrases beginning with "not" resume, as
what appeared to belong to the story of Actaeon now belongs
equally to that of Vidal. The goddess, who was Diana, is now
Diana/Loba. Because Vidal knows his Ovid, he is aware of the
parallel between his own story and that of Actaeon, and we are
reading not only Pound's presentation of the Actaeon story but
Vidal's transformation of it as well. Vidal is poet and protagonist;
his mind, like Pound's, produces a shorthand of correspondences,
as the pool in which Diana bathed suggests other Ovidian pools
associated with tales of passion and transformation.

The final line of the passage, "The empty armour shakes as the
cygnet moves," from another story by Ovid, serves as a gloss on
what has come before. We witness, but we are not to moralize or
allegorize; we are aware of the tragic powers of the gods, who
are, Pound says, "irresponsible." One thing ends (the armour is
empty/Troy falls) as another begins (the metamorphosed swan
flies to safety/Rome is founded). Beauty, this canto, springs from
horrors; all four of its principal stories tell of people being eaten
(though Vidal is saved in the nick of time). Ovid, mistakenly
thought of as a prettifier, never turns away from horror or from
passion. We are not to judge these transformations by our standards
of ethics or decency. Tereus is shameful in every way; yet, Ovid
tells us, he is subject to forces larger than himself: "Men of his land
are quick to fall under the spell of Venus: his own and his nation's
passion burnt within him." Is his evil entirely his fault? His
marriage to Procne had a curse on it from the start: The gods re-

fused to bless the marriage (why, Ovid does not say), and the Furies brandished funeral torches over the marriage bed. Actaeon is guilty of nothing more than surprising Diana by accident. And what advice could one have given Soremonda or Vidal? That they pull themselves together and think of the consequences of their passions? "A narrative is all right," Pound says, "so long as the narrator sticks to words as simple as dog, horse, and sunset. His communication ceases almost entirely when he writes down 'good,' 'evil,' and 'proper.' " He will hardly follow that rule at all points in the *Cantos,* but he does in Canto 4. Something "whirls up," takes form, like Aphrodite rising from the sea in Canto 1, and we are asked to behold, not to judge.

If these interwoven stories, "ply over ply," do not supply a moral, they are still a demonstration of something, as we hear from the heavily accented *Thus* with which the poem resumes after the space of a line. What is being demonstrated is the presence of a force, a divine energy underlying and unifying all metamorphoses. The images come rushing, as close to simultaneity or montage as words spread across a page can be, a foretaste of the light-crystal-water images in later cantos: "That the crystal wave mount to flood surge" and "The light there almost solid" (C.95). It is a force that is irresistible:

> Shall the comet cease moving
> or the great stars be tied in one place!

This liquid, rushing crystal, full of transformations, carries with it all phenomena, however beautiful: "Brook film bearing white petals"; "The peach-trees shed bright leaves in the water"; "One scarlet flower is cast on the blanch-white stone." (By juxtaposition, the last becomes a symbol of Aurunculeia, whose virginity is destroyed as the marriage and its renewals take place.)

If the energies dramatized in Canto 4 are beyond morality, they are also, or should be, beyond the powers of individuals to monopolize them, as we see in the debate between the poet Sō-Gyoku and King Hsiang. (There is a suggestion of the poem's economics here: Certain forces, *bankers* in shorthand, have convinced us that they have a special relationship to the issue of credit. It is as if they claimed the right to issue, or to control the value of, sunlight or wind.) Sō-Gyoku's opening speech is touched with a slight chinoiserie, perhaps a shade too formal, implying flattery. The king's reply is in straightforward English, for his thought is less "twisty." When Sō-Gyoku resumes his argument, that there is a king's wind, different from the common people's wind, he is firmly interrupted by the voice of the poem itself: "No wind is the king's."

Hsiang is wise in knowing that he cannot capture the wind in his gauze curtains, wiser than Danaë's father, King Acrisius, who schemes to prevent the fertility of nature by shutting her in a "gilded tower." The "god's bride" in the recapitulation of the story becomes not only Danaë (she lay not "once" but "ever") but all who have ever awaited the Light, waited for revelation, or who share the impulse of Père Henri Jacques to climb a sacred mountain and communicate with the spirits of the air.

The camel drivers look down on the ruins of Ecbatan: They seem to be modern camel drivers, in the same position as "we" who sit on the steps of the crumbling Roman arena. Not even Deioces, a civilizing force (like Cadmus) and a legendary figure of justice, has been able to build a city to withstand metamorphosis: Today, Ecbatan is the city of Hamadan in West Iran, its terraces no longer the color of stars. "Plotted," precisely chosen as too strong a word, emphasizes the futility of any attempt to plot—against the arrival of Zeus or toward the subdivision of the wind.

The light effects in the canto begin as "smoky"; become a "dew-haze" of "green cool light" in the dawn; increase to "Blaze, blaze in the sun" and to the pouring light that makes the forked branch-tips appear "flaming"; and as the canto closes, become smoky again in "evening haze." The rushing light is not constant; we are being prepared for the sudden withdrawal of color and energy as the canto concludes in the twentieth century. We are brought to a quiet landscape in which we hear no dancing nymphs, only a bark scraping at the ford. The decreasing light is concentrated in "gilt rafters" of a building at the water's edge. [It is, or was in an early draft, a temple of the Buddhist goddess Kwannon (Kuanon), who now does not enter the poem until Canto 74.] Then stone steps and posts set mysteriously in an open field, but the ellipsis prevents us from discovering where the steps may lead. We will find them again in Canto 16 and see that they descend into the earth, to a kind of anteparadise. Rather than follow the steps at this point, the poem shifts suddenly to the top of the Chinese sacred mountain, Rokku. Or, to be precise, Père Henri Jacques "would" speak there with the Sennin, spirits of the air. Much later, in Canto 88, we find that his wish has been granted:

> Père Henri Jacques still
> speaks with the sennin on Rokku

The mention of the priest is the first Christian suggestion in the *Cantos,* acting as a leading tone held in suspension for seven lines, until the Christian development of the canto's themes in "sa'ave Regina!" and in the madonnas of Stefano and Cavalcanti, after which the centaur returns us briefly to the pagan world. Finally, Christian and pagan elements, the continuity of which is being demonstrated, are brought together, by implication, in the Roman arena where they once met.

The sudden movement from pagan and troubadour tales to the three appearances of the Virgin in the final lines is less abrupt than it may seem. Pound sees the impulse by which men have approached godhead through the image of a beautiful woman as a common impulse moving, in religious practice and in the lyric tradition, through Greece and Provence to the Tuscany of Cavalcanti and Dante. James J. Wilhelm, writing of the troubadour and Tuscan traditions, says:

> Yet to view this love poetry in its total form as a one-dimensional hymn to an earthly lady is to ignore both its provenance, which is religious, and its essence, which is ambiguous. . . . These lyric voices speak from a romantic twilight that shrouds the shrines of Aphrodite, Persephone, Venus, and the Great Lady of Christianity, Mary, Star of the Sea.

In the 1912 essay "Psychology and Troubadours," we saw Pound working out his sense of that tradition, speaking of the "pagan lineage" of Mariolatry. (The general outlines are hardly original, and Pound was well aware of Frazer.) In short, the encounter with the divine may come through Venus or Mary, Diana or one's own Lady. Peire Vidal had written:

*Bona domna, Deu cug vezer*
*Quan lo vostre gen cors remir.*

[Fair lady, I think I see God,
When I look at your fair person.]

One's impulse toward the Lady, however, to adopt troubadour terminology, may be a *fals'amors* (profane love, mistaking the creature for the Creator) or a *fin'amors* (leading, through an idealized Lady, a Beatrice, toward the contemplation of the Light).

As Canto 4 concludes, the complexities of the tradition, freed from chronology, are glimpsed in the procession in honor of the Virgin (in which folk memories of pagan elements remain), in Stefano's painting of the Madonna, and in Cavalcanti's sonnet about another painting of the Madonna. The sonnet is ambiguous, parallel lines of double entendre receding into a perspective beyond "false" and "refined" love. The sonnet says that the poet's Lady resembles, and so is worshipped in, the face of a miraculous Madonna at Or San Michele. The surface of the poem blandly protects the poet's orthodoxy: It may be read simply as a homage to the Virgin, with only a passing compliment to the Lady. A less orthodox reading is possible: Cavalcanti worships his earthly Lady and ascribes "miraculous" powers to her. The poem ends curiously, its own ambiguous motives projected wittily upon the clergy:

Her voice is bourne out through far-lying ways
'Til brothers minor cry: 'Idolatry',
For envy of her precious neighborhood.

Pound thinks the sonnet's "blasphemous intention is open to the simplest capacity," and the implication here is that when Cavalcanti "had seen her" he was aware of the tradition with which Canto 4 is concerned.

◊   ◊   ◊

The interweaving of themes, epochs, and images is carried out with such mastery of phrasing that we may not have noticed that the entire canto contains almost no "complete" sentences in the normal sense. Everything flows along on commas, colons, semicolons, ellipses—syntax expressing content. The liquid crystal energy cannot be forced into a pattern of subject-verb-object. The syntax is its own marvel of metamorphosis. In the scene in the dark valley through which Actaeon passes toward his fatal encounter, the syntax allows cinegraphic effects, cutting from the valley thick with leaves to a shot in which we look up on a roof of trees catching the light, then back to the valley from which direct sunlight is so firmly excluded, illumination being provided by the presence of the goddess. Everything is in motion: the air, the water, Diana and her nymphs. Against these shaking light effects, the hypnotic repetitions stop time.

With the exception of a few lines in the Soremonda/Procne passage ("And she went toward the window"), the entire canto moves in the present tense. The effect is to make us "present" at the events, to suggest that the force that manifests itself in them is a "present" force. The canto is not an exercise in the exotic nor in scholarship. It is a remarkable display of technique, not only to have brought these stories together in a single poem, but to have made them all contemporary.


◊   ◊   ◊


*Page 6 (16)*

Anaxiforminges! / "Lords of the lyre," from Pindar's *Olympian* 2: "Hymns that are lords of the lyre, what god, what hero, and what man shall we praise?" Although Pound thought Pindar pompous and rhetorical and used the opening of *Olympian* 2 ironically in *Mauberley,* there is no need to seek irony here. Cadmus also appears in Pindar's ode.

Aurunculeia / The bride whose marriage is celebrated in Catullus's epithalamium, *Collis o Heliconii.*

Cadmus / Legends of Cadmus present him as a civilizing force: He founded Thebes and introduced the alphabet to Greece. The epithet "of Golden Prows" appears to be Pound's invention. The story of Cadmus's line, much of which is told in *Olympian* 2 and in Ovid, has rich associations throughout the *Cantos.* The tales of his four daughters and their children form a complex of madness and destruction, often produced by an encounter between gods and men: (1) Through the union of his daughter Semele with Zeus, Cadmus was the grandfather of Dionysus, whose rites are important in the *Cantos.* (2) A second daughter, Ino, became the nurse of Dionysus. Hera, jealous of Semele, and thus angry at her entire family, drove Ino mad, and she killed her own children. Relieved of her madness by Dionysus (in some stories, by Aphrodite), Ino was transformed into the sea-goddess Leucothea, who comes to the rescue of Pound/Odysseus in Canto 95. (3) A third daughter, Agave, was the mother of King Pentheus, whose story is told in Canto 2. Together with her sister, Autonoe, she tore Pentheus limb from limb for violating the Dionysian rites of which she was an initiate. (4) Autonoe was the mother of Actaeon, whose violent death is one of the subjects of Canto 4. The stories of Cadmus and his line reinforce the tragic theme of the canto (and of the longer poem) in which splendor and savagery, civilization and destruction are inextricably mixed.

Choros nympharum / Nymphs dancing. *Choros,* "a circling dance," by extension a group of dancers.

Ityn / The accusative of Itys, whose name is echoed in the swallows' cry "It is!" He was the son of Tereus and Procne. When Tereus raped Procne's sister, Philomela, and cut out her tongue, the sisters revenged themselves by killing Itys and cooking him in a dish, which they served to Tereus. When they told Tereus what they had done (in stories like this there's no point to revenge unless your enemy knows what's happened to him), he attempted to kill them, but the sisters were changed into birds (swallow and nightingale, but stories differ) and Tereus into a more warlike bird.

Et ter flebiliter / "And three times tearfully." The *ter* (thrice) is imitated in the three repetitions of *Ityn* and in " 'Tis. 'Tis. Ytis!" *Flebiliter* is from an ode by Horace (4.12), which refers to the tale.

Cabestan / Also, Cabestanh, Cabestaing. From the Provençal *vida* of the troubadour Guillem da Cabestanh. He and the Lady Soremonda fell in love with each other. Her jealous husband killed Cabestanh, cooked his heart in a dish, and served it to his wife. When she discovered this, she said: "My Lord, since you have given me the best to eat, I shall taste nothing else." And she went to the window "and cast her down." Her husband was punished by having his castles razed, so that, as at Troy, not a stone was left upon a stone.

## Page 7 (*16–17*)

Rhodez / Like the other French towns mentioned in the canto, Poitiers and Gourdon, it belongs to the part of France associated with the troubadours.

Actaeon/ After a morning's hunt, Actaeon wanders into the shady valley of Gargaphia, sacred to Diana-Artemis, who is bathing naked in a pool. When Actaeon sees her, she splashes him with water, transforming him into a stag. His own dogs set upon him: "It was not until he had died from a multitude of wounds that the wrath of Diana the Huntress was appeased."

Poictiers / Pound recalls the overlapping tiles on a church roof, looking like fish scales, perhaps the church of Saint Hilaire praised in Canto 45, or Notre Dame in the same city. Poitiers was the seat of the first troubadour, Guillaume, ninth duke of Aquitaine, who (C.8) "brought the song up out of Spain."

Vidal / Peire Vidal, troubadour, loved a lady named Loba (she-wolf). Her love drove him mad, or drove him at least to a gesture near to madness: He dressed in wolfskins and inhabited the woods, where, his *vida* says, "he had himself hunted by shepherds and dogs." Loba and her husband brought him half dead to their castle, laughed at his folly, and cared for him until he was well. Pound saw both folly and splendor in Vidal, who was a "mad poseur," yet one of the company of poets who "lived" their verse. In an early poem, "Piere Vidal Old," Pound has him bitterly regretting that his days of folly and passionate gesture are over. The reference here in Canto 4 leads through a complex series of metamorphoses: from a name, Loba; to the literal meaning of the name, wolf; to Vidal's attempt to turn himself into a wolf; to word and melodramatic gesture becoming reality, as he is hunted; to his reading of Ovid and recognizing the parallel between himself and Actaeon; and finally to his transformation of his experience into poetry.

*Page 8 (17–18)*

Pergusa . . . Gargaphia . . . Salmacis . . . the cygnet / Pound brings together in Vidal's mind a series of pools from Ovid, all scenes of transformations: (1) It was near Pergusa that Persephone was gathering flowers when Hades ravished her and carried her off to the underworld kingdom we have just visited in Canto 1. (2) Gargaphia is where Diana was bathing when Actaeon saw her. (3) Salmacis is a pool named for the nymph who fell in love with Hermaphroditus, who spurned her; she dived into the pool after him, "possessed" him, and their two bodies became one. (4) Pound captures the moment of transformation when Cygnus, an almost-invulnerable son of Neptune, is slain by Achilles. As Achilles is about to strip the body, the armor suddenly is empty, as Neptune transforms Cygnus into a swan. Pound suggests not only the stories but the Ovidian flavor: glamorous surfaces for tales of rape, murder, destructive passions.

*e lo soleills plovil* / "And the sun rains." That is, the sun is so "tensile" that it seems like crystal water. The phrase is adapted from a poem by Pound's (and Dante's) favorite troubadour, Arnaut Daniel, about getting free from the entanglements of *fals'amors.* Pound's translation of *"Lancan son passat li giure"* is in his essay on Daniel (*Literary Essays*).

Takasago . . . Isé / *Takasago* is a Noh play based on a Japanese legend about twin pines, one of which grows at Takasago, the other at Sumiyoshi (somehow Pound has turned Sumiyoshi into Isé, the oldest of the Shinto shrines). Each night the spirit of one pine, an old man, travels a great distance to visit his wife, the spirit of the pine at Takasago. Thus the pines, beyond the universal symbol of the evergreen, represent enduring conjugal love (like that invoked in Catullus's marriage hymn and like that of Cadmus and his wife) in contrast to the destructive passions that dominate the canto. The passage beginning "Thus the light rains" is a "magic moment," with its evocation of an active, divinity-infused nature.

the Tree of the Visages / This is clearly related to the story of humans metamorphosed into trees but is not from *Takasago.*

Gourdon / Near Toulouse.

## Page 9 (*18–19*)

Hymenaeus Io! / The refrain from Catullus's marriage hymn, invoking the god of marriage. Hymen's feasts are usually accompanied by dancing and torches.

Sō-Gyoku / Japanese name of the Chinese poet Sung Yü (fourth century B.C.). Pound, having depended on the notes of Fenollosa, who studied Chinese under Japanese instructors, uses transliterated Japanese versions of names.

Hsiang / King of Ch'u, with whom the poet is discoursing in the *fu,* the prose poem on which these lines are based. Pound is not translating the *fu* here but is creating a small poem of his own from it. The king says, "How pleasant a thing is the wind which I share with the common people." Sō-Gyoku defends the proposition that the king's wind and the people's wind are different.

Ecbatan / Deioces ("Dioce" in the *Cantos*), the legendary first king of the Medes, built or "plotted" his capitol city of Ecbatan, as

Herodotus describes it, "of great size and strength fortified by concentric walls, there so planned that each successive circle was higher than the one below it. . . . The circles are seven in number, and the innermost contains the royal palace and treasury." In the Pisan cantos, Ecbatan is a symbol of Pound's dream: "To build the city of Dioce whose terraces are the colour of stars."

Danaë / Daughter of Acrisius, king of Argos, and mother, by Zeus, of Perseus. Acrisius, faced with a prophecy that a child born to Danaë would kill him, shut her away—Pound suggests in a "gilded tower" to correspond to the golden inner circle at Ecbatan. But Zeus arrived as the shower of gold, Perseus was born, and Acrisius met his fate. He committed the same sin, incidentally, as did Pentheus in Canto 2, the denial of the god Dionysus.

Père Henri Jacques / A French Jesuit. The meeting of East and West and the exchange of cultures through Jesuits in China is a theme that returns at several points in the poem.

Sennin / "Chinese spirits of nature or of the air."

Rokku / One of the five sacred mountains of China.

*Page 10 (19)*

Polhonac / The viscount of Polignac, who assisted his wife and the troubadour Guillaume de Saint-Leidier in a love affair.

Gyges / In Herodotus, a few pages from the story of Deioces, Pound discovered this tale of unseemly sexual behavior resulting in murder and political disorder. King Candaules "conceived a passion for his own wife, and thought she was the most beautiful woman on earth." He urged his bodyguard, Gyges, to hide in their bedchamber so that he might admire the naked body of the queen. Gyges protested but was forced to obey. Like Actaeon, he saw "what he had no right to see." The queen, consumed by shame, forced Gyges to kill the king, and he succeeded both as husband and as ruler. There is no connection between Gyges and Thrace: the "Thracian platter" is a means of weaving together the stories of Gyges and Tereus.

Garonne / River in southwest France, in troubadour country.

Saave! / A modern religious procession in honor of the Virgin is singing (or screaming almost savagely, as Pound recites this canto) the hymn "Salve Regina."

Adige / River flowing through Verona. A connection is suggested between the modern worship of the Virgin by the Garonne, her image by the painter Stefano da Verona, and the ruined Roman arena at Verona.

Stefano / Guido Cavalcanti had seen "her," but not Stefano's painting of her, the *Madonna in Hortulo,* in which a pensive, fair-haired North Italian woman with a restless child on her lap, and a gem-encrusted starry halo radiating from behind her head, sits before a rich pattern of flowers and curving arbors laced with vines.

Cavalcanti / Dante's friend, whose canzone "Donna mi pregha" is translated in Canto 36. The reference here is to Cavalcanti's Sonnet 35, in which (Pound says in a headnote to his translation) "he explains the miracle of the madonna of Or San Michele, by telling whose image it is." The translation begins, "My Lady's face is it they worship there. / At San Michele in Orto. . . ." Pound is deliberately violating chronology to convey his sense of the continuity of vision that inspires Cavalcanti's poem, the miraculous image at Or San Michele in Florence, and Stefano's painting. The two Madonnas are also connected through "garden" (*or*/*orto*/*hortulo*).

Centaur / Ovid always insists on their "double nature."

arena / At Verona, the third largest of extant Roman arenas. The visit to the arena recurs in later cantos, notably in Canto 78, where it is again juxtaposed with a reference to a sonnet by Cavalcanti (Sonnet 7) in which, as in Sonnet 35, a profane love leads toward a sacred one: *E la beltate per sua Dea la mostra,* "She being beauty's godhead manifest."

◊  ◊

## CANTO 9

THE TWO SCHOLARS, Basinio and Pandone ("the anti-Hellene"), were debating the revival of Greek in the courtyard at Rimini in 1456, surrounded by the trappings of feudal war games—lists and palisades set up for tourneys. The image presents Canto 9 in miniature, as Renaissance humanism flourishes in the midst of perpetual warfare. The lists and palisades were soon dismantled; the words of the debaters may or may not be preserved in an archive. Yet something remains of the energy expended that afternoon: Basinio and his cause won the day, and we have Milton, Monticello, and courses in Greek backgrounds to literature.

There is no point in unscrambling the time sequence of the Malatesta cantos (8–11), which Pound has so deliberately shuffled; he wants to place us in the midst of events, so we may see them as Rimini saw them. "We do NOT know the past in chronological sequence. It may be convenient to lay it out anesthetized on the table with dates pasted on here and there, but what we know we know by ripples and spirals eddying out from us and from our own time." Today, only a handful of specialists in fifteenth-century Italian history know in what year—or on what day of a given year, events moved so swiftly—Venice was supporting Milan, or Milan the pope, or which *condottieri* were working for whom. It is confusing, and the confusion itself and its attendant barbarism and lack of order are an important part of Pound's Renaissance. He is not interested in untangling *that* history, but rather in how "a conspiracy of intelligence outlasted the hash of the political map."

The Renaissance, briefly interrupted by twentieth-century munitions makers and by a contrasting Confucian ethic, dominates Cantos 5 through 30. It is the dark forest or the purgatory of human error, its "picturesqueness" merely something to be "survived." We are familiar with the picturesque horrors of Pound's

Renaissance from Browning and from Jacobean plays: Borgias are poisoning each other; government is being conducted on distinctly non-Confucian principles; people are being tossed from windows of *palazzi;* worldly popes preside over a Church in which (to translate Padre José's remark in Canto 81) "there's a lot of Catholicism, but not much religion." Yet barbaric as that Renaissance may have been, there was another Renaissance mixed with it, a civilization, as Pound saw it, not yet entirely given to usury. It produced moments of high culture in which the conversation of Gemisthus Plethon inspired Cosimo de Medici to subsidize Ficino's life work of translating Plato and "the greek neoplatonists. Porphyry, Psellos, Iamblichus, Hermes Trismegistus." (The neoplatonic tradition is important in the later cantos.) Malatesta's Tempio was another such moment, with its portrait of Sigismundo in fresco by Piero della Francesca, its mysterious carvings by Duccio, and its synthesis of the pagan and the Christian.

For this other Renaissance in which pagan gods returned, and in which princes not only supported but conversed with the greatest scholars of the age, Pound had no need to go to obscure sources. It was there in a book that was standard reading for any young literary man born in 1885, Pater's *The Renaissance* (1873):

> Even the mysteries, the centers of Greek religious life at a later period, were not a doctrine but a ritual; and one can imagine the Roman Catholic Church retaining its hold through the "sad mechanic exercise" of its ritual. . . . There is scarcely a wildness of the Roman Catholic Church that has not been anticipated by Greek polytheism.

> In the *Doni* madonna in the Tribune of the Uffizi, Michelangelo actually brings the pagan religion, and with it the unveiled human form, the sleepy-looking fauns of a Dionysiac revel, into the presence of the Madonna . . . and he has given to that Madonna herself much of the uncouth energy of the older and more primitive mighty Mother.

Pound's Renaissance and Pater's have much in common, although Pound's is earthier, more shocking, and more fun. Pater claimed

the essence of humanism is . . . that nothing which has ever
interested living men and women can wholly lose its vitality—
no language they have ever spoken

but he reported nothing like those two patrons of the arts, Malatesta and Urbino, talking to each other (in Canto 10) at a peace
conference:

*"Te cavero la budella del corpo!"*
*El conte levatosi:*
   *"Io te cavero la corata a te!"*

["I'll rip your guts out!"
The Count arose:
   "And me, your heart!"]

Burckhardt, the great historian of the Renaissance, found it
difficult to believe of Sigismundo Malatesta "that a monster like
this prince felt learning and the friendship of cultivated people to
be a necessity of life." Pound does not find that hard to believe, and
he sees that if Sigismundo's own poetry is "doggerel," it is also
representative of its culture. He translates a sample of it in Canto 8:

"Ye spirits who of olde were in this land
Each under Love, and shaken,
Go with your lutes, awaken
The summer within her mind,
Who hath not Helen for peer
        Yseut nor Batsabe."

The choice of Sigismundo as hero, in light of his reputation as a
monster, is no stranger than Dante's placing Cunizza in Paradise.
But the *Cantos* are not melodrama (though at times Pound can
tempt us to forget they are not), and if Sigismundo is a hero, he is
far from exemplary in every way; he is a man of his time in whom
order and disorder contend, as they do on every page of the *Cantos*.

Pound's history is not always correct, but he made great efforts
to get it right, spending days in the Rimini archives and Vatican
library, taking trips along the routes Sigismundo took, "to see
how the land lay." But the "truth" was no easier to find than was

the "real" Sordello (a problem posed at the beginning of Canto 2),
and most of all, one was writing a poem:

> Am reading up historic background for Canto IX . . . shall
> probably only get more bewildered; but may avoid a few historic
> idiocies, or impossibilities.

> Authorities differ as to whether Sigismundo Malatesta raped a
> german girl in Verona, with such vigour that she "passed on", or
> whether it was an italian in Pesaro, and the pope says he killed her
> first and raped her afterwards; also some authorities say it was
> Farnese and not Malatesta who raped the bishop of Fano, and in
> fact all the *minor* points that might aid one in forming an historic
> rather than a fanciful idea of his character seem "shrouded in
> mystery" or rather lies.

> I suppose one has to "select". If I find he was TOO bloody
> quiet and orderly it will ruin the canto. Which needs a certain
> boisterousness and disorder to contrast with his constructive work.

> Francesco Sforza, whom I had first cast for the villain seems also
> to have had good reason for etc. etc.

> Hang it all it is a bloody good period, a town the size of Rimini,
> with Pier Francesca, Mino da Fiesole, and Alberti as architect.
> The pick of the bunch, all working there at one time or another.

Sigismundo's life, accurately interpreted or not, makes a very
good story, good material for a poem about the possibilities of
*directio voluntatis,* the directed will. The figure of Malatesta fights
its way through the jumbled details that are, in Hugh Kenner's
words, "not the applied color but the reality itself in which the
will and intelligence of Malatesta are to be discerned like the
iron filings that reveal the contours of the magnetic field." For
all his faults and failures, Pound sees Malatesta as corresponding
to Jefferson, who was "trying to set up a civilization in the wilderness." Pound's intentions are clear:

> There is no mystery about the Cantos, they are the tale of the
> tribe. . . . No one has claimed that the Malatesta cantos are ob-
> scure. They are openly volitionist, establishing, I think clearly,
> the effect of the factive personality, Sigismundo, an entire man.

If you consider the Malatesta and Sigismundo in particular, a failure, he was at all events a failure worth all the successes of his age. He had in Rimini, Pisanello, Pier della Francesca. Rimini still has "the best Bellini in Italy". If the Tempio is a jumble and a junk shop, it nevertheless registers a concept. There is no other man's effort equally registered.

Sigismundo's Rimini belongs among "examples of Civilization":

> The Tempio Malatestiano is both an apex and in a verbal sense a monumental failure. It is perhaps the apex of what one man has embodied in the last 1000 years of the occident. A cultural "high" is marked.
>
> In a Europe not YET rotted by usury, but outside the then system and pretty much against the power that was, and in any case without great material resources, Sigismundo cut his notch. He registered a state of mind, of sensibility, of all-roundness and awareness.
>
> He had a little of the best there in Rimini. . . . All that a single man could, Malatesta managed *against* the current of power.

Forty years later, Pound's own career, having moved against the current of power, would come to resemble that of his fifteenth-century *condottiere;* his own life's work would appear to him a jumble and a junk shop,

> a tangle of works unfinished

and:

> Tho' my errors and wrecks lie about me.

Yet at the same time, in the same canto (116), he cannot help but boast that an effort had been made, a sensibility and awareness "registered." There is always another side to the story:

> These concepts the human mind has attained.
> To make Cosmos—
> To achieve the possible—

The verse and structure of the canto imitate the inner shape of Sigismundo's life. It begins lyrically, with clear cadences established by open rhyme (*rose*/*snows*), off rhyme (*hail fell*/*walls*), variations of phrasing (*off him*/*find him*/*end of him*), and repetitions (*One year*/*one year* and *Down here*/*down here*). It drives its way through floods, hail, and marshes; through the deaths of two wives and a union with his beloved Isotta; through treacheries and confused battles; through Sigismundo's own sins. It follows the decline of his fortune, from being "Captain for the Venetians" to fighting for "a man with a ten-acre lot." Then, from the rubble of dead documents, there arises the form of the Tempio and the lyrical apotheosis of Isotta, which is itself entirely metamorphosed from fragments of documents.

Pound had surely read, for he borrows his narrative point of view from it, Edward Hutton's popular, slightly fictionalized life of Malatesta (1906). Hutton imagines a scene in which the great humanist, Leon Battista Alberti, discourses to the Rimini court. Alberti's reply to Sigismundo, and the narrator's comment, make a good epigraph to the Malatesta cantos, and to the *Cantos:*

> Mass being over, and Messer Leon Battista about to begin his lecture, Sigismundo, smiling at Madonna Isotta, who stood beside him, turned to the company, and presenting Messer Battista to us with many friendly words added, as though by way of explanation: "To raise the dead—that is what we are trying to do."
>
> To raise the dead! but Messer Battista would not have it so. "Not to raise the dead, but rather to awaken the living," he began; and certainly among much that was abstruse, difficult, or merely technical, this was the refrain, as it were, that ran through his whole discourse.

*Page 11* (*20*)

Astorre Manfredi / An ally of Malatesta's great enemy, Federigo d'Urbino. The attempt to ambush Sigismundo took place in 1447, when he was thirty.

Fano / Port about thirty miles south of the Malatesta seat at Rimini, in the possession of the Malatestas since the mid-fourteenth century. Sigismundo struggled all his life to retain or to regain his territories. Fano, one of his last possessions, was finally taken from him by papal forces a few years before his death.

the Emperor / Sigismund V, crowned Holy Roman Emperor at Rome in 1433. Returning from his coronation, the emperor visited Rimini, where a Latin ode was recited by Basinio, and triumphal "Roman" arches were erected. The emperor knighted Malatesta, then sixteen.

Basinio / Humanist, one of the remarkable assemblage of writers and artists who formed "the great humane culture that went into Rimini." The anti-Hellene, Pandone, had contended that "one may be an excellent Latin poet without having studied assiduously the Greek authors."

Rocca / Sigismundo had torn down his family castle where, a century and a half before, his ancestor, Giancotto, had stabbed to death his wife and her lover, his brother, the Paolo and Francesca of Dante's *Inferno*. Sigismundo replaced the castle with a great fortress, the Rocca.

Madame Ginevra / The first of Malatesta's two political marriages was to Ginevra d'Este, daughter of Niccolo d'Este, lord of Ferrara. Sigismundo was sixteen. After her death seven years later, Pope Pius II, a bitter political enemy and an unreliable witness, accused Sigismundo of having poisoned her.

Monteluro / Near Florence, site of one of Sigismundo's innumerable battles.

*Page 12 (20–21)*

Sforza / Francesco Sforza, one of the remarkable figures of the Italian Renaissance, rose from humble origins to become a powerful *condottiere,* then duke of Milan. He is the "old bladder" and "old Wattle-wattle" mentioned below (his portraits show a considerable paunch and jowls). After Ginevra's death, Sigismundo sought to form an alliance with him by marrying his daughter, the Polixena mentioned here. However, Sforza "bitched" him in the Pesaro affair, probably the greatest disappointment of Sigismundo's life.

Pesaro / Port city between Rimini and Fano. With Fossembrone, it had been part of the Malatesta holdings since the fourteenth century. Later, the family split, and Pesaro came under an independent line of Malatestas. It was Sigismundo's ambition to return all the territories to his own command. Pesaro and Fossembrone were controlled by his cousin, Galeazzo ("the Inept"), whom Pound calls Galeaz. Sforza promised to have Pesaro returned to Sigismundo, but engineered the "wangle" in which he was betrayed. Galeazzo, pressed for cash, was forced to sell his lands; Pesaro went to Sforza's brother, Alessandro; Fossembrone, to Sigismundo's rival, Federigo d'Urbino, whom Pound calls Feddy. The loss of these cities and the strengthening of his enemies marked the beginning of the decline of Sigismundo's power over the next ten years and "finished our game."

*per capitoli* / Sforza's oath that Sigismundo should have Pesaro had been sworn "by the chapters" (of the Bible?).

Marches / Territory between Florence and Rimini. Alarmed at the growth of Sforza's power, the pope, the king of Aragon (who had become king of Naples and wanted Milan for himself), and the duke of Milan (Sforza's father-in-law) formed a league against him. Sigismundo, who had been at odds with the pope, became the papal captain general, achieved a victory over Sforza (*his* father-in-law), and "drove them out of the Marches." He did not, however, regain Pesaro.

King o' Ragona, Alphonse le roy d'Aragon / Who betrayed whom in the relations between Alfonse and Sigismundo is hard to say. Malatesta was supposed to be in Aragon's service, but at the council mentioned below, he decided to switch sides and fight for Florence, then under seige by Aragon. (Pound translates *haec traditio* as "change-over" but it suggests treachery.) At any rate, he did save the Florentine state (*rem eorum saluavit*).

Valturio / Engineer and advisor to Malatesta. His *De re militari* came to represent, for Pound, the catalogs of munitions-makers:

The one history we have NOT on the news stands is the history of Usura. . . . Who paid for such and such wars, what save poverty prevented so and so from making more wars, with more splendid equipment? Malatesta and the late condottieri, their mouths watering over the designs, in Valturio, of war engines, tanks, superior catapults, as damn'd froust now letches after a Vickers' advertisement.

"Florence our natural ally" / In the language of modern military diplomacy.

TEMPIO / Slipped almost unobtrusively into this string of *and*'s, the Tempio, and what it represents, most attracted Pound to Malatesta, and it becomes a recurring symbol in the *Cantos*. When he was about thirty, Malatesta began a complete remodeling of the old gothic church of San Francesco. The high-Renaissance "neoclassical" Tempio, built like a shell around the older church, remained uncompleted at Sigismundo's death in 1461; like the *Cantos* it turned out to be a monument coextensive with the life of its creator. In every way, its architecture and decoration were given high humanist significance. It is a monument both to Christian and to pagan gods; to Sigismundo's own fame; and to his great love for his mistress, later his wife, Isotta, who appears in many guises in the carvings on its walls. The intertwined letters *I* and *S* are everywhere.

Polixena / The building of the shrine to his "goddess" Isotta was going on while Sigismundo was still married to Sforza's daughter. She died in 1449. Twelve years later, Sforza and the pope, both of whom were out to crush Malatesta, accused him of having her strangled.

*Page 13 (21–22)*

Feddy / Federigo d'Urbino, like Malatesta one of the great *condottieri* and patrons of the arts of his age. The two clashed throughout their lifetimes.

Foscari / Francesco Foscari, Doge of Venice during the height of Venetian power and prosperity. Malatesta from time to time hired himself out to Venice.

Classe / The beautiful Sant'Apollinare in Classe (Pound's "Apollinaire," one of his favorite churches), outside Ravenna. Sigismundo bribed the cardinal of Bologna to allow him to despoil Sant'Apollinare of its stone, which was smuggled away at night, to be used for the Tempio. Malatesta was later forced to make restitution to Ravenna.

*Casus est talis* / "The case is such."

Ill^{mo} D° / *Illustrissimo Domino,* "Most Illustrious Lord." Pound liked to give the flavor of the orthography of the documents he was working from.

Ariminum / Latin name for Rimini.

Santa Maria in Trivio / The Church of San Franscesco, now being turned into the Tempio, had formerly borne this name and before that may have been a temple of Venus.

## Page 14 (22–23)

German-Burgundian female / Another of the many scandals in Malatesta's life. The story, one of the many crimes Pius II accused him of, was that a German lady, visiting Rimini, resisted Sigismundo's advances and that he killed and then raped her.

Poliorcetes / Taker, or besieger of cities, epithet given to Malatesta by Pisanello, who cast superb portrait medals of Sigismundo and Isotta.

Polumetis / "Of many contrivances," Homer's epithet for Odysseus. Sigismundo is an Odyssean figure—alert, clever, a "receiver of all things"—but here the *polumetis* is slightly ironic: He is interested in so many things, principally work on the Tempio, that he wants time off from his job as Venetian commander. But, as the Venetians asked him on the preceding page, "Did he think the campaign was a joy-ride?"

Broglio / Malatesta's lieutenant, who wrote a *Chronicle* from which Pound has taken details.

*m'l'ha calata* / "He put that over on me" or "he got me." In a
last attempt to take Pesaro, Malatesta besieged Alessandro Sforza.
Urbino came to Alessandro's rescue and badly defeated Sigismundo's forces.

Istria / The quarries at Istria provided the "salt-white stone"
used extensively at Venice and for the Tempio's facade.

Silk War / A Venetian campaign for commercial and maritime
dominance of the Adriatic.

Vada / In Tuscany, site of another campaign. Sigismundo set
up his *bombarde* (a kind of cannon) in the swampy land below
the town. In Canto 41, we hear that, after two thousand years of
being useless, these marshes have been drained and are producing
grain.

Siena / The decline of Malatesta's fortunes is shown by his
having to take this small job in Siena's campaign against its
neighbor, the count of Pitigliano. Sigismundo, former captain
general of the papal and Venetian forces, is now a star reduced to
taking bit parts, as Pitigliano points out to him in a letter quoted
in Canto 10:

> ". . . but if you will hire yourself out to a
> "commune (Siena) which you ought rather to rule than
> "serve . . ."

## Page 15 (23–24)

his post-bag / The Sienese, not entirely trusting their hired
commander, grabbed his post-bag to look for evidence of treachery.
The contents of the post-bag are still at Siena. They are concerned
only with domestic affairs and with the building of the Tempio.
Excerpts from Malatesta's intercepted mail make up the next four
pages.

*Ex Arimino,* etc. / "From Rimini 20 December. 'Magnificent
and powerful lord, my most excellent lord.' "

master Alwidge / Craftsman working on the Tempio. His name
appears below as "Master alwise."

*Magnifico, etc.* / "Magnificent and most excellent. My lord." The letter is from Isotta, and Pound gives an English equivalent of the semiliterate Italian in which it is written.

**Mr. Genare** / Petrus Genariis, Malatesta's secretary, who wrote the long final letter beginning on page 17.

**Albert** / the great architect-humanist, Alberti, whose work Sigismundo had admired at Florence and whom he imported to design the Tempio.

**Sagramoro** / One of Malatesta's counsellors.

**Messire Battista** / Alberti.

## Page 16 (24–25)

**Sr. Galeazzo's daughter** / Sigismundo's devotion to Isotta did not keep him from other women. He got into a scrape over a citizen's daughter, and Isotta had to smooth things out. His correspondent says, *"Mi pare che avea decto hogni chossia"* [It seems to me she said it all].

**Madame Lucrezia** / Malatesta's daughter by Isotta, to whom he was not married when these letters were written.

**Messire Malatesta** / His son by Isotta, Sallustio, who writes the thank-you letter on the next page, signing himself Malatesta de Malatestis. At twenty-two, two years after his father's death, he was murdered by his older half brother, Roberto. In a power struggle over Rimini, Roberto, who became a famous *condottiere* in his own right, overthrew Isotta, whom Sigismundo had named regent.

**Rambottom** / Georgio Ranbutino, a stonemason engaged to work on the Tempio. This "comic" nameplay throughout the *Cantos* often seems sophomoric, but Pound wants constantly to remind us that we are not reading a "historical reconstruction," but a poem written in and about the twentieth century.

**Lunarda da Palla** / Probably Sallustio's tutor.

*Page 17 (25–26)*

*Malatesta de Malatestis,* etc. / The six-year-old Sallustio writing to his father: "Malatesta of the Malatestas to his Magnificent Lord and Father."

Ex<sup>so</sup> D<sup>no</sup> (*Excellentissimo Domino*), etc. the salutation: Most Excellent Lord and Lord without Lord, Sigismundo Malatesta, Son of Pandolfo, Captain General."

*Magnifice ac potens domine,* etc. / "Magnificent and powerful lord, my most excellent lord, permit me this humble recommendation."

*Page 18 (26–27)*

Antonio degli Atti / Isotta's brother.

The tomb / It is Isotta's. Less a tomb than a monument to his love, Malatesta had begun it as early as twenty-four years before her death. Hovering above it, in lordly protection, is the carved figure of a crowned helmet; it is surrounded by elephants (Malatesta's emblem), roses (Isotta's emblem), and shields with the intertwined initials *I* and *S*. On the wall above are scrolls with the motto *Tempus Loquendi, Tempus Tacendi* [a time for speaking, a time for silence], which appears again at the opening of Canto 31—and on the dedicatory page of *Selected Cantos.*

*Page 19 (27)*

*et amava perdutamente,* etc. / In 1456, Malatesta made Isotta his third wife. So far she has only been mentioned twice in the canto, and then almost casually. Yet the whole canto is about her, in a sense, for she stands at the center of the complex art-love-humanism-religion that makes Sigismundo's effort heroic. Pound has composed this lyrical tribute to her out of assorted documents and inscriptions: "and he loved Isotta degli Atti to distraction, and she was worthy of him, constant in purpose, pleasing to the eyes of the Prince, beautiful to look at, beloved by the people, the grace (or honor) of Italy."

"and built a temple so full of pagan works" / Quoted from the edict issued by Malatesta's enemy, Pius II. The pope charged him with heresy, ordered him to appear at Rome to be burned at the stake, and when Sigismundo failed to show up, had him burned in effigy on the steps of Saint Peter's. As proof of heresy, the pope pointed to the Tempio, saying, *"templum aedificavit,"* that is, a *pagan* temple. In Canto 89 we hear, of another hero, that

> Andy Jackson
> POPULUM AEDIFICAVIT
> which might end this canto, and rhyme with
> Sigismundo.

"Past ruin'd Latium" / The allusion is to Walter Savage Landor's "Past ruin'd Ilion Helen lives." Pound has changed Ilion to Latium in tribute to Sigismundo and Isotta. Landor's poem is about the power of art to give "Immortal Youth to mortal Maids" when "Verse calls them forth." So Helen survives the ruins of Troy; Isotta, the ruins of Sigismundo's ambitions; and Landor's Ianthe, the "peopled Hills" now hidden in "Oblivion's deepening Veil." Isotta, a mortal maid who became Sigismundo's goddess, carved in stone on the Tempio's walls, remains a goddess throughout the *Cantos*. In Canto 74 we see exactly the movement of the tradition:

> stone knowing the form which the carver imparts it
> the stone knows the form
> sia Cythera, sia Ixotta, sia in Santa Maria dei Miracoli

In Canto 76 she appears to the poet in his prison:

> Dirce et Ixotta e che fu chiamata Primavera
> in the timeless air

> that they suddenly stand in my room here
> between me and the olive tree

the old sarcophagi / The sarcophagi along the outer wall of the Tempio form part of its total concept. They were to hold the bones of all the artists and humanists Sigismundo had brought to Rimini. He plundered the grave of the Platonist, Gemistus Plethon, to have the ashes for the Tempio—a gesture of piety that combines Sigismundo's rapacity, learning, idealism, and sense of drama.

San Vitale / The imitation of antique sarcophagi on the Tempio resembles the Roman sarcophagi that may still be seen outside the Church of San Vitale in Ravenna. The canto ends, like Canto 4, with modern eyes observing the remains of ruined Latium.

◊　◊

# CANTO 13

THE POPULAR IMAGE of Confucius in the West is as a purveyor of fortune-cookie wisdom and as the founder of one of the "religions" of China, one largely devoted to ancestor worship. Pound, studying closely the Confucian texts, took Confucius for his guide as he was to take no other philosopher. If we had to choose between reading the *Cantos* and reading Confucius ("Kung" in Canto 13), Pound, I believe, would prefer that we read Confucius. In 1937 he concluded an essay, "Immediate Need of Confucius," with the sentence, "Men suffer malnutrition by millions because their overlords dare not read the *Ta Hio* [the *Great Digest* or *Great Learning*]." When Pound's friend Eliot asked in print exactly what Mr. Pound believed, he replied, "I believe the *Ta Hio*."

He believed a good deal more than that, of course: for one thing, that the gods exist and that we must seek harmony with "the vital universe." But the point of the *Ta Hio* (the first chapter of which "you may treat as a *mantram*") was precisely that centuries-old disputes over metaphysics and religion need not be settled before a man, or group of people, and with luck the leader of a government, could agree on standards of sanity and social responsibility. If philosophers and theologians, like historians, were to leave blanks in their writings "for things they didn't know," that would not prevent a man from getting up and doing something useful. Confucius did not deny a life after death; he merely said nothing about it. There were more important things to talk about, things one knew, things close at hand, small disorders that lay within one's scope to rectify. "It is perhaps more true of Confucius than of any equally famous thinker," H. G. Creel writes, "that he divorced ethics from metaphysics." The *Ta Hio* suggests a place to begin (at home), and a scale to work on (modest).

Canto 13 suggests the major themes in Confucianism, but is hardly an exposition of them. Or rather, it is an exposition in the musical, not the rhetorical, sense. The *Cantos* continues to work out, in hundreds of fragments from history, its Confucian and non-Confucian gestures; it intends to sensitize our minds to recognize them. We come to think of John Adams as Confucian in his sense of public responsibility and in his concern for balance and the precise word; and of Sir Basil Zaharoff, munitions salesman and financier, as not. When in Canto 52 Lord Palmerston says, "Begin where you are," and goes on to fight the smoke nuisance in London and to dredge the harbor at Sligo, he is being Confucian; those who want to "bust out of the kosmos" (C.105) are not. A black soldier at an army prison near Pisa displays the Confucian virtue of "brotherly deference" to his prisoner, an aging poet. And on every page of the *Cantos,* there is the concern for *ching ming,* the precise definition of terms, which is the fulcrum of the system proposed in the *Ta Hio.*

Looking at the heart of that system, we may wish to reconsider the word *modest* used above to describe the individual's scope. It has two parts. First:

The men of old wanting to clarify and diffuse throughout the empire that light which comes from looking straight into the heart and then acting, first set up good government in their own states; wanting good government in their states, they first established order in their own families; wanting order in the home, they first disciplined themselves; desiring self-discipline, they rectified their own hearts; and wanting to rectify their hearts, they sought precise verbal definitions of their inarticulate thoughts; wishing to attain precise verbal definitions, they set out to extend their knowlege to the utmost. This completion of knowledge is rooted in sorting things into organic categories.

The *Ta Hio* presents a demanding program, somewhat puritanical in the scrupulous vigilance with which it seeks the moral implication of the smallest gesture. Then it considers the fruits of such vigilance, as it moves outward in a widening spiral:

> When things had been classified in organic categories, knowledge moved toward fulfillment; given the extreme knowable points, the inarticulate thoughts were defined with precision. Having attained this precise verbal definition, they then stabilized their hearts, they disciplined themselves; having attained self-discipline, they set their own houses in order; having order in their own homes, they brought good government to their own states; and when their own states were well governed, the empire was brought into equilibrium.

It is a path equally open to "the Emperor, Son of Heaven" and to "the common man."

Canto 13 is an image, however, not an argument, suggesting, as poetry, that the Confucian clarity and sensibility are more productive of individual and social good than are the confusion and perverted sensibility presented in Canto 14. The two cantos are juxtaposed to achieve the sharpest possible contrast between ways men relate to natural law. They are extremes, and the rest of the poem is sufficiently concerned with the human complexities and contradictions (Malatesta, for example) that are the ambiguous ground that lies between them. There are, and this is good Confucian teaching, "gradations" and "distinctions in clarity" (C.84).

The emphasis in the Confucianism of Canto 13 is on ethical wisdom; its function in the poem at this point is to remind us of alternatives to the greed and disorder that dominate the chronicles of the West in the first thirty cantos. Later, we will see the ethical Confucianism of Canto 13 supplemented by another more "religious" wisdom, as Pound attempts to bring his Confucianism, his paganism, and his Christian neoplatonism into harmony. Here, he is content to note that Kung "said nothing of the 'life after death.'" As he wrote in *Guide to Kulchur*, "The concentration or emphasis on eternity is not social. The sense of responsibility, the need for coordination of individuals expressed in Kung's teaching differs radically both from early Christian absolutism and from the maritime adventure morals of Odysseus or the loose talk of argumentative greeks."

Canto 13 first appeared in 1924, when Pound's study of the Confucian writings had hardly begun. He is still an outsider visiting a spiritually exotic country; yet he is aware that Confucius will be useful in the struggle against the forces he opposes. Of course, Confucius, like everything else Pound brings from the past into the present, has to be made new, as one of his favorite passages in the *Ta Hio* teaches:

> In letters of gold on T'ang's bathtub:
>
> AS THE SUN MAKES IT NEW
> DAY BY DAY MAKE IT NEW
> YET AGAIN MAKE IT NEW.

Equivalents had to be found for whatever Confucius meant by "the Odes," "brotherly deference," the "lord of a province." And what would it mean to "stand fast in the middle" in terms of life in the twentieth century?

The restless, irritable bard who is telling this "tale of the tribe" can spend a short while walking by the dynastic temple and into the cedar grove, but something in his temperament is attracted to that other temple, the one we have just left in Canto 9. Eccentric, not wearing its learning lightly, restless, "almost sacrilegious in its boldness," the Tempio had been built around and over a plain dynastic temple, the old Church of San Francesco. It is as much a gesture of contempt for its surroundings as it is an act of love. We leave the quiet and wisdom of Canto 13 for the noise and evil of Canto 14, and the *Cantos* continues as the record of its epic speaker's search for a point of rest. In the modern age it is difficult to find a dynastic temple that is just *there* to walk by or to worship in.

A story in the *Analects* reflects the simultaneous awareness of human failure and of an imperative for constructive action, an awareness central to an understanding of the *Cantos*:

> Tzu Lu happened to pass the night in Shi-men. The gatekeeper asked: "Where are you from?" "From Master Kung's" was the reply. "Is he not the one," said the man, "who knows that what he does is in vain yet keeps on trying to do so?"

The last three lines of Canto 13 (the only lines with no direct source in the Confucian Classics) give Confucius an elegiac, perhaps tragic note that is not usually his:

> The blossoms of the apricot
> > blow from the east to the west,
> And I have tried to keep them from falling.

It foreshadows Pound's understanding, which becomes dramatically explicit in the Pisan cantos, that the empire will not be brought into equilibrium, and that the city whose terraces are the color of stars will be built only in the mind. Yet to know that is not to be relieved of the effort to build it.

◊   ◊   ◊

Canto 13 requires few notes. Its luminous clarity is a poetic gesture: The tonality of Kung's mind and teachings, the order he creates around him, are not "interesting" in the manner of the chronicles of the Odyssean West.

Khieu, Tchi, Tian, Tseu-lou, and Thseng-sie are disciples of Kung/Confucius.

Yuan Jang is said to have been an old acquaintance who had become a Taoist. Kung's attack is not on one man's laziness, but on a mystical quietism. Pound's Confucianism is aggressively opposed to that strain in Taoism, the only strain he recognized, that produces statements such as, "Therefore the sage keeps to the deed that consists in taking no action." The long history of China in Cantos 52 through 61 attempts to demonstrate that the empire was healthy when Confucian principles were respected, decadent when "taozers" and Buddhists held influence.

In mentioning Wang as model ruler, Confucius follows the practice, important throughout the Confucian texts, of invoking exemplary rulers of the early Chou dynasty (about six centuries before his lifetime) and the earlier legendary rulers Yao, Chun, and Yu. In his own decadent age of "Warring States," he found no princes to match them. In Canto 53 we hear him saying, "I am pro-Tcheou . . . [Chou] in politics."

Confucius was born in 551 B.C., in the small state of Lu, in a period when all central authority had broken down in the empire; a combination of high civilization and barbarism prevailed, similar to that portrayed in the Malatesta cantos. The teachings of Confucius were first addressed to the immediate disorders of his age. He never meant to spend his life as a teacher. Ideas were not to be discussed for their own sake but to be put into action, and Confucius wanted a ministerial post. He never achieved a responsible government post (though in time his students did), and in his fifties he left the state of Lu for ten years of wandering. The years of exile brought further disappointment, as he and his disciples went from state to state seeking a ruler who might adopt the Confucian point of view. Such a ruler was never found, and Confucius returned to Lu, where he taught in semiobscurity ("we are unknown") until his death in 479 B.C.

It is generally agreed that Confucius, like Socrates and Jesus, wrote nothing (the bo leaves are legendary), so that what we know of him comes through his disciples and their disciples, followed by centuries of emendations and legends. Pound made little effort to thread his way through the intricacies of Confucian textual scholarship; his Confucianism is that part of the Confucian classics he considered important. Other Confucians have heard other things. Yet Pound's Confucius is by no means the construct of his fancy. Amateur as he was, he was guided by the work of older scholars such as Pauthier, Legge, Couvreur, and Lacharme, and it is only in insignificant detail that his Confucius differs from that of one of the leading modern authorities on the philosopher, H. G. Creel. For readers who are interested in going beyond Pound's translations and discussions I recommend Creel's *Chinese Thought from Confucius to Mao Tse-Tung* and his more detailed study, which has appeared under two titles, *Confucius: The Man and the Myth* and *Confucius and the Chinese Way*. The best introductions to Pound's Confucius are first his translations of *Ta Hio* (*The Great Digest*) and *Chung Yung* (*The Unwobbling Pivot*); then the *Analects,* which are somewhat harder to read because fragmentary and loosely arranged; then his essays "Immediate Need of Confucius" and "Mang Tsze (The Ethics of Mencius)" in *Selected Prose*.

◊　◊

# CANTO 14

CANTOS 13 AND 14 are mutually exclusive worlds, as sharp a contrast as any in the poem. The hell of Cantos 14 and 15 becomes more grotesque, more deprived of Confucian "benevolence" or "humanity," as the memory of the walk by the dynastic temple remains in the mind. The falling apricot blossoms at the end of Canto 13 are the last mention of organic nature, or of anything noble or beautiful, for the space of the two hell cantos.

We are in a landscape from which every possibility of natural increase has been excluded, a landscape of coal, ooze, shit, dry dust, acid, an unproductive soil of pus and decrepitude. It is a landscape appropriate for its inhabitants, because in life—although this *is* their life—they stood against natural increase. Their sex life is limited to masturbating; a condom is filled with black beetles. The condom is merely waved, the masturbating is done on a tin whistle, for they deny themselves even perverted pleasures of the senses. The connection between social and sexual perversion is Dantesque, and we are reminded that in the *Inferno* Dante found usurers and sodomites in the same circle, each the reverse image of the other: the sodomites making the naturally fertile infertile; the usurers making the naturally infertile (money, coin) to "grow." "Metal is durable, but it does not reproduce itself," Pound reminds us. "Fascinated by the lustre of metal, man made it into chains. Then he invented something against nature, a false representation in the mineral world of laws which apply only to animals and vegetables."

The figures in Canto 14 are anonymous, for if they had displayed a trace of Confucian responsibility, which would imply individuality, the pilgrim could not stare at them, as he does, without compassion. Yet the scatological landscape invented for them implies no lack of humanity on the part of the poet. "Only the fully humane man," says the *Ta Hio,* "can love another: or can really hate him." Pound quotes from Spinoza: "The love of a thing consists in the understanding of its perfections," and comments that "Spinoza's statement distinctly includes knowing what they (the perfections) are NOT." Cantos 14 and 15 are the poem's most concentrated image of that NOT.

Given what Pound saw in Dante, it became almost inevitable that his own hell would be modeled on the *Inferno.* Dante's "whole hell reeks with money. . . . Deep hell is reached via Geryon (fraud) of the marvellous patterned hide, and for ten cantos thereafter the damned are all of them damned for money." "Dante MEANT *plutus,* definitely putting money-power at the root of Evil, and was not merely getting muddied in his mythology." (The name *Plutus,* associated with Hades, derives from the Greek for "wealth.") If the *Divine Comedy* and the *Cantos* are poems including history, it follows for Pound that they must include economics, for no one but a "sap-head can now think he knows any history until he understands economics." The state of mind presented in Canto 14 is the "grab-at-once state of mind," which is "predatory, not statal." To identify it is, for Pound, to begin to recapture something we have lost in our time, "the medieval discrimination between productive and destructive investment."

If Canto 14 is like the *Inferno* in some ways, it is unlike it in others. Dante's hell is vast, varied, and not "without dignity, without tragedy." Dante's pilgrim is moved at times to contempt, at times to compassion, as he meets with individuals, personalities, a wider range than in either Purgatory or Paradise. The most intense suffering reserved for Dante's damned is something Pound denies his: awareness of the state to which they have brought themselves.

The souls Dante meets still seek news from home and beg him to bring back messages to the living. Pound has deliberately stripped his minihell of all but a grotesque pantomime of humanity. We are asked to feel no more for its inhabitants than we do for the figures in a Bosch.

This is satire without the aim of reforming its immediate subjects. We feel no impulse to approach these men, to discuss anything with them. That there is even an "I," a pilgrim who sees them there, is suggested only by the *Io* of the opening quotation from Dante; then the pilgrim himself disappears until in Canto 15, guided by Plotinus, he emerges "Panting like a sick dog," into the sunlight.

It is clear to *us* that the denizens of Canto 14 are suffering, or should be. *They* are unaware of it; their hell is a world they make and take for granted. What suffering they know is the same they would have had back at the office. They howl, not in physical or spiritual pain, but in frustration that diamonds (say, works of art) will not be stained in their mud. Their noisy howls are merely an extension of the obscuring din they set up to distract their fellow citizens from perceiving what is going on. In hell, they go about their normal business, addressing crowds, running printing presses, preaching sermons, obscuring texts that might reveal uncomfortable truths. The awareness of the stink, the rot, the shit dripping through the air is all the poet's and ours. In Canto 15, the conservatives, unaware of their surroundings, go on "chatting, / distinguished by gaiters of slum-flesh."

Pound presents them as nameless grotesques within a scatological landscape in "bad taste," precisely because these people have, in Cambridge or in the City, at the Hamptons or in Wall Street, the trappings of respectability. They are not, we note, the great profiteers and financiers, but their underlings—press lords, bishops, professors, politicians—the point being that Usura is smart enough to employ the voices we should most expect to hear raised against it. The common denominator for the members of this corporation is presented in the slowing cadence of the last two lines:

monopolists, obstructors of knowledge,
    obstructors of distribution.

The corporation is nothing as narrow as "bankers," but a gigantic conspiracy, not always aware of its own complicity. The monopoly, as Pound sees it, may be in gold or on God. The knowledge may be of the full implications of the words printed on our money, or of the classics, increasingly removed from the curriculum. The obstructed distribution may be of purchasing power, or of writers Pound thinks should have wider circulation. The darkness here is not physical (for we see quite clearly) but of that Spirit which, when it "enters the rational spirit, it inflames it with its own divine ardour and transforms its qualities into its own likeness, so that it shows forth the love of its author, as is fitting."

There are those who object to the combine of darkness in the hell cantos as projecting a shallow or inadequate vision of Evil. T. S. Eliot's most famous complaint, in *After Strange Gods,* is clever word play ("a Hell without dignity implies a Heaven without dignity also"), but some of his other complaints are more just:

> Hell, for all its horrors, is a perfectly comfortable one for the modern mind to contemplate, and disturbing to no one's complacency: it is a Hell for the *other people,* the people we read about in the newspapers, not for oneself and one's friends.

That is so. At least in cantos written before 1945, there is nothing like the sense of separation from the Good, or from God, that we find in *The Waste Land* or in *Four Quartets. After Strange Gods* reflects Eliot's search for a tradition that includes Original Sin, a term not in Pound's vocabulary. When Pound quotes from Christian theologians, he never selects passages about the Fall or Depravity; rather, phrases about the Light and Right Reason. The Dantean *directio voluntatis,* "direction of the will," seems naturally available to all men, if few avail themselves properly of it. Eliot is right, too, in suggesting that Pound flatters his readers, although that is more true of his prose than of his poetry. Like a good teacher, he makes us aware that we have not done our homework, have not fought the good fight intensely enough, have allowed stale formulations and imprecise definitions to clog our understanding; yet the conspiratorial rhetoric makes us feel the mere fact that we are reading Pound means that we are, after all, on the right side, heading in the right direction.

D. S. Carne-Ross, writing in 1950, and in a much larger context than a criticism of the hell cantos, extended (in an opinion later modified) Eliot's central complaint:

> Pound's good is excellent but never radical. And his evil is of the same sort. Primarily monetary, issuing in usury and the corruption of the will which usury produces, it gives no hint of permanent essential Evil underlying this or that manifestation. And yet the Vision of Evil is perhaps the most searching test of a writer's quality. . . . But it does not appear in the Cantos.
> Their fundamental weakness is that they do not show any real religious comprehension. Lacking it, Pound has not been able to dispose of sufficiently powerful forces to move a mighty poem; he presents a vision of good, which does not satisfy our deepest demands, checked and thwarted by an evil which is never radical enough.

In 1950, of course, the later cantos had not been written, and in them the religious comprehension deepens considerably. Yet it remains true for Pound, as has been said of Confucius, that the secular is sacred and that, as he wrote in 1940, "the idea of good government is perhaps the highest idea we can ever translate into action." That is not the same as saying that the secular is all there is nor that good government is the highest idea of which we can be aware, or by which we can be inspired.

I had always taken it for granted that Pound's usury was not a technicality but a manifestation of something permanent in human nature. Yet Pound, in one of his last published statements, dated 4 July 1972, felt impelled to deepen his definition:

> re USURY:
> I was out of focus, taking a symptom for a cause.
> The cause is AVARICE.

Yet agreeing, at least in respect to Cantos 1 through 71, that the poem lacks the profoundest emotional and philosophic power, we should not consider Cantos 14 and 15 in isolation nor place the burden of Pound's vision of evil entirely upon them. "Their function in the poem," Suzanne K. Langer says, "is that of a violent dissonance." They are a savage comic book, aimed at producing disgust; a cartoon whose justification, at this point, is the artist's revulsion. We look at certain drawings by Bosch, Posada, or Gillray, with no obligation to find a summa in them. In a copy of Dürer's prints, *The Four Angels Holding the Winds* and *The Four Horsemen of the Apocalypse* stand on facing pages, forming a diptych like Cantos 13 and 14, part of a life's work, but not all of it.

◊   ◊   ◊

### Page 23 (*31*)

Io venni in luogo d'ogni luce muto / *Inferno* 5.28: "I came to a place where every light was dumb." Dante has arrived at the Second Circle, but Canto 14 does not correspond exactly to any circle of the *Inferno*. The perverted money-lust of Pound's damned has muted the light of nature and reason.

. . . . . . . . . e and . . . . . n / Their names are *"not* worth recording as such. . . . My 'point' being that not even the first but only the last letters of their names had resisted corruption."

### Page 24 (*31–32*)

ΕΙΚΩΝ ΓΗΣ / *Eikōn Gēs,* "Image of the Earth." Not Pound's image, but what these people would have it.

THE PERSONNEL CHANGES / These individuals are not themselves the source of Evil but are in the pay of Usura. That they are safely in hell is no comfort, for they are easily replaced. The system itself is the Great Beast, greater than the individual greed of its members.

Pearse and Macdonagh / They were executed by the British for taking part in the Irish uprising of 1916. Yeats paid them memorial tribute in "Easter, 1916."

Verres / The time shift reminds us that the subject is a perennial force with changing personnel. Verres, Roman governor of Sicily, was notorious for corruption and greed. As Cicero pointed out at Verres's trial in 70 B.C., the question was not his corruption, which was clear, but whether or not corrupt gains can reach a point of critical mass, accumulate enough power to lie beyond justice.

Calvin / Pound saw him as an "arch-heretic," encouraging the bigotry that leads to military and economic warfare. "The Church slumped into a toleration of usury. Protestantism as factive and organised, may have sprung from nothing but pro-usury politics."

St. Clement of Alexandria / An early father of the Church, he attacked paganism and was an earlier "explainer" of Christ's words about selling what you have and giving it to the poor. "Clement," says a historian of the primitive Church, "was at pains to show that wealthy pagans should not turn away from the Church because of the mistaken impression that it was the religion of the poor only." In short, Calvin and Saint Clement participated in making Christianity not uncomfortable for the rich.

*Page 25 (32–33)*

frigging / Masturbating.

pets-de-loup / Wolf-farts; slang for university scholars.

corruptio, foetor / Corruption, stink.

◇  ◇

## CANTO 16

WITH CANTO 16, the poem arrives firmly in the twentieth century, as it moves through references to Ovid, Augustine, Dante, Blake, Byron, and the Franco-Prussian War, into the Europe of 1914–1918—or more precisely, 1914–1918 seen from the point of view of postwar disillusion. As Hugh Kenner points out, the war casts its shadow throughout the *Cantos:* "Wars, ruins, destruction—a crumbling wall in Mantua, smoke over Troy—these are never far out of mind. . . . This is postwar poetry, as much so as *The Waste Land*."

The central theme of the canto is clear: a deromanticized view of war. The landscape, however, is more confusing than it need be. Its local precisions seem to demand allegorization, yet the clues are not strong enough. The overriding image is the Dantesque emergence from hell and arrival at the lower slopes of Mount Purgatory, but while Pound goes to some trouble not to imitate the first cantos of the *Purgatorio* slavishly, the magnetism of Dante's pattern may be too strong for the divergences from it. Why is Augustine here? Why "limbo"? Why two mountains?

The first part of the resumed journey leads through an unattractive landscape, with an acid lake in which criminals are being purified, and a swamp (an image of history?) in which an embryonic, eellike humanity writhes and from which an arm briefly emerges with its "fragment of marble," a symbol of civilization, only to be submerged again. We then find ourselves in a more pleasant district, an "oasis" of "light air," trees, a "blue banded lake," only to return *under* the earth again. The descent, however, leads not back to hell, but to a quiet place with nymphs and fountains, clearly a "good" place, inhabited by heroes and founders of cities, probably modeled on the Elysian Fields in Book 6 of the *Aeneid*. In that quiet place, the pilgrim seems to lie down to rest and hears, in a dream, voices speaking of war. At this point we may find ourselves puzzled, wondering why we have come to a region that may strike us as "paradisal," only to find ourselves suddenly back in the "infernal."

Our difficulty in seeing that Canto 16 is a Purgatory may have two sources. First, at this point in the poem, Pound has not established the nature of his Paradise, which is filled with images of light and flashing transfers of energy quite unlike this restful, pastoral region with its diffused "light as after a sunset." A second difficulty comes from the readiness with which we associate "war" and "hell." Yet Canto 16 does not take us into the war itself; rather, we hear purgatorial voices remembering the war. The dreamer and the speakers in his dream are in a Dantesque Purgatory that has been, perhaps confusingly, syncretized with Virgil's Elysian Fields. The important distinction is that Pound's hell is reserved for the men who *make* war, while the Purgatory of Canto 16 is reserved for those who have had to endure it. The warriors here have participated in the "hell" of war, but they are not responsible for the causes of war.

*Mauberley* contains lines more biting than anything in the *Cantos,* dissecting the false rhetoric and romantic gestures that brought men to the trenches:

Died some, pro patria
               non "dulce" non "decor" . . .
walked eye-deep in hell
believing old men's lies, then unbelieving
came home, home to a lie,
home to many deceits,
home to old lies and new infamy;
usury age-old and age-thick
and liars in public places

The Great War, as it has become a commonplace to say, was the hardest war yet to romanticize: the swagger of the war-loving troubadour Bertrans de Born, Pound thought, had been "much more impressive before 1914 than it has been since 1920." The men who were killed, wounded, shell-shocked were no longer members of a military caste only; they were one's friends: Lewis, Hulme, Gaudier-Brzeska.

Of all the names in the World War I passage, Gaudier's is the most important. The impact of his death in battle, and the waste of his talent influenced the shape the *Cantos* would take. Pound kept his memory alive, beginning in 1916 with *Gaudier-Brzeska: A Memoir*. In 1918 Pound wrote, "He is irreplaceable"; and in 1934:

> For eighteen years the death of Henri Gaudier has been unremedied. The work of two or three years remains, but the uncreated went with him.
>
> There is no reason to pardon this either to the central powers or to the allies or to ourselves. . . . With a hundred fat rich men working overtime to start another war or another six wars for the sake of their personal profit, it is very hard for me to write of Gaudier with the lavender tones of dispassionate reminiscence.

Canto 16 is less about the horrors of war than it is an astringent attempt to deromanticize war and revolution, to show men behaving unheroically and with no clear purpose. The anonymous veteran who speaks in French tells us that men behaved as usual, bringing their vices to the trenches. Hulme goes on reading and receives an overdue notice from the London Library. Lewis escapes death because he is in the latrine when shells strike his unit. Hemingway's touch of out-of-date bravado is mocked, "too much in a hurry."

The introduction to the passage is neatly constructed as romantic remnants of other wars fall away before the war that will not lend itself to romance. First there is the double vision of a moment from the Franco-Prussian War. A seven-year-old boy watches a swashbuckling charge "for the honour of the army," and thinks, as only a boy should think, "This is pretty bloody damn fine." But the story is being told by the boy grown up, remembering the rotting corpse in the street.

The four-line coda is handled with a delicate irony Pound does not often control. As Paul Fussell points out in *The Great War and Modern Memory*:

What makes experience in the Great War unique and gives it a special freight of irony is the ridiculous proximity of the trenches to home. Just seventy miles from "this stinking world of sticky trickling earth" was the rich plush of London theater seats and the perfume, alcohol, and cigar smoke of the Café Royal. The avenue to these things was familiar and easy: on their two-week leaves from the front, the officers rode the same Channel boats they had known in peacetime, and the presence of the same porters and stewards ("Nice to serve you again, Sir") provided a ghastly pretence of normality. One officer on leave, observed by Arnold Bennett late in 1917, "had breakfasted in the trenches and dined in his club in London."

In the final lines, we find ourselves suddenly removed from war and revolution, back in London at the opera. The "we" are the ruling class, safely out of it for a while, those whose economics have caused the war and against whom the revolution is aimed. They are insiders, with privileged gossip to exchange about the next offensive—"It" was going to begin in a week—but the implication is that things are about to begin that these opera-goers do not suspect. Unheroically, soberly, Lenin is forcing his will on a mob in the streets of Petrograd; Gaudier is dead in France; "we" return to our boxes for the next act.

◊   ◊   ◊

*Page 27 (34)*

And before hell mouth / The landscape is Dantesque without duplicating the carefully subdivided geography of the *Purgatorio*. Both Pound and Dante (their pilgrims, if we must) emerge from hell and are purified, Pound ridding himself of ticks in a lake of acid, Dante cleansing his face with dew. After a journey, each arrives at a resting place, an antepurgatory.

Blake / Portrayed in the posture of Cain in his *The Body of Abel Found by Adam and Eve,* in the Tate. The steel mountain and road like a "screw's thread" suggest the industrialism Blake protested against, as he did usury, banking, war, and colonial plunder. What David Erdman says of Blake is equally true of Pound, that he "sees all these matters as interrelated. War grows out of acquisitiveness and jealousy and mischanneled sexual energy, all of which grow out of the intrusion of possessiveness into human relations."

Peire Cardinal / Troubadour and satirist, "extremely lucid on the imbecility of belligerents and the makers of war," Pound says. He saw "the world, blind with its ignorance, its violence, and its filth."

Il Fiorentino / Dante.

lo Sordels / Dante finds Sordello brooding in the antepurgatory, and he becomes Dante's guide upward to the valley where his first day's journey ends. The encounter with Sordello occasions Dante's tirade against Italy as the home of war and dissension; Pound's denunciation of war occupies the second part of his canto. Sordello's shield and Dante's mirror are their art, in which they can look upon horrors without turning to stone, as Perseus looked at the Medusa.

Augustine / If we read the geography literally, as we should not, Pound would be demoting Augustine, whom Dante places in the highest realm of Paradise. "Gazing toward the invisible" may be intended as irony. The line does not seem very well thought through.


*Page 28 (34–35)*

flames patterned in lacquer / Dante's Purgatory is not a place of fire, except for the lustful. Here, Pound's flames seem painted in the manner of a Japanese screen. The complex of associations may be: (1) The flames attached to Cain's body (in the Blake painting that seems to be Pound's model above) are highly stylized and (2) an early influence on Pound's aesthetics was Laurence Binyon's essay on oriental art, *The Flight of the Dragon* (1911), which insists that art is not "a reproduction of the actual," and emphasizes "pattern." Pound is indicating that this is not a realistic purgatory, but what he would call an equation.

crimen est actio / "The action is the crime." Is the suggestion that, in some cases, an action is sufficient proof of guilt, without regard to motivation? The slogan appears to be inscribed on the wall containing the lacquer flames.

limbo of chopped ice / "Limbo" should not be taken too literally here; Dante's limbo is an antecircle of hell, not of Purgatory. Few readers will remember what an old-fashioned icehouse looked like: Blocks of ice were chopped or sawed from ponds in winter, then stacked, separated by layers of sawdust.

Palux Laerna / The swamp of Lerna, home of the Hydra, whose destruction was one of the labors of Hercules. After the lake of acid, the pilgrim seems to proceed along a dry path from which he observes the swamp of dead water ("aqua morta") in which generations of men rise and submerge.

clutching a fragment of marble / Donald Davie comments:

Where "marble" appears, or "stone," it is a sign of resurgence and renewed hope. The most striking example is in Canto 16, where the first glimmer of convalescence after the passage through infernal regions . . . is a hand clutching marble. After the marble comes the new inflow, the embryonic, the new potential; and twelve lines later in Canto 16 a new amplitude and tranquility. . . .
    It is this casing in hewn and chiselled stone that, in the *Cantos*, justifies Sigismundo Malatesta.

Indeed, Malatesta as builder appears within a few lines.

the tree of the bough / In the *Aeneid,* the hero must pluck a golden bough before he descends to the underworld.


*Page 29 (35–36)*

patet terra / The earth lies open, that is, for the descent that follows.

Sigismundo, and Malatesta Novello / The presence of Sigismundo is clear: As hero and builder, he displayed enough light to warrant salvation; yet he was no saint and, like most men, must bide his time in purgatory. But why his younger brother, whose nickname was Novello? He is mentioned in the Malatesta cantos, but nothing is said about him to give him this place of honor in Canto 16. The answer lies in a Poundian habit the reader may find playful, illuminating, or maddening. An inhabitant of Dante's antepurgatory is one Federico Novello, who died more than a century before Sigismundo's brother was born. There is no connection other than the name, but Pound enjoys finding these verbal correspondences, which at times (as I think here) seem pointless but at other times suggest significant recurrences that transcend chronology.

one man . . . went off into the plain / Because his time in these Elysian Fields and/or antepurgatory is over? Or does he become the one who, in the following lines, sleeps in the grass and hears voices telling of modern wars?

et j'entendis des voix / "And I heard voices."

Plarr's narration / An eyewitness account of a charge led by the French general, Gallifet, against the Prussians at Strasbourg in 1870. Victor Plarr (the "M. Verog" of *Mauberley*), born in Strasbourg, was seven when he saw the "swashbuckling" action. He became a minor English poet whom Pound knew and respected.

*Page 30 (36–38)*

Brother Percy / Puzzling. The *Annotated Index to the Cantos* suggests Lord Algernon Percy, a British naval officer who died in 1865. Shelley has also been suggested, given the presence of Byron, but this seems far-fetched. In the context of the canto, which is about the collapse of possibilities for seeing war as romantic, another candidate might be the most famous Percy in literature, Shakespeare's Hotspur, though he is always "cousin Percy," not "brother."

Silk War / Canto 9: "And we sent men to the Silk War." The Venetian forces in this fifteenth-century struggle over trade routes were led by Malatesta's father. The suggestion is that imperialist nations have been sending forces to Ragusa over a period of four hundred years.

Franz Joseph / Emperor of Austria, who died in 1916. Pound always emphasizes him as one of the men responsible for the Great War.

Napoléon Barbiche / Napoleon III, *barbiche* because of his goatee. In Canto 38 he is presented as a warmonger dealing with international munitions salesmen.

Aldington, etc. / Gaudier and T.E.H. (Hulme) were killed in the war; the others survived. All the reader must know is that these men were friends of Pound's, who is putting together a pastiche of war experiences based on oral history. Richard Aldington: one of the original Imagists of 1912. Henri Gaudier-Brzeska: young sculptor and Vorticist, killed in France in 1915. T. E. Hulme: poet and philosopher who had considerable influence (on Pound and Eliot among others) in prewar London. B. C. Windeler: a writer connected with Pound's Paris circle in the early 1920s. Captain Baker: probably an acquaintance from Pound's London years. John Gould Fletcher: American poet Pound knew in Paris and London. Hemingway: Pound often scolded that part of Hemingway that seemed eager for violence; whatever the story was, about being buried for four days, it is apocryphal, though Hemingway had been wounded in the war.

*Page 32 (38–40)*

Et ma foi, vous savez / The long passage in slangy French is another voice from the trenches. A working-class Frenchman is talking to someone he addresses as "vous," perhaps the poet. The passage is Joycean, the meticulously reported language containing its own gestures, a mixture of received opinion and of genuine insight. It may be a monologue, although possibly the four lines beginning "C'est le corr-ggras" are an interruption by the speaker's friend, the one who stayed working in the factories. My translation is very free:

And really, you know, / a lot of them were nervous. No, / There's a limit; animals, animals aren't / Made for that, a horse isn't worth much. / Thirty-four-year-old men down on all fours / crying "Mamma." But the tough guys, / At the end, over at Verdun, only the big boys were left / And they saw the whole thing very clearly. / What are they worth, generals, a lieutenant. / You can weigh them by the centigram, / they're only wood, / Our captain, everything, kept everything shut up inside himself / an old graduate from the Polytechnic, but solid, / Had a good head. Out there, you know, / Everything, everything was going on, thieves, all the vices, / But the greedy ones, / we had three in our Company, all killed. / They'd go out to rob a dead body, for nothing, / and that's all they'd go out for. / And the Krauts, say what you will about them, / militaristic, etc., etc. / All of that, but, BUT, / your Frenchman, he won't fight until he's had something to eat. / But *those* poor guys, / At the end they attacked so they could get some food, / No orders, like wild animals, we took some / Prisoners; the ones that could talk French said: / "What *for?* Come on, we attacked so we could get something to eat." / It was the grease, the grease, / their trains could only move three kilometers an hour, / And they squawked, they creaked, you could hear them five kilometers away. / (That's what ended the war.) / Official list of the dead: 5,000,000. / He tells you, well, yeah, the whole thing was about oil. / But, No! I bawled him out. / I told him: You're an idiot! You missed the war. / Oh, yeah! all the people of "taste," I admit it, / They were all in the rear. / But a guy like you! / That man, a guy like that! / What he couldn't have pocketed! / He was in a factory. / Hey, burying squad, gravediggers, with their heads / twisted around, so they could watch, like this. / They risked their life for a shovelful of dirt, / It had to be squared off, nice and even . . .

## Page 34 (40)

Dey vus a bolcheviki dere / The rest of the canto, except for the last four lines, is made up of voices talking of revolution, especially the Russian Revolution, which was going on during the last days of the war. Once again, Pound might have clarified his history or made it chronological, but he chooses to convey a sense of the confusion as well as of the threat of revolution. Much of the material is drawn from the conversation and reportage of Lincoln Steffens. Pound is presenting Steffens's view that revolutions were started, inadvertently, by the governments which were to be overthrown, rather than by the revolutionists. Essentially this passage adds to a sense of modern Europe's violence and confusion.

### Page 35 (40–41)

There was a man there talking / In Steffens's account, Lenin. After the overthrow of the czar, crowds were milling in the streets listening to speakers from many parties and factions. Lenin kept making a short, quiet speech to just a few people at a time, his theme being that the other parties could talk but only the Bolsheviks could act.

"Pojalouista" / "If you please" or "Excuse me." The much-feared Cossacks were sent out to control the crowds. Instead of charging, the Cossacks moved gently through the people, saying, "Please," an indication that they had joined the people. Forces were in action that became a "revolution" only when it was decided to call it the Revolution.

Nobody knew it was coming / The point is that the "old gang" itself, the controlling elite, fearing revolution and preparing for it, were the ones who set it off. The leaders who didn't know it was coming were the leaders of the revolution itself.

### Page 36 (41)

Haig / The final voice, representing the cultured Establishment of London, contrasts sharply with the other voices. Haig was the commander of the British forces in France.

◇

# Eleven New Cantos (1934)

◇

BETWEEN THE PUBLICATION OF *A Draft of XXX Cantos* and *Eleven New Cantos*, Pound wrote *ABC of Economics* and *Jefferson and/or Mussolini*, their titles indicating themes that become increasingly apparent in the poem. For *Selected Cantos*, he has chosen two sections from the eleven new ones: Canto 31, based on the Jefferson-Adams correspondence, and a page from Canto 38, giving the gist of his Social Credit economics.

Each new installment of the *Cantos*, from *Eleven New Cantos* through the final *Drafts and Fragments*, contains important new themes that are hinted at in earlier installments; recapitulates material from earlier volumes; and compares the past, directly or implicitly, with the twentieth century, the "blackness and mess and muddle of a 'civilization' led by disguised forces and a bought press." The new material in *Eleven New Cantos* is primarily Pound's vision of American history. The volume begins with the ideals of Adams and Jefferson and their warnings against banks and a national debt; moves to the fight against the second Bank of the United States during the administrations of Jackson and Van Buren; and ends with a contemporary investigation of the Federal Reserve System, a system that reflects the triumph of Hamilton, as "Usury ruined the Republic." The volume, dated "ad interim 1933," closes with a contrast between Jefferson and modern warmongers:

> Independent use of our money . . . toward holding our bank.
>     Mr Jefferson to Colonel Monroe
> 120 million german fuses used by the allies to kill Germans
> British gunsights from Jena

In other cantos, Pound returns to Odysseus (C.39) and, briefly, to Renaissance evils (C.35). Contrasting material includes the important Canto 36, a translation of Cavalcanti's *canzone* on the philosophy of love:

> Custom of the soul,
>     will from the heart;
> Cometh from a seen form which being understood
> Taketh locus and remaining in the intellect possible

and suggests, in Canto 40, the neoplatonism that will become increasingly important as the poem approaches Paradise:

> the NOUS, the ineffable crystal

But it is essentially Jefferson and the Adamses, John and John Quincy, who dominate *Eleven New Cantos* (which became "Jefferson—Nuevo Mundo" in *Selected Cantos*). Before 1920, Pound had shown only a superficial interest in American history, but about that time another exiled American poet, T. S. Eliot, gave him a set of the Memorial Edition of the works of Jefferson. The volumes found their way to Paris, the city from which the letters that begin Canto 31 were written. Soon, Pound was saying that Jefferson was "perhaps the last American official to have any general sense of civilization" and that Jefferson supplies an example of "the public utility of accurate language." From his study of Jefferson, Pound went on to the writings of the Adamses and Martin Van Buren.

The first suggestion that the Founding Fathers will appear in the *Cantos* is at Canto 21, first published in 1928. There, a long letter of Jefferson's is quoted, interrupted by a phrase from a letter by another "factive" personality, Malatesta. It was in the Malatesta cantos that Pound first experimented with turning documents and the contents of a postbag into poetry. In Canto 31 he continues his documentary method and tries to fit his cuttings together as carefully as he would the words of a lyric poem.

◇ ◇

## CANTO 31

*Tempus loquendi, tempus tacendi.* It had been a time for silence since 1801 when John Adams made his "midnight appointments" of Federalist judges, then departed Washington in a huff, refusing to attend Jefferson's inauguration. Ten years later it was a time for speaking again, and the two retired Presidents began the extraordinary correspondence that passed between Monticello and Quincy until their deaths on the fiftieth anniversary of the Declaration. To Ezra Pound, it seemed an outrage that almost no Americans had read that exchange of letters. It was "a Shrine and a Monument" that "ought to be in curricula." In the letters, Adams and Jefferson display minds that are curious, practical, passionate, generous, and learned. Through them the best of the Enlightenment, undistorted by impractical ideologies, shines upon possibilities for government at a particular time and place.

Pound measures the letters against the teachings of Confucius, which had, in fact, inspired the men who in turn inspired Adams and Jefferson. As rulers, the two Presidents displayed humanity and were concerned with order and equity in the State; now in retirement they are like Confucius's "real man," who "perfects the nation's culture without leaving his fireside." They have the Great Learning that is rooted in watching the way things grow. The letters show them as men who understand that, as Confucius said, "research without thought is a mere net and entanglement," while "thought without gathering data, a peril." Throughout the correspondence, they are concerned with the precise definition of terms, which lies at the heart of the Confucian ethic.

*Mutatis mutandis,* the Adams-Jefferson correspondence is in many ways like the *Cantos.* The writers survey all ages and the nature of God and man. They leap from theology to history to philosophy to the classics to economics to contemporary anecdote. They measure their wide reading against what they themselves have seen and heard, and they find connections among all their disparate subjects. Everything comes to serve the one subject on which their minds are focused: the possibilities for human happiness within an ordered society. Their entire conversation is really about good government, whether Jefferson is analyzing Greek roots or making plans for the University of Virginia; whether Adams is discussing astronomy or remembering something he heard in a Paris *salon* four decades earlier. Moreover, their sharply expressed views on banks and the nation's money confirm Pound's.

Excited by the discovery of the correspondence, Pound heard in the clarity and rhythms of its prose almost a kind of verse. In *Guide to Kulchur*, after discussing Johnson's *London* and *The Vanity of Human Wishes*, he adds:

> Johnson's verse is not as good prose as that often found in Tom Jefferson's letters. There is probably no couplet in the two reprinted poems that has the quality of Jefferson's,
> "No man has the right to be a moneylender save him who has the money to lend." Or any other of the citations on p. 116 and following of my *Jefferson and/or Mussolini*.

In the Malatesta cantos Pound had experimented with making poetry from documents, and in Canto 31 the documentary method is boldly extended. With the exception of the final *"Hic Explicit Cantus,"* the entire canto is composed from other men's language; Pound has not "written" a word but has selected, edited, and arranged Adams's and Jefferson's writings to form a pattern of his own. Their diction, prose rhythms, and tones of mind are concrete "things" from which he shapes an ideogram and a new kind of lyric poem.

Canto 31 confronts us with perhaps the most difficult problem we have yet encountered in the poem. There are, as it were, two structures, one apparent on the surface—what one can discover simply by reading carefully—and the second, a deeper structure that can be understood only when we turn to the original documents. However closely we attend to the surface of this canto itself, we are likely to remain unsatisfied, to sense that something else is going on; but we cannot know exactly what it is until we study the Adams-Jefferson letters. I am convinced that by arranging his snippets into a tightly organized "hidden" poem (somewhat in the manner of the troubadours' *trobar clus* or "obscure style"), by providing us with maddeningly cryptic fragments, Pound is trying to get us to do just that. But before turning to the documents and attempting to clarify the deeper structure of the canto, we should see what we can discover on the page itself.

The quotations are not selected merely to give the flavor of an era nor merely to suggest the qualities of Adams's and Jefferson's minds; nor is there much communicated about American history, for all the great events take place off stage and are suggested only by indirection. The Adams-Jefferson correspondence itself would ordinarily be thought of as a minor, or ancillary, contribution to an understanding of American history. Pound has arranged phrases and passages from the letters as carefully as one might arrange words and sounds in a lyric, creating patterns that provide thematic unity beneath the apparent disarray of the documentary cuttings.

The canto opens and concludes in Latin. The first Latin phrases are from the Bible (Ecclesiastes), and the last page contains a reference to Holy Scripture. "Tempus loquendi" announces a time for speaking; then the first English word is "Said." The antecedent of the "It" (in what is then said) is buried somewhere in the twenty volumes of Jefferson's writings but does not matter, for the emphasis is on "time." *Tempus* runs throughout the canto, not only in the nine specified dates and in the care with which the canto records exactly when something was said or happened, but in repetitions of "time" and in words or phrases that suggest time: *modern, prior discovery, so short a warning, worthy of former time, long live, in a few years, years before that, at the same time, tomorrow, a month, future, circumstances of times.*

The theme of *tempus tacendi* is similarly developed: Madison wryly refuses to look too deeply into human nature; Jefferson masks a dangerous word with code; Adams sits "silent" through a

conversation in his Paris hotel; Mr. Barlow must see that the enclosed letters remain secret. We are also given examples of times
when it would have been better for men to have remained silent
than to have written or spoken as they did: the English papers;
the *philosophes* whose conversations display "ignorance"; and the
generations of legal commentators who "continue this error."

The point is that Adams and Jefferson understand time; that
"circumstances of times" change; that they know how and when
to speak, when and how to keep silent. An understanding of time
is implied in the cryptic ". . . this was the state of things in
1785. . . ." The antecedent of "this" may be discovered by a
painstaking search of Jefferson's correspondence but does not, I
believe, matter here, for the emphasis is on knowing the "state
of things" at any particular moment, so that one may act with
Confucian propriety, rather than follow ideology, which tram-
ples the particular. Thus there is no contradiction between Jefferson opposing a classical model for Washington's statue and his
adopting a classical model for the Virginia capitol. The ideologue
would force an abstract question: Should the art of the new nation
be classical or *not?* But in the Confucian *Analects* we read:

> He said: a proper man is not absolutely bent on, or absolutely
> averse from anything in particular, he will be just.

Jefferson understands that a toga for Washington would be in-
appropriate but that neoclassical columns would be suitable for
Monticello. The style of a statue may seem a trivial question, but
the point, again Confucian, is that one cannot correctly understand
large affairs if one cannot understand small ones. The attention
to detail, the understanding of "circumstances of times" that Adams
and Jefferson display in small matters, are the same that enabled
them to found a nation.

Other patterns may be found in the canto in reference to commerce, political economy, and communication. More central is the
suggestion that the good ruler must understand human nature,
the way things are rooted, the way things grow (Jefferson wants
to know how that flower vegetates in the air). We hear about

other rulers and theorists of government who simply do not know enough; but Adams and Jefferson, in addition to their learning, have a kind of knowledge that theorizing *philosophes* do not, as Adams insisted, actual "experience in the nature of free government." He wrote:

> The political and literary world are much indebted to Napoleon for the invention of the new word IDEOLOGY. . . . And a very profound, abstruse, and mysterious science it is. . . . It is the bathos, the theory, the art, the skill of diving and sinking in government. It was taught in the school of folly, but alass [*sic*], Franklin, Turgot, Rochefoucauld and Condorcet, under Tom Paine, were the great masters of that Academy!

In 1815, when Adams said that the *philosophes* had "shewn themselves as incapable of governing mankind, as the Bourbons or the Guelphs," he was aware of his old friends' fates. Turgot had died in 1781 and so escaped the Terror. But Lafayette was forced to flee France; Rochefoucauld was stoned to death; Condorcet was put to the guillotine. It was grim proof of his argument.

Franklin's sprightly anecdote about the scholar who refuses to eat contains in miniature the folly against which Adams and Jefferson struggled to form a government that, if not a full realization of their dreams, might yet endure. The world, as the canto firmly reminds us, is a place of slavery, lying newspapers, scheming ministers, ignorance, and stupidity, where men have "kinks" and find it easy to "continue in error." Understand that, and you may take steps toward building a new civilization, but you will not establish practical government if, like Franklin, you "suppose a rational man."

Something like this, rooted in the particular language of Adams and Jefferson, is what we may find in Canto 31, to be modified and extended by our sense of the whole poem. But now we have a problem: In studying this canto, I have read and reread, with an enthusiasm equal to Pound's, the Adams-Jefferson correspondence. Having read the letters, it is hard for me now to imagine what a reader who has not read them will find, unaided, in the canto. It is harder for me to know what weight such a reader may be willing to give to each detail. Donald Davie, writing of

Cantos 31 through 33, points to a similar problem: "It is kindest, therefore, to suppose that Pound intended by these cantos to do no more than tease the reader into looking up his sources."

Davie's "to do no more" may overstate his case; at least, I have tried to show that there are themes running through Canto 31 that can be perceived merely by attending to the words. Yet he is right in suggesting that Pound's editing of the fragments is often puzzling. In fact, I am convinced that Pound, at times but not always, wants to draw our attention not only to the parts of letters he quotes but also to parts he does not quote, and that some of his meaning (which is what I meant by *trobar clus*) is reserved for the few who will follow him into the arcanum.

For example, the story about the rational man and his ham breaks off with an "etc.," but the sentence, in Adams's letter, continues:

. . . thus the exalted dignity of human nature would be annihilated and lost. And in my opinion, the whole loss would be of no more importance, than putting out a candle, quenching a Torch, or crushing a Firefly, *if in this world only we have hope.*

The next fragment makes a cryptic reference to Epicurus, which is surely intended to do more than make a witty juxtaposition with "appetite." Here is a problem, then, with Pound's allusive method: The reader often has no way of knowing when to stop. I suspect the reference to Epicurus is meant to indicate Adams's and Jefferson's (and Pound's) consistent opposition to materialism as well as to indicate the Confucian view that metaphysical questions are unanswerable and have little to do with practical ethics.

Finally, let us look at the two lines beginning ". . . church of St. Peter. . . ." Following his attack on the Church, Adams goes on to discuss contemporary European politics, and then:

Your Question "How the Apostasy from National Rectitude can be Accounted for" is too deep and wide for my Capacity to answer. . . . I can only say at present, that it should seem that human Reason and human Conscience, though I believe there are such things, are not a Match, for human Passions, human Imagination and human Enthusiasms.

The canto concludes with examples of failures of human reason and conscience; but without the unprinted continuation of Adams's letter, his affirmation is somewhat misleading.

With *Hic Explicit Cantus,* Pound parodies the medieval practice of marking the end of a section of manuscript, as if to recognize that the canto is "documentary" and that he has merely functioned as a scribe. He means, if I am correct, the opposite: that, although every word is transcribed, he has made his own poem from the transcriptions. I am suggesting, in fact, that he has made two poems—one that we can read without further research, one that we discover only by finding the context of each fragment—and for that reason I have supplied such contexts in the annotation on the following pages.

On the surface, then, the canto is a presentation of Adams and Jefferson as nation builders, giving a sense of their minds and prose, and working out the themes of time, speech, and silence stated in "Tempus loquendi / tempus tacendi." The deeper structure is probably more than the surface can bear. It connects the canto with a larger theme of the poem, a theme most movingly expressed in the Pisan cantos and in *Drafts and Fragments:* that although history is a purgatory from which mankind will not be released in time, that although the New Jerusalem will not appear on earth, we should rejoice at the examples of those, like Adams and Jefferson, who work toward it; rejoice, too, that limited, temporary successes are possible. Such a success, for Pound, is the Constitution, even though, as we discover in later cantos, it has been largely subverted.

Canto 31, then, mirrors the themes of Ecclesiastes, from which its opening words are taken. First, the vanity of human endeavor in the face of time:

> I have seen all the works that are done under the sun; and, behold, all is vanity and vexation of spirit. That which is crooked cannot be made straight: and that which is wanting cannot be numbered.

Yet mixed with that wisdom is another:

> Then I saw that wisdom exceedeth folly, as far as light excelleth darkness. . . . Whatsoever thy hand findeth to do, do it with thy

might; for there is no work, nor device, nor knowledge, nor wisdom, in the grave, whither thou goest. . . . Let us hear the conclusion of the whole matter: Fear God, and keep his commandments: for this is the whole duty of man.

The letters of Adams and Jefferson have something of the same conflicting impulses, full of pride and hope on the one hand, and on the other, full of despair at human depravity and folly. They are aware that the nation they founded has endured and is valuable; yet they know that it is far from what they had envisioned. The two themes can be heard in the last letters they wrote each other. Jefferson is sending his grandson on a visit to Quincy:

> Like other young people, he wishes to be able, in the winter nights of old age, to recount to those around him what he has heard and learnt of the Heroic age preceding his birth, and which of the Argonauts particularly he was in time to have seen. It was the lot of our early years to witness nothing but the dull monotony of colonial subservience, and of our riper ones to breast the labors and perils of working it out. Theirs are the Halcyon calms succeeding the storm which our Argosy had so stoutly weathered.

Adams replied:

> Your letter is one of the most beautiful and delightful I have ever received.
> Public affairs go on pretty much as usual: perpetual chicanery and rather more personal abuse than there used to be. . . . Our American Chivalry is the worst in the World. It has no Laws, no bounds, no definitions; it seems to be all a Caprice.

## Page 37 (45)

Tempus loquendi / Tempus tacendi / From Ecclesiastes: "A time to speak, a time to be silent." Malatesta had the words inscribed on Isotta's tomb.

"modern dress for your statue . . ." / These and the next lines are from a letter (17 August 1787) from Jefferson, representing the new nation in Paris, to Washington, who was presiding over the Continental Congress in Philadelphia. The statue was to be made in Europe; the question was whether it should display Washington in a toga. Jefferson thought "a modern in an antique dress as just an object of ridicule as a Hercules or Marius with a periwig." The lines following show Jefferson's farsighted plans for the Erie Canal, not to be completed until thirty-eight years later.

no slaves north of Maryland / Jefferson to Dr. Price, author of an antislavery pamphlet (7 August 1785): "Emancipation is put into such a train that in a few years there will be no slaves northward of Maryland. . . . This Virginia is the next State to which we may turn our eyes for the interesting spectacle of justice in conflict with avarice and oppression. . . ."

flower found in Connecticut / The three samples of Jefferson's range of interest—justice, botany, and technology—show him as *polumetis,* many-minded. "When the nit-wits complained of Jefferson's superficiality it merely amounted to their non-perception of the multitude of elements needed to start any decent civilization in the American wilderness. . . . [He had] the dynamism of the man who did *get things* DONE."

## Page 38 (45-46)

"English papers . . . their lies . . ." / By 1945, as Pound saw it, the medium had changed, but not the message (C.76):

and Bracken is out and the B.B.C. can lie
    but at least a different bilge will come out of it
        at least for a little, as is its nature
can continue, that is, to lie.

"Their tobacco . . ." / Jefferson as economist. In a letter to the count of Vergennes, 15 August 1785, he argues that lower tariffs will increase trade.

the Maison Quarrée / Jefferson as architect, designing, in Paris, a capitol for Virginia. The Maison Quarrée, a Roman temple with Corinthian columns, had been restored by Louis XIV.

Mr. Robert Smith / An ambitious member of Madison's cabinet, his factionalism threatened to tear the government apart. Jefferson was brought in to solve the crisis.

XTZBK49HT / Pound has hit the keys of his typewriter to create the word in cypher. His source, the Lipscomb-Bergh edition of Jefferson's letters, uses asterisks for the cyphered passages; a more recent edition reads the cypher here as "a bankruptcy." Jefferson, writing from Paris to Madison, 2 August 1787: "Mr. Adams adds, that . . . Congress may borrow enough in Holland to pay off their whole debts in France, both public and private, to the crown, to the Farmers, and to Beaumarchais. Surely it will be better to transfer these debts to Holland. So critical is the state of that country, that I imagine the moneyed men of it would be glad to place their money in foreign countries. . . . This country [France] is really supposed to be on the eve of a * * * * *. Such a spirit has risen within a few weeks, as could not have been believed."

*Page 39 (46–47)*

Beaumarchais / The author of *The Marriage of Figaro* devoted years of his life and a substantial part of his fortune to the American cause. In 1787, when Jefferson made this remark, Beaumarchais was attempting to collect his money, but in spite of contracts and assurances, he was never repaid. In threatening to "make himself heard" he was an embarrassment to delicate financial and diplomatic negotiations.

Lafayette . . . Turgot, La Rochefoucauld, . . . Condorcet / Adams had no personal animosity toward these men, though he had some toward Franklin. In Paris, Adams was welcomed by the radical *philosophes,* but he found their ideas impractical and ignorant of history and human nature. His tart pen scurried down the margins of their books, refuting in exasperation point after point. Turgot, Louis XVI's liberal comptroller general, had just been turned out of office when Adams met him in 1778. Turgot's criticism of the constitutions of the American states inspired Adams's magnum opus, *A Defence of the Constitutions of Govern-*

*ment of the United States of America.* The duc de la Rochefoucauld was a member of Turgot's circle and a leader of liberal
politics in France. The marquis de Condorcet, youngest of the
*philosophes,* greatly admired Americans: "They are the only people
among whom the teachings of Machiavelli are not erected into
political doctrines, and whose leaders do not profess the impos-
sibility of so perfecting the social order as to harmonize prosperity
and justice."

Gallatin / Jefferson's secretary of state.

Adair / English author of a *History of the American Indians*
(1775). Jefferson liked the book but found this theory strange.

paying on it an interest / Jefferson's remarks on the national debt
contain, by implication, much of Pound's economics. The question
is: If a nation's sovereignty is the ultimate guarantee of its money,
why should a nation have to borrow that same money at interest
from private lenders? Jefferson saw the debt and its service as a
mortgage imposed by one generation on the next.

*Page 40 (47–48)*

"Man, a rational creature!" / Adams is remembering a morning
in 1775 when Franklin was "unusually loquacious."

Gosindi's Syntagma / From a letter of Jefferson's to Charles
Thomson, 9 January 1816: "I, too, have made a wee-little book
from the same materials, which I call the Philosophy of Jesus;
it is a paradigma of His doctrines. . . . And I wish I could sub-
join a translation of Gosindi's Syntagma of the doctrines of Epicurus, which, notwithstanding the calumnies of the Stoics and
caricatures of Cicero, is the most rational system remaining of the
philosophy of the ancients." Pierre Gassendi, a contemporary opponent of Descartes, attempted to reconcile the teachings of Epicurus with the doctrines of the Church.

". . . this was the state of things in 1785 . . ." / Jefferson is
writing to Benjamin Austin, 9 January 1816. The point of the
letter is that in 1785, when the oceans were open freely to Ameri-

can ships, it was reasonable to oppose, as he had in his *Notes on Virginia,* the growth of "manufactures" in the United States; but he recognizes that in 1816 conditions have changed and "We must now place the manufacturer by the side of the agriculturalist."

Patrick Henry / Jefferson recalls events on the eve of the Revolution, when he and Henry established Committees of Correspondence among the States. The Virginians named here all became delegates to the Continental Congress in 1774.

*Page 41 (48)*

church of St. Peter / Adams to Jefferson, 2 February 1816: "That stupendous Monument of human Hypocricy and Fanaticism the Church of St. Peter at Rome . . . excited the Ambition of Leo the tenth, who believed no more of the Christian Religion than Diderot. . . . Your Question 'How the Apostacy from National Rectitude can be accounted for' is too deep and wide for my Capacity to answer. . . . I can only say at present, that it should seem that human Reason and human Conscience, though I believe there are such things, are not a Match, for human Passions, human Imaginations and human Enthusiasm."

A tiel leis . . . en ancien scripture / These two lines and "and they continue this error" are from Jefferson to Adams, 14 January 1814, a lengthy technical discussion of law. A chief justice of the reign of Henry VI had written that "to such laws [*a tiel leis*] of the church as have warrant in ancient writing [*en ancien scripture*] our law giveth credence." But an early commentator began "the business of falsification by mistranslating and mistating" the original to read "to such laws of the church as have warrant in *holy scripture.*" Jefferson goes on to show how one commentator after another has passed on the error for two centuries, until "who can question but that the whole Bible and Testament are a part of the Common Law?"

Bonaparte / Jefferson (to Adams, 5 July 1814) thought Napoleon "a cold-blooded, calculating unprincipled Usurper, without a virtue, no statesman, knowing nothing of commerce, political economy, or civil government." The line about English paupers is from a letter to Thomas Cooper, 10 September 1814, in which he protests the economic oppression of laborers and paupers by the English aristocracy.

*Hic Explicit Cantus* / "Here the canto ends."


◊    ◊


*from* CANTO 38

> The Pentagon has told a Senate subcommittee that American manufacturers of military equipment paid more than $200-million to sales agents in foreign countries over the last two and a half years. . . . "My common sense tells me that fees as high as $45-million for a single deal have a potential for abuse," the official said. "It's hard to imagine what work would justify such a fee."
>
> *The New York Times,* 22 June 1975


IN 1918, MAJOR C. H. DOUGLAS, the prophet of Social Credit, the Third Resolvant Force (the other two being the extreme left and the extreme right), met and converted A. H. Orage, editor of the lively London weekly the *New Age* and its successor the *New English Weekly*, which became the leading vehicles for Douglasite discussion. Pound, who had been writing for Orage since 1911, soon met the major and saw the light that was "so bright and so blindin'."

Douglas was a thorny personality with a mysterious background (though Pound and his contemporaries seem to have taken him at face value), and Pound never tries to make him personally charming or even interesting. Yet the encounter with Douglas turned Pound into a lifelong student of money in history and a propa-

gandist for monetary reform. The passage Pound has chosen from
Canto 38 is a paraphrase of Douglas's central proposition, the
$A + B$ Theorem.

Here, I attempt only a brief comment on Pound's economics.
In his prose works on the subject (most of them collected in
*Selected Prose,* pp. 187–355), Pound speaks clearly enough for
himself and in such a lively and entertaining way that a summary
is in danger of returning the subject to dullness.

Clearly, Pound does not want us to read the *Cantos* tossing its
economics aside as some impure element to be tolerated for the
sake of more "poetic" passages. The long poem was always to
have been an epic, therefore a poem including history, but it
seems to have been the meeting with Douglas that crystallized
Pound's sense of what history is and what it is not: "An epic is
a poem including history. No one can understand history without
understanding economics. Gibbon's History of Rome is a meaningless jumble till a man has read Douglas."

In *Selected Cantos,* Pound has omitted most of the parts in-
corporating his more technical interest in economics, the "sufficient
phalanx of particulars" (C.74) he needs to support his generali-
ties. He draws the particulars from anywhere and everywhere,
from the classics as well as from contemporary muckraking
journalism. Below is a representative passage from earlier in
Canto 38, its unstopping syntax pointing to the tangled operations
of those who, as the last line of the canto says, "faire passer ces
affaires / avant ceux de la nation" [put their own business before
that of the nation]. The passage begins with the salesmanship of
Sir Basil Zaharoff, then moves on to the international oil cartel,
which was held together in 1933 by an agreement negotiated by
Andrew Mellon, ambassador to the Court of St. James, whose
family happened to control Gulf Oil, a member of the cartel:

> Don't buy until you can get ours.
> And he went over the border
> and he said to the other side:
> The *other* side has more munitions. Don't buy
> until you can get ours.

And Akers [Vickers] made a large profit and imported gold into
England
Thus increasing gold imports.
The gentle reader has heard this before.
And that year Mr Whitney
Said how useful short sellin' was,
We suppose he meant to the brokers
And no one called him a liar.
And two Afghans came to Geneva
To see if they cd. get some guns cheap,
As they had heard about someone's disarming.
And the secretary of the something
Made some money from oil wells
(In the name of God the Most Glorious Mr D'Arcy
is empowered to scratch through the sub-soil of Persia
until fifty years from this date . . .)
Mr Mellon went over to England

But it is not this lively kind of reportage Pound has chosen for
*Selected Cantos*. Rather, he insists on a perversely dry passage—
though it mocks its own dryness. The passage loses much by being
removed from its context in Canto 38, where it serves as a sharp
paradisal contrast to an international hell of Krupps and Mellons,
but its choice is an indication of Pound's own sense of the poem's
"main elements."

The language is an overlayering of Douglas's own (notoriously
plodding) prose with Poundian syntax and American go-getter
exasperation ("damn blast your intellex," "any damn factory").
Douglas, of course, hardly originated radical economic discussion
in England; it had been going on in the writings of, to name a
few, Cobbett, Carlyle, Mill, Ruskin, and (closer to Douglasite
analysis) Arthur Kitson. But it was his own $A + B$ perception
that inspired Douglas's economic studies and became the foundation of Pound's.

The $A + B$ Theorem is simple—most economists would say
too simple—though Douglas and his followers elaborated and
qualified it in detail. Douglas, looking over the books of firms for
which he worked, thought that, in an age of potential abundance,

the financial practices of industry (and of the financiers behind industry) prevented that abundance from being fairly and freely distributed because the total of wages generated could never keep up with the total of prices charged for the goods purchased. The difference between wages and prices is accounted for not by fair profits of managers and entrepreneurs (that is, fair payment for productive contribution) but by an unfair drain of profits into unnecessary activities, primarily in the form of interest charged by banks. The difference between wages and profits is in "nonexistent values," and the alchemy, producing the unproductive profits, lies in convincing society that the nonexistent exists.

Pound is working from one of Douglas's expositions of the $A + B$ Theorem, compressing and dislocating the language, as he always does with his documents, in an effort to elevate it just enough for the sake of his poem (and adding his own voice: in effect, "Yes, I know you think this is dull, that it doesn't belong in a poem"). Here is Douglas's early (1920) statement of $A + B$:

A factory or other productive organization has, besides its economic function as a producer of goods, a financial aspect—it may be regarded, on the one hand, as a device for the distribution of purchasing power to individuals through the media of wages, salaries, and dividends; and on the other hand as a manufactory of prices—financial values. From this standpoint its products may be divided into two groups:

Group A: All payments made to individuals (wages, salaries, and dividends).
Group B: All payments made to other organizations (raw materials, bank charges, and other external costs).

*Now the rate of flow of purchasing power to individuals is represented by A, but since all payments go into prices, the rate of flow of prices cannot be less than A+B. The product of any factory may be considered as something which the public ought to be able to buy, although in many cases it is an intermediate product of no use to individuals but only to subsequent manufacture; but since A will not purchase A+B, a proportion of the product at least equivalent to B must be distributed by a form of*

*purchasing power which is not comprised in the descriptions
grouped under A* . . . this additional purchasing power is provided by loan-credit (bank overdrafts) or export credit.

Note the *rate* of flow. In each instance, the drain on, or clog in,
the system may appear relatively small, but it is enough cumula-
tively to produce very large profits for one class and very large
shortages for the many. Indeed, the whole system (Pound's
Usura) depends on the success capitalists have had in persuading
mankind that the unnatural is natural, that there should be, must
be, shortages. The central shortage, which can be monopolized
and manipulated with great leverage, is that of money or credit.
From this perception, it follows for Pound that:

1. Money itself should not be treated as a commodity (though
TV commercials urge us to "Come to the Money Store"). Rather,
it should be a device, a means of establishing the just price of a
real commodity, of seeing that the abundance of nature is distributed to all.

2. Because money is central to civilization, a perversion of the
money system leads to perversions in everything else—the quality
of our bread, philosophy, art, and so forth—and ultimately to wars.

3. The real source of credit is, or should be, the "process," nature
itself, and the heritage of man's inventions through the ages. These
sources of credit should be public, not private.

4. Much of modern history is the story of how what should be
public has in fact fallen into private hands and of the ends to
which those private hands will go to keep it.

This is a mere abstraction of the poem's "economics," which is
underlined, dramatized, annotated, at times gaily, at times tedi-
ously and obscurely, through hundreds of particulars.

Pound refers to the rhetorical trinity of *ut doceat, ut moveat, ut
delectet* ("that it teach, that it move, that it delight"). Here, for
the first time in *Selected Cantos,* the baldest of *ut doceat*'s prevails.
Pound is aware of the risk he takes in including specific economic
material in his poem. Indeed, it appears that for many readers he
violates some deep taboo in going beyond satire and denunciation,

the traditional encounters between literature and economics, and moving into technical questions on the nature of money.

He enacts, with good humor, his frustration in getting our attention: "damn blast your intellex." We can hear that frustration again in *ABC of Economics:* "I shall have no peace until I get the subject off my chest, and there is no other way of protecting myself against charges of unsystematized, uncorrelated thought, dilettantism, idle eclecticism, etc., than to write a brief formal treatise. . . . Not one man in a thousand can be aroused to an interest in economics until he definitely suffers from the effects of an evil system. I know of no subject in which it is harder to arouse any interest whatsoever." When Pound tried to get Douglasite economics into the program of the Irish Sinn Fein movement, Arthur Griffith, its leader, replied, "Can't move 'em with a cold thing like economics." So we find, in Canto 103:

"Not with a cold thing"
                    said Griffith,
                    "can't move 'em"
                    ut delectet

That "ut delectet" is ironic, suggesting not only the traditional requirement that poetry should please, but that most men are concerned only with their pleasures, and will not strain their minds to move very far toward charity or *compassione.*

Whatever one thinks of Social Credit, Pound was not quite the isolated crank on the subject that he may appear. That is, most of us only hear about Douglas and Social Credit because we are reading Pound, and it may look as if among the poet's many interests this is a very odd one. To us, Douglas is a footnote to Pound; but as soon as one turns to the extensive literature on Social Credit, Pound becomes the footnote. In numerous guises and variations, Social Credit was widely considered by intelligent people in the 1920s and 1930s. For a while, it appealed to those on the Left as well as to those on the Right, although it offered a radical moral solution for a world becoming polarized between Left and Right authoritarian systems. The story of the Social

Credit movement, interesting in itself, shows Pound as one of many intelligent people who were offering homemade programs for a sane civilization. In fact, we may see him not as a man who picked up an obscure crackpot idea but as one standing well within the tradition of nineteenth-century moral-economic writing. Few of us are equipped to deal technically with the history and theory of money. Was the civilization of Byzantium indeed, as Pound claims, so high and so stable because the interest rate was kept low? Is it true that, in painting, when usury increases "the line thickens"? We cannot know. It is more profitable to look at the questions Pound asks than at the answers he proposes; he always claimed that he never heard those basic questions answered.

The economics in the *Cantos* are primarily moral, notes toward a vision of the New Jerusalem. The poem itself conveys only a general idea of what Pound thinks of as a sane and sacred economic program. Enlightenment optimism, the faith that, given help in defining terms, men will grasp truth, reflects only one side of Pound. He also knows that one will not escape the dark forest without direction of the will. Thus in *ABC of Economics:*

No economic system is worth a hoot without 'good will'. No intellectual system of economics will function unless people are prepared to act on their understanding.

People indifferent to the definition of liberty as *'le droit de faire tout ce qui ne nuit pas aux autres'* will not DO anything about their economic knowledge, whatever be the degree of that knowledge. . . .

Give a people an almost perfect government, and in two generations they will let it run to rot from sheer laziness (*vide* the U.S.A. where not one person in ten has the faintest idea of the aims and ambitions of the country's founders and lawmakers. Their dung has covered their heads.)

It is nevertheless one's duty to try to think out a sane economics, and to try to enforce it by that most violent of all means, the attempting to make people think.

Proof of this last statement is very obscure. I suppose the only warrant for it is the capacity to think and the sense of obligation thereby conferred.

Pound's concept of the effective didacticism of his poem is much subtler than an effort to convince us that the $A + B$ Theorem is correct. The poem is an attempt less to provide practical instruction than to prepare the mind, by irritation if necessary, for an awareness, a perception of relations necessary for making us want to put our ideas into action:

"Doceat, moveat" should be fused in the delectet in any great work of art. Separate, they belong to action and as action they pass in time, with the day or the hour contingent. The need of teaching goes when the scholar has learned, the need of moving, with the mass action intended. But begun at the wrong end or hind end, the delectet is prone to mean mere literature of escape.

In the last two lines of this passage from Canto 38, language that burlesques the *doceat* suddenly and wittily leaps into language that burlesques the *delectet,* leaps from the most "mundane" into Paradise. Like Dante in the first canto of the *Paradiso,* we did not even know we were there. Beatrice tells him, "You are not now on earth, though you may think so." Dante cannot bear the blinding light. Though Beatrice explains where he is, his mind is bewildered: "If I was disencumbered of my first doubt . . . I was now more ensnared within another." Then Beatrice begins her discourse on Paradise: *"Le cose tutte quante / Hann' ordine tra loro"* [All things have a relation to each other].

Just before the presentation of the $A + B$ Theorem in Canto 38, one Mr. Blodgett (discussing the textile industry in the nineteenth century) is heard to say that "Sewing machines will never come into general use." But that is exactly how Douglas saw himself, as the inventor of a device so *clearly* useful that its adoption was as inevitable as the abandonment of hand stitching. He could only account for resistance to it as a conspiracy of self-interested financiers and their bought economists and politicians.

Pound, though he spent a lifetime elaborating the major's ideas, saw Douglas, as early as 1920, as "a Don Quixote desiring to *'Make democracy safe for the individual.'*" But of course Quixote does not see himself as Quixote. The major preferred to compare himself to Galileo and went on muttering, quite literally, *E pur si muove.*

◇ ·

# The Fifth Decad
# of Cantos (1937)

◇

IN THE THREE YEARS he was writing these ten new cantos, Pound continued to live at Rapallo, where he created a small, personal vortex of culture. Aside from his poetry and his economic-political propaganda, he put much of his energy into organizing concerts and reviving the music of Vivaldi and other early composers. *Jefferson and/or Mussolini* (1935) had been written in 1933, and *Social Credit: An Impact* was pamphleteering on familiar themes. The title of *Polite Essays* (1937) is a wry comment on the "blue china and slush boys" at his publisher's, Faber and Faber. Eliot, now a director of Faber and Faber, "won't print me either, except when I am harmless (they have been trying to find something harmless for a year.)" The impulse that would lead to the wartime radio broadcasts resulted in over three hundred contributions to periodicals—letters to editors, articles, and doggerel verse—and in letters to bankers and politicians in several countries. There were letters to American senators and congressmen, and even to President Roosevelt. Through Fascist officials, he attempted to make an impact on the Italian government. But the letters of this period by no means ignore literature and include the fine series to H. D. Rouse and Laurence Binyon on their respective translations of Homer and Dante.

"It takes a while to get your bearings," he said years later, "—like a detective story—and see how it's going to go. I hit my stride in *The Fifth Decad of Cantos.*" It is not just a collection of recent cantos but a carefully composed volume with its own unity.

Pound was increasingly aware both of the singular demands he was putting on readers and of the problems he was creating for himself. He wrote to a puzzled correspondent:

Fair questions. When I get to the end, pattern *ought* to be discoverable. Stage set à la Dante is *not* modern truth. It may be O.K.
but *not* as modern man's. . . . Take a fugue: theme, response,
contrasujet. *Not* that I mean to make an exact analogy of structure.

But the intricacies of fugue and the ever-expanding ideogram, he
added, would be "mere matter for . . . Harvud instructors *unless* I pull it off as reading matter, shouting matter, the tale of the
tribe."

In 1936 he gave a new definition of the ideogram, one that
comes closer to describing the *Fifth Decad*:

> the clamping of words to groups of objects not necessarily of the
> same species, that is to say the ideogrammic method (for the
> purpose of poetry)

At first glance, the groups of objects and their several styles come
from different species indeed. The volume moves from an obscure
Sienese bank and an almost-forgotten period of Tuscan history,
through a medievalized chant on Usura, and a chatty twentieth-
century version of the usury theme, to profoundly beautiful pages
on Greek myth and mystery religions and Taoist quiet. It embraces the minutely particular:

> Eunited States of America, a.d. 1935
> England a worse case, France under a foetor of regents.
> 'Mr Cummings wants Farley's job' headline in current paper.

(C.46)

and cosmic metamorphosis:

> That the grass grow from my body
> That I hear the roots speaking together,
> The air is new on my leaf,
> The forked boughs shake with the wind.

(C.47)

The unifying effort in the *Fifth Decad* is to connect specifics of
modern history (in particular, economic policy) both with the
natural rhythms of life, the "process," and with deep-rooted wisdom of folklore, myth, and ritual.

Pound has omitted from *Selected Cantos* most of the more

immediately poetic passages (Cantos 47, 49, and 51), leaving the famous Canto 45 and selections from three historical cantos under a new section-title, "Siena—The Leopoldine Reforms." My purpose in the following pages is not only to provide a background for these cantos but to see what case can be made for, what sorts of poetry can be found in, their documentary methods.

◇   ◇

## *from* CANTO 42

IN THE MONTE DEI PASCHI OF SIENA, Pound discovered a historically verifiable example of what a bank "built for beneficence, for reconstruction" could be. Likewise, dukes Leopold and Ferdinand, whose actions were reported in the same Sienese documents that recorded the founding of the Monte, were models of humane rulers. Documentary cantos, on the Monte and on the Leopoldine reforms, combined with lyrical cantos on the themes of usury and the abundance of nature, dominate this section of the poem.

The documentary method can be forbidding—and surprisingly confusing. For most readers of the *Cantos,* the documentary stretches are only sporadically successful. George Dekker, for example, in approaching Canto 42, distinguishes between "the prose of Pound's bread-and-butter cantos, interesting perhaps, but remote from poetry," and what he considers "poetic interruptions," such as the four lyrical lines (*Selected Cantos,* p. 44) beginning "wave falls and the hand falls." Dekker finds that the canto begins "unpromisingly enough with a pastiche and paraphrase of documents" and that only "four lines of poetry cannot bring pages of Poundian economics to life." Hugh Kenner, too, has problems with Pound's method here, objecting to the fact that we have to go to Pound's prose to find a real explanation of the meaning of the Bank of Siena:

> In the Canto it is virtually hidden amid the picturesque details, and while the facts are all present it is doubtful if an uninstructed

reader could be sure he had assembled them correctly. . . . the Sienese Bank Cantos conserve the vigor of actual documents, to convey a *senso morale* and a purpose. But they convey less well what the *senso morale* is engaged on: no . . . such vivid image for the Sienese bank as the prose pamphlet offers: ". . . on the growing grass that can nourish the living sheep." . . . So a poetic opposed to generalization is thwarting its own didactic purpose.

Donald Davie makes an interesting defense of the material in the opening section of the *Fifth Decad:*

The measured and ominous condemnation of usury in Canto 45 has been much anthologized and much admired; but the case there stated has been argued through the three preceding cantos, which forbiddingly accumulate the necessary documentation. Our admiration and sympathy for Canto 45 is worthless because it is unscientific unless we see how the conclusions to be drawn arise unavoidably from the case in point there documented from Tuscan history—the case of the reforms instituted by Leopold, Grand Duke of Tuscany from 1765 to 1790. Righteous indignation is worse than worthless, it is a vicious self-indulgence, unless it is indeed "righteous," unless we have earned the right to it. And so after Canto 45 the reader is forced back into the circles of Pound's hell, the snapping and snarling voices of recorded history, before in Canto 51 he has once again earned the right to join in with measured condemnation.

It is true that, after we have read the Siena bank cantos, we have only a general idea of how the bank worked and why Pound thought it so important. Certainly, in order to feel competent to discuss Canto 42 in detail, one must go to Pound's prose—indeed, for the notes that follow, I have gone well beyond it. But let us consider what we can find in Canto 42 without notes, before we turn to an exposition of the Monte dei Paschi.

First, we find a mimesis of the act of research itself, of someone skimming through documents, not always understanding them, taking notes, but not always notes that are completely intelligible when he tries to use them. The canto reproduces Pound's activity in the archives: Details, the style of the period, impress themselves

on the mind but are not essential—" Soffici, Marcellus de? Illuri, /
no, Marcellus Austini"; "(in what wd. seem to have been 1622)";
"Johnny something or other de Binis." Well, if it really mattered,
one could have stopped to find out if it *was* 1622, and what
Johnny's middle name was. The documents are interesting for their
flavor, and they prove that all this really happened; but the skim-
mer in the archives is not centrally concerned with accuracy or
with the picturesque. He is looking for the real nuggets of meaning to be found there, not for "history" in any normal sense. "Assigned on the office of grazing"; "ob pecuniae scarcitatem." Yes,
something can be made out of this; there's something here. The
beauty of the idea itself springs to life from the neglected, slightly
disordered documents. Pound is trying to avoid conveying, "I
have figured this out at some time in the past, and now I am
going to tell you about it"; rather, he wants to plunge us into
the act of discovery itself, as we were plunged in Canto 9 into the
midst of confusing events at Rimini.

Moreover, he wants us to know, as Davie suggests, that meaning-
ful or beautiful actions, political or aesthetic, are not lightly
achieved. The poet, down there in the archives, must put in a good
deal of drudgery (but "All of this is important") in order to get
at facts obscured by usury and laziness. Odysseus did not get home
without a struggle; nor was the Tempio easily built; nor the
American Constitution swiftly arrived at; nor is a work of art
merely a matter of "inspiration":

> And Brancusi repeating: je peux commencer
>     une chose tous les jours, mais
>                     fiiniiiir
>
>                                           (C.86)

So four centuries ago someone in Siena, no one remembers who,
perhaps one of the names on these documents, conceived the
idea of a bank that would be beneficent, but it took the people of
Siena, and two grand dukes and their advisors, ten years of hard,
persistent, detailed work to get the idea into action.

Perhaps the researcher's drudgery and confusion is worth it if from time to time, as Kenner says, "The rhetoric, still documentary, shifts towards exultation. Here is something promising, something new. Yet how does it work exactly?" Pound's explanation:

> Two kinds of banks have existed: The MONTE DEI PASCHI and the devils. . . .
>
> Three centuries of Medici wisdom went into the Monte dei Paschi, the *only* bank that has stood from 1600 till our time.
>
> Siena was flat on her back, without money after the Florentine conquest.
>
> Cosimo, first duke of Tuscany, had all the Medici banking experience behind him. He guaranteed the capital of the Monte, taking as security the one living property of Siena, and a certain amount of unhandy collateral.
>
> That is to say, Siena had grazing lands down toward Grosseto, and the grazing rights worth 10,000 ducats a year. On this basis taking it for his main security, Cosimo underwrote a capital of 200,000 ducats, to pay 5 per cent to the shareholders, and to be lent at 5½ per cent; overhead kept down to a minimum and all excess of profit over that to go to hospitals and works for the benefit of the people of Siena. . . .
>
> And the lesson is the very basis of solid banking. The CREDIT rests *in ultimate* on the ABUNDANCE OF NATURE, on the growing grass that can nourish the living sheep.
>
> And the moral is in the INTENTION. It was not for the conqueror's immediate short-sighted profit, but to restart the life and production of Siena, that this bank was contrived.

Again, in *Gold and Work:* "The basis was, and is, the abundance, or productivity, of nature together with the responsibility of the whole people."

It was simple. The grazing lands were the prime source of income to Siena. In good times or bad they would be there, producing real wealth. That real wealth could serve as a guarantee to the duke, who in turn guaranteed the *luoghi,* the shares. Now, at least 200,000 *scudi* were in circulation, allowing people to buy goods produced; yet no usurious interest charges were created to clog the system. No one could lose anything, except the opportunity for usury. It worked so well, in fact, that across the centuries the income from the pasture lands never had to be touched. The guarantee remained, says a modern chronicler of the bank, "moral and nominal." Pound would have been delighted with the pronouncement of the anonymous modern chronicler: "The organic principles on which the 'Monte' were based were actually a very solid and unfailing guarantee."

Note the slight strain in the verse, some sort of mixed figure, that results from the word *bottom* in the fourth line: "A mount, a bank, a fund, a bottom. . . ." That, I believe, springs from Pound's compulsion to use a term he found in Jefferson, in a passage that seemed to him one of the most valuable statements he had found in any archive:

> and if the national bills issued, be bottomed (as is indispensable) on pledges of specific taxes for their redemption within certain and moderate epochs, and be of *proper denomination* for *circulation,* no interest on them would be necessary or just, because they would answer to every one of the purposes of the metallic money withdrawn and replaced by them.

Jefferson was unaware of the Monte and its *luoghi,* but something like it is what he is proposing for America.

The operations of other banks, the devil banks, are described in other cantos. Rather than being rooted in nature, in natural increase, they are perversions of nature, men abrogating to themselves the power of God to create something out of nothing (or at least to fool us into thinking they have created something) so that they may then "rent" it for profit. Thus in Canto 46 we hear Paterson, the inventor of the Bank of England (a private venture), saying that his bank

<u>Hath benefit of interest on all</u>
<u>the moneys which it, the bank, creates out of nothing.</u>

A Rothschild, centuries later, nods his head in agreement:

"Very few people
"will understand this. Those who do will be occupied
"getting profits. The general public will probably not
"see it's against their interest."

Today, as Pound saw it, the Federal Reserve System, the general public hardly knowing what it is, still operates on Paterson's principle.

The documentary method can produce some drama after all, even if at first it appears dry and confusing. The language of Canto 42 is more durable than one might think; it stands up to rereadings, perhaps because one never quite knows how it is going to move syntactically, nor into what language or level of diction, nor quite when it may burst into "poetry." There is an occasional failure of tone. "Have you a place on the Hill, sir" sounds like someone soliciting for the United Fund, and

> (to be young is to suffer.
> Be old, and be past that)

is a shade too glib and portentous.

But two other points at which document springs into lyric are exciting, made more so by their contexts, and by the fact that they arrive syntactically unannounced. First:

> wave falls and the hand falls
> Thou shalt not always walk in the sun
> or see weed sprout over cornice
> Thy work in set space of years, not over an hundred.

Were the waves suggested to the poet in the archives by Livio's manuscript? At any rate, Livio's hand has fallen, as the grand duke and the members of the Bailey have fallen, and as the busy poet/researcher knows that his own hand will fall. George Dekker comments, "The simplicity of the language is striking, as is the absoluteness with which Pound identifies human life and death with the primordial motion of the sea. That man's destiny is bound up with the motions and seasons of the natural world is a source of joy for him . . . but it also makes man terribly vulnerable."

The language and emotion of this brief passage return in later cantos, as in Canto 47:

By this gate art thou measured
Thy day is between a door and a door
.  .  .  .  .  .  .  .
Thus was it in time.
And the small stars now fall from the olive branch,
Forked shadow falls dark on the terrace
More black than the floating martin
          that has no care for your presence,
His wing-print is black on the roof tiles
And the print is gone with his cry.
So light is thy weight on Tellus
Thy notch no deeper indented
Thy weight less than the shadow
Yet hast thou gnawed through the mountain

Likewise, the documentary method allows the fine moment (*Selected Cantos,* p. 47) when the capitalized "WHEREFORE" and "MOUNT" suggest the rising excitement as the long negotiations seem finally completed, and the researcher's mind suddenly leaves the library and sweeps across Italy:

so that the echo turned back in my mind: Pavia.
Saw cities move in one figure, Vicenza, as depicted,
San Zeno by Adige . . .

Years later, at Pisa, some of these things assembled again in the prisoner's mind: beloved cities, churches that come not by Usura, and the beauty that arose from another manuscript (of Cavalcanti's Sonnet 7) in another library. The poet/prisoner, allowing himself a rhyme, almost a couplet, longed to see:

          Pavia the romanesque
        being preferable
and by analogy the form of San Zeno the
      columns signed by their maker
         the frescoes in S. Pietro and the madonna in Ortolo
e " fa di clarità l'aer tremare "
as in the manuscript of the Capitolare

                       (C.74)

◊   ◊   ◊

*Page 43 (53–54)*

nell'anima / The document from which Pound was working reads *animo,* which would have the force of "mind" rather than "soul." The change may be an error in transcription, but Pound probably wants to emphasize "soul," connecting civic and religious impulses, as he does throughout the canto.

Illustrious College / The Collegio di Balia, a Sienese institution that Pound calls "the Bailey." Most of the canto is assembled from records of the Balia's dealings with the grand duke of Florence.

Monte / The Monte dei Paschi, "the mount of the pastures," the name of the bank that is the subject of the canto.

banco di giro / The sense is that the Monte lent out only funds it actually had on deposit. A *banco di giro* can transfer credits between accounts, at the same time using the deposits to make loans, thus drawing interest on money that does not belong to it. The Monte dei Paschi was not "yet" doing this but would have joined mainstream banking procedures by the time Pound was writing. *Giro* means "turning," "circling" and contrasts with the solidity of *mount, fund, bottom.*

S. A. / *Sua Altezza.* Here the Bailey appears to be addressing the grand duke.

dei ministri / Of the administrators (of the bank).

*id est, più utilmente* / "That is, most usefully."

*Page 44 (54–55)*

contrade / The *contrade,* or wards, of Siena are important in the civic structure. In the race described in Canto 43, the contest is not among individual horsemen but among the *contrade* to which they belong.

Loco Signi / "Place for the sign."

Consules, Iudices / "Consuls, judges."

pro serenissimo / "For his Most Serene," the grand duke.

AA VV / *Altezze Vostre,* "Your Highnesses."

## Page 45 (55–56)

Luoghi / Shares in the bank. Literally, places, positions.

"The Abundance" / The *abbondanza* was a magistracy regulating commodity prices and controlling the revenues from the Maremma or pasture lands that were the guarantee for the bank. Pound is interested in the primary meaning of the word, suggesting the "abundance of nature."

## Page 46 (56)

Antille, Gionfiglioli, Cellesi / Representatives of the Bailey.

Maria Maddalena Tutrice / The original petition for the Monte was submitted to the Medici grand duke, Cosimo II. (Siena had lost its independence in the sixteenth century, and was incorporated into the Grand Duchy of Tuscany.) Cosimo II died in 1629, and his heir, Ferdinand II, who was in his early teens, ruled under the guidance of the "she-tutrices" or regents, Maria Christina of Lorraine and Maria Maddalena of Austria. Thus the plural TTheir HHighnesses. Horatio della Rena was secretary or aide to the regents, his name appearing under that of Maria Maddalena on the documents.

## Page 47 (57)

Fabbizio bollo vedo Governatore / Translates the words just above.

Cenzio Grcolini / This and other names on the page are merely "documentary" and need not be identified.

ACTUM SENIS / "Done at Siena." Pound wants to emphasize *act,* an idea put into action, his "volitionist" economics.

Pavia . . . Vicenza . . . San Zeno / The civilizing, constructive force behind the Monte brings to mind other admired cities and churches that, the suggestion is, could not have been built under a usurious system. The Church of San Zeno in Verona, with its signed capital (see Canto 45) was particularly important to Pound.

Senatus Populusque Senensis / "The Senate and the People of Siena." The emphasis throughout is on the whole people acting together through their representatives.

*Page 48 (57–58)*

ob pecuniae scarcitatem / Pound repeats the phrase in Canto 43, where he translates it, "because there was a shortage of coin." The Monte will increase the amount of money in circulation.

Monte non vacabilis publico / Literally, "a bank never to be vacated." *"Non vacabilis"* is printed on the *luoghi,* the shares or bonds that established the bank. That is, a person depositing funds, thereby contributing to the bank's capital of 200,000 *scudi,* was given a paper representing *luoghi* or shares. The *luoghi* were transferable and did not expire, like an annuity, at the death of the original depositor. The holder of one of these papers, however, could not withdraw his capital, and so the bank could not be "vacated" or emptied. Thus the *luoghi* became permanently circulating, nonusurious money.

Don Ferdinandus Secundus Dux Magnus / "The Grand Duke Ferdinand II."

*Page 49 (58–59)*

MOUNTAIN / The figure formed of heraldic mounts appears on the *luoghi* and on official documents of the bank (it is still in use). Sometimes the Virgin, the patroness of Siena, was portrayed standing on top of the mountain.

Chigi, etc. / Again, the names are unimportant, establishing documentary flavor and authenticity. Lord Mt Alban is a playful anglicizing of Montalbano, a member of the Balia.

Loca Montis / Emphasizing the literal meaning of *luoghi* as "places on the hill."

ex certe scientia et / Translated in the line above (the document reads *certa*). The point is that the plan for the Monte (a plan that in essence could be used by any people at any time) is foolproof, resting on the will of the whole people and on the abundance of nature.

de libris septeno / The document reads *de libris septem*, "of seven pounds."

◊   ◊

*from* CANTO 43

THE COMPLETE CANTO 43 contains several more pages assembled from the Monte dei Paschi documents and continues to mimic the researcher's interior monologue:

> guarantee of the income from grazing
> up to (illegible) said to mean, no . . .
> libris septem, the sum of, summam, scutorum

Themes are repeated, underlining the discovery that the will of the whole people, finding "legitimate consumption impeded" by shortage of coin and usury, has acted "for the common good." The harmony between sound economics and religion is stressed:

> thus deliberated in full meeting
> in the name of the OMNIPOTENT, and of the glorious Virgin

The passage in *Selected Cantos* needs little comment, only a context. It is a comic parenthesis, a description of something Pound observed at Siena: preparations for the procession that precedes the great Sienese public festival, the running of the *palio*. Named for the *palio*, or banner, which is the prize, the twice-yearly event remains one of the leading tourist attractions of Siena. The *carroccio* (a festooned and painted wagon drawn by oxen) brings up the rear of the procession. The climactic horse race itself is somewhat dangerously run on the sloping central *piazza*. The riders represent their *contrade*, or wards, of which there are seventeen (thus the "17 banners").

The introductory "to the end:" both departs suddenly from the preceding documentary material and indicates the continuity of tradition: This same *palio* was being run in the years when these documents were being written. But tradition, as we find in Canto 83, can be both good and bad; sometimes it becomes a parody of its own origins, and it can represent the reluctance of people to change their ways, even when change is for their benefit. "To the end:" is also ironic, suggesting that this is what it has all come to, a pageant whose significance the participants no longer understand. The Imperial Roman origins of the purple stoles and gold eagles are undoubtedly forgotten, and St. George and the unicorn rest on "hokey-pokey stands," their pagan origins also forgotten. A box with "200 LIRE" on it has been plunked down in the midst of a religious ceremony, and the docile oxen may be an ironic echo of the pagan bull race that was in time turned into a horse race. (As in *The Sun Also Rises*, the pagan origins of the running of the bulls have largely been forgotten, transformed into a tourist attraction.)

So it has come to this end, and the Monte dei Paschi, as well, both incorporates and has forgotten its origins. But the tone of the passage is genial, for Pound always delights in finding instances of Mediterranean folk customs that include the old religion, even when they have been given an official Catholic facade.

The oxen, still used to plow the hills around Siena, form a link with the past; they return in a more serious context, with echoes of Hesiod, in Canto 47:

Begin thy plowing
When the Pleiades go down to their rest,
Begin thy plowing

.　.　.　.

Thy day is between a door and a door
Two oxen are yoked for plowing
Or six in the hill field

The oxen also connect Canto 43 with the opening lines of Canto 44, where the grand duke Leopold, understanding both economic perversion and the basis of natural increase, commands:

> 　　　　　　　　　　　　　　thou shalt not
> Sequestrate for debt any farm implement
> nor any yoke ox nor
> any peasant while he works with the same.

◊　◊

# CANTO 44

IN CANTOS 42 THROUGH 44, Pound conveys his excitement at discovering, in the same nine-volume work, two monuments of civic intelligence: the Monte dei Paschi and the Leopoldine reforms in Tuscany during the eighteenth century. He is always delighted to discover and to rehabilitate members of the "conspiracy of intelligence" who have been forgotten or deliberately ignored in the "historical blackout." There are, he says, "whole beams and ropes of real history" that have been buried as "the thought of Van Buren, A. Johnson, A. Jackson and the story of Tuscany under Pietro Leopoldo, have been buried." The best of the Enlightenment had informed the two revolutions, Leopoldo's and Jefferson's, and in Canto 50 we hear them brought together for a moment, as a Tuscan writer sings: "Te, admirabile, O VashinnnTTonn!" But in twentieth-century America, "the traces of the Leopoldine Reforms have been lost. . . . It can be said with certainty that the same current towards the liberation from the shackles of the guilds

made its appearance in Tuscany and in the American Colonies.
The return to a controlled economy in Tuscany was wrecked by
the Napoleonic Wars."

Canto 44 begins with the Sienese excitement over Ferdinand's
controlled economy, which is abruptly interrupted by the "Napoleonic flurry"—and it is precisely as a flurry that the canto presents half-intelligible glimpses of the French occupation. In the
final lines, after the fall of Napoleon ("And 'Semiramis' 1814
departed"), the verse becomes more lucid as it recites examples of
good government.

Pound refuses, however, to turn history into melodrama (Leopold and Ferdinand good, Napoleon bad). The French cause taxes
to rise, which in turn brings civil turmoil, and they install the
king of Etruria, who is a burden to the people. Yet on the other
hand, it is members of the Napoleonic forces who stop the attack
on the ghetto, urge someone to distribute the sums in his cash
box to the community, and criticize the Etrurian taxes. "Respectons
les prêtres" contains both Confucian and Machiavellian possibilities.
Napoleon's letter to the queen regent of Etruria is a mixture of
civility and barbarism, official suavity masking ambitious determination. His praise of artists is noted with a mixture of admiration
and skepticism. The canto then sums up its mixed attitudes toward Napoleon in the epitaph that marks his fall:

> "Thank god such men be but few"
> though they build up human courage.

After which, the conqueror and lawgiver fades out on the anti-
climactic mention of "the ex-emperor's mother."

The long verse paragraph on the last page of the canto, spiraling
upward in a series of expanding relative clauses, makes it clear
that the return of Ferdinand III, after the fall of Napoleon, is to
be celebrated, and the tone of celebration returns us to the beginning of the canto. Yet the achievements of Napoleon-as-ruler
remain (the Code, improvements in agriculture and in the mortgage system), outlasting Napoleon-as-adventurer.

The first long episode of the canto, ending with the departure of Ferdinando, is shrewdly constructed to make verse of its prose. It contains little sections of hidden rhyme and assonance, as chains of repeated sounds lead from one line to the next. Note, for example, the first seven lines, with their short *e* sounds: *Firenze, sequestrate, debt, any, implement, any, any, peasant*. The *p* of *peasant* leads to *Pietro* in the next line, as the *old* in *Leopoldo* leads to *unsold*. There is a concentration of sixteen sibillants (five in "1766") reaching from *shalt* to *specie*.

This is more than prose given an unorthodox syntax and cut up to look like poetry. There is great concentration of repetition and alliteration in the lyrical opening and closing episodes (and markedly less during the Napoleonic interruption), such as *intermission/procession* and the concentration of *p*'s, *r*'s, and *o*'s in "motu proprio / Pietro Leopoldo." In the passage beginning "Evviva Ferdinando il Terzo" (*Selected Cantos*, top of p. 53) clusters of consonants (*f*'s, *w*'s, *s*'s, and *d*'s) and interior rhymes (*drumming/trumpets/hunting; wood/goods; stayed/day*) are threaded on a repeated sound leading from *torch* through *mortaretti, torches, warned, straw*, and *for*, to *disorder* and *doors*, the final syllable catching up all the *o* and *r* sounds before it:

> with the torches
> or with wood fires and straw flares
> and the vendors had been warned not to show goods for
> fear of disorder and stayed all that day withindoors

The first two-and-a-half pages present a pleasant balance of eighteenth-century prose against the noises of the unrestrained celebration described. The passage is full of sound effects: shouts of VIVA and EVVIVA, trumpets, horns, drums, carillons, singing, bells, and the hullabaloo of grenades, gunshots, and mortars— leading up to the phrase "unforseen jubilation." (The use of gunpowder to celebrate an act of constructive government is in contrast with the use to which a Napoleon puts it.)

The last line of the canto, marked by a concentration of *p*'s and *o*'s (the name is pronounced Piccolómini), closes the story of the bank of Siena and the Leopoldine reforms, and the last of the nine volumes in which Pound discovered so much *ben dell' intelletto.*

*Page 51 (61)*

Pietro Leopoldo / During the eighteenth century, the Medici line in Tuscany was succeeded by the house of Hapsburg-Lorraine. Leopold II was grand duke from 1765 to 1790, and Pound, for all the VIVA's and praise, scarcely conveys the splendor and variety of his reign. In 1790, when Leopold became Holy Roman Emperor, his son, Ferdinand III, became grand duke, continuing and extending his father's liberal programs.

the Mount / Pound is viewing Tuscan history through the Monte dei Paschi documents in Siena. Not only did the Monte never lack for specie, but one of Leopold's first official acts was to increase its capital.

motu proprio / A legal term: "of one's own accord, of one's own will" (now used only for papal decrees). It was through hundreds of decrees *motu proprio* that Leopold instituted his reforms.

*Page 52 (61–62)*

St Catherine / The fourteenth-century Sienese mystic died at Rome, but a few years later her head was piously severed from her body and returned to Siena, with great ceremony, in a golden reliquary.

e di tutte le qualità / "And of all sorts."

*Page 53 (62–63)*

Dovizia annonaria / Abundance of food or provisions. The celebration here recorded marks Ferdinando's return to his father's economic programs after a period of experiment with more restrictive measures. The "Yoke of License" refers to "coercita de annonaria" in the Latin inscription below. The name of the price-regulating body, the *Abbondanza,* had turned ironic, for its controls were not producing abundance. In Canto 50, Leopoldo calls it *" 'Un' abbondanza che affamava' "* [an abundance that starves].

Frumentorum licentia, etc. / "Freedom, or distribution, of grain, relaxation of restrictions on commodities, for both the poor and the rich, he maintained the good."

il più galantuomo del paese / "The finest gentleman of the land." Two days after French Republican troops invaded Tuscany (in 1799, not, as Pound suggests, in 1796), Ferdinand was forced to flee, in spite of the citizens' appeal that he was not a monarch but "the first gentleman of the state, the first subject of its laws." His final act of beneficence, until his return after the Napoleonic occupation, seems to have been his refusal to take state property with him into exile.

citizen priest Fr Lenzini / The rest of the canto supplies a rapid, impressionistic survey of Tuscan history during the Napoleonic period. It might be helpful to sort out the different governments: After the invasion of 1799, the French only remained for a few months, but they returned in 1800, when Tuscany was declared part of Napoleon's Cisalpine Republic. In 1801, Napoleon incorporated Tuscany into the kingdom of Etruria, under Louis, duke of Parma. In 1805, Napoleon was crowned king of Italy, and in 1807 Tuscany became part of the kingdom of Italy, then in the following year it was incorporated into the French empire. The emperor's sister, Elisa, was made grand duchess of Tuscany. When Napoleon was exiled in 1814, Ferdinand III returned.

men of Arezzo / City in Tuscany. Arezzo resisted the French rule, probably (Pound suggests by the arangement of detail) because the price of grain had gone from 7.50 to 12 in a month. The French ordered the total destruction of Arezzo. The suggestion is that the men of Arezzo do not understand the true reason for the rise in prices and, allowing their antisemitic prejudices to break out, blame the rise on the Jews. Tuscany, under Leopold and Ferdinand, had an enlightened attitude toward its Jews and allowed no overt antisemitism. In time of hardship, however, the people had been known to attack the ghetto and had to be put down by the government.

*Page 54 (63–64)*

the liberty tree / The French had raised the liberty tree in the piazzas of Tuscan towns. Pound is emphasizing the irony of the burnings next to the symbol of equality and fraternity.

Respectons les prêtres / The phrase in fact is in a letter from Napoleon to Talleyrand: "Let us respect the priests; it is the only way to live in peace with the Italian peasants."

Brumaire / One of the new names given the months by the Republican French.

Vous voudrez citoyen / "You will be willing, Citizen." Pound takes the opportunity of this cutting to remind us that good government is concerned with letting money circulate in the community.

Delort / A French officer, aide to the Napoleonic general Dupont de l'Etang.

Louis / Duke of Parma, whose reign was not enlightened.

Clarke / Napoleonic general. During the first French occupation in 1799, the Monte dei Paschi was injured by the invaders' policies, but later it thrived under Napoleon's reforms.

Madame ma soeur et cousine / "Madame, my sister and cousin." The letter, which continues for most of the next page, is from Napoleon to Marie-Louise, "Reine Régente d'Etrurie." It indicates that the kingdom of Etruria was having trouble; Napoleon was in fact about to dissolve it and install his sister as grand duchess.

*Page 55 (64-65)*

Lisbon / Pound has made a slip of the pen, seeing "Lisbon" in the next line of the text he is copying from. The letter reads "Livorno," the port of Etruria.

Bandini / He seems to be a chronicler Pound finds inferior to those he is drawing upon.

*Page 56 (65-66)*

"Semiramis" / The ship on which Elisa Bonaparte left Tuscany after her brother's fall from power.

monumento di civile sapienza / "Monument of civic wisdom."

*gabelle* / "Taxes."

Val di Chiana / Fertile valley in Tuscany.

porto franco / "Free port." Napoleon had violated the traditional neutrality of Livorno and its status as a free port; Ferdinand, on his return, restored the privilege.

Madame Letizia / She passed through Tuscany on her way to Elba, where she joined her son.

Piccolomini / President of the committee that authorized the compilation of the nine-volume work from which Pound has taken his notes, *Il Monte dei Paschi di Siena e la aziende in esso riunite* (Siena, 1891–1925).

◇   ◇

## CANTO 45

WRESTING SONG OR CHANT from its subject, Canto 45 moves firmly forward in anger, leaving no room for sympathy toward, or qualification of, Usura. The relentless litany or exorcism, however, is modulated with fine detail and subtle transitions, displaying the craftsmanship it praises.

It bears relation with Canto 14, but there the speaker/observer remains at a sardonic distance from the scene, his anger somewhat diminished by contempt for his subjects, the inhabitants of his hell, who are beyond the use of castigation. They are merely hirelings, a changing personnel. In Canto 45, we approach more closely their employer, and the speaker/chanter assumes an intimacy with and affection for the people and landscapes through which the blighting "murrain" of Usura moves. There is a finer balance than in Canto 14, which is composed entirely from negative elements. The dry bread, rust, palsey, canker, whores, and corpses of Canto 45 are counterbalanced with rich suggestions of achieved or potential beauty and fertility. The whores who desecrate the mysteries of Eleusis are measured against the concubines who have produced heirs for Gonzaga and for whom he has such healthy affection that he brings them into a family portrait.

Usura is not morally ambiguous, but it is linguistically metaplastic: at times a personified malevolence (moving the active verbs *blunteth, rusteth, slayeth, lyeth*), and at other times a generalized force or state. Lying between bride and bridegroom, Usura is a single figure, but elsewhere it is an ubiquitous "murrain" (related to *mortus, muerte, morte*). For most of the canto, it moves alone, as through the panels of a medieval Dance of Death; not until the final lines do we see that it commands a legion of servants. Feminine only by courtesy of grammar, it is essentially a sexless figure and lies in the marriage bed to enjoy neither bride nor bridegroom but to prevent fertility and pleasure. Even its name is ambivalent, a perversion of its basic meaning, which begins in the *use* of things. It now stands in the way of proper use, leaving us with adulterated bread and stopping the stonecutter's and the embroiderer's hands. So would it have stopped those of Fra Angelico, the stone carver Adam, and the architects of Saint Hilaire, if they had not worked before usury broke down the last defenses of the medieval traditions that condemned it.

One of the unifying elements in the canto is that all the painters and sculptors mentioned (and Villon) worked in the fifteenth century, before, as Pound thought, the quality of art began to be influenced by its salability. The point of division was about the middle of the sixteenth century, its *locus classicus* a letter from John Calvin to Claude de Sachin: "If we wholly condemn usury, we impose tighter fetters on the conscience than God himself." The central text on which the canon law had been based (Deut. 23:19) no longer held, Calvin maintained; God was speaking only to the Jews in laying down that prohibition. Calvin effectively ended the long debate brilliantly recorded in Benjamin Nelson's study, *The Idea of Usury: From Tribal Brotherhood to Universal Otherhood*. "Calvin on Deuteronomy," Nelson says, "became a Gospel of the modern era. Everyone from the sixteenth to the nineteenth century who advocated a more liberal usury law turned to Calvin for support."

So men's sense of how things should be *used* changed, and the root meaning of *usura* gave way to its present meaning. Pound is less concerned with quibbles over interest rates than with the perversion of *use*—of a man's time, of the fruits of the earth. The usurer wants more than he can decently use, and to get it he "stoppeth" other people's use of things.

The craftsmanship of the canto is itself a gesture of defiance toward Usura. (Pound worked fifty years on the *Cantos,* deriving from it an income that probably could not have supported him for two of those years.) The latinate coloration given the canto by the names and by the fragments of French, Latin, and Italian is counterpointed by suggestions of Anglo-Saxon alliteration: *hath/ house; virgin/message/projects; bride/bridegroom; banquet/be-*

*hest.* Note, too, the sound effects as in "Azure hath a canker," in which *a*'s both enclose and stand at the center of *e* and *r* sounds; in the echo of *Emerald* and *Memling;* and in the strong internal rhymes of *whores* and *corpses.* In the final line, *behest* picks up the *b*'s in the preceding lines, as well as the initial sound of *whores.* Strongly positioned words with Anglo-Saxon roots play against the Italian, Latin, French, and Greek: *house, stone, live, sell, sin, bread, wool, rust, craft, whores, behest.* (Never is Pound's mixture of tongues more appropriate: Usura is not local.)

The final passage beginning "None learneth to weave gold in her pattern" is particularly rich in suggestion, although by now the momentum of the chant is such that the reader is unlikely to pause consciously for complications. First, *gold:* its paradox is woven throughout the *Cantos,* where it appears as a useful commodity perverted, and as one of the colors of Paradise. The mention of gold then leads to a cluster of pure colors—azure, cramoisi (crimson), and emerald—words in which nature and art meet. Gold would have been used for the painting of the Annunciation where "halo projects from incision," and emerald is a pigment for Memling, whose "sparkling color, still as fresh as the day it was painted, fills each panel with a beautiful luminosity, almost as if it were sunlight." Yet if the colors belong to art and craft, *azure* is also sky, *emerald* a gem, and *cramoisi* extends its roots to blood, berries, and an insect.

The momentum of the chant takes us quickly over verbal resonances, but they are there. In the final lines, obsolete words enter the canto for the first time, chosen not only for their sounds, but because, without distraction of current denotation, they can harbor so many suggestions. *Behest* holds not only "command," but "promise, vow"—which resonates against the Annunciation of the first page, and against bride and bridegroom. *Cramoisi* is crimson cloth, but it begins with the scarlet grain insect (long thought to be a berry), which produced the first red dyes, and so connects with the wheat mentioned on the first page and with the agricultural ceremony of the Eleusinian mysteries. (Compare, in Spenser's marriage hymn, "Like crimsin dyde in grain.") *Canker* is perhaps the finest choice of all, not only a malignant tumor and spreading sore, but also rust ("It rusteth the craft"), anything that frets, consumes, corrodes.

" 'Eleusis' is *very* elliptical," Pound wrote to his Italian translator in 1938. "It means that in place of the sacramental — — — — in the Mysteries, you 'ave the 4 and six-penny 'ore. As you see, the moral bearing is very high, and the degradation of the sacrament (which is the coition and *not* the going to a fatbuttocked priest or registry office) has been completely debased by Xtianity, or misunderstanding of that Ersatz religion." It is indeed elliptical, and to work it out in relation to the *Cantos* would take many pages. But why is the pagan Eleusis in a canto otherwise colored by Christian references? Precisely because Christianity is not *entirely* Ersatz for Pound, to the extent that it has not completely obscured "the Light from Eleusis," which still shines in the Christian art he cares for. So Usura's public, paid (and presumably infertile) whores, violate the mysteries of Demeter, who is associated with agriculture and natural increase; but Demeter's mysteries may be harmonized with the mystery of the Annunciation earlier in the canto.

Although we might expect the language and allusions to distance the canto, giving it a medieval tone, Usura here comes closer to our twentieth-century lives than at any point in the *Cantos*. These are not other people's houses, bread, churches, art, sexuality, which are marred by Usura, but *ours,* and we are addressed with a familiar "thy." The final image is vivid, as Usura, having refused strong mountain wheat to the common man, perversely provides a banquet for corpses.

*Page 57* (*67*)

*harpes et luz* / From François Villon's ballade written for his mother to say as a prayer to the Virgin: "In my parish church, I see a painted paradise where there are harps and lutes."

Gonzaga his heirs and his concubines / Pound's title for Mantegna's mural of the Gonzaga family in the Ducal Palace at Mantua.

## Page 58 (67–68)

Pietro Lombardo / The architect and sculptor, Lombardo; the sculptor Agostino di Duccio (who worked on Malatesta's Tempio); and the painters Pier della Francesca, Giovanni Bellini, Botticelli, and Hans (Jean) Memling are all artists Pound admires, all fifteenth-century, and all Italian except for Memling, who had, however, close associations with Tuscany.

"La Calunnia" / An allegorical painting by Botticelli. Truth stands at the left, while Calumny, accompanied by Hate, Deceit, Fraud, and Suspicion, drags a helpless man along the ground by his hair.

*Adamo me fecit* / A stonecutter working on the church of San Zeno at Verona has signed his work, "Adam made me."

St Trophime . . . Saint Hilaire / The admired churches are at Arles and Poitiers.

CONTRA NATURAM / "Against Nature."

Eleusis / The Eleusinian mysteries were celebrated at Eleusis, near Athens, since prehistoric times. The rituals enacted Demeter's sorrow and joy at the disappearance and return of Persephone and reflected the agricultural cycle. A "sacred marriage" may have been performed during the ceremonies, human sexuality expressing the divine (Pound's letter, quoted above, would indicate that he thought so).

Usury / The prose note was added to later American editions only.

◇

# Cantos LII–LXXI (1940)

◇

A NEW SET OF TWENTY CANTOS was completed at Rapallo just as the war broke out. They form the longest, least read, and least admired of the separately issued sections of the poem. These cantos have been harshly treated by critics; and clearly the concentration, energy, and surprise of cantos such as 1, 4, 9, 13, 45, and even 31, are missing except for short passages. The 1940 volume is constructed around a conceit, and a good one, a play of time and space: ten cantos on Chinese history, in which time is vastly expanded (about five thousand years); then ten on American history, in which time is contracted to about thirty years, from the Boston Massacre to the end of John Adams's administration. There is a nice play of symmetry against asymmetry in this, for each "time" occupies the same number of pages. The two parts form a diptych, and the most exciting moment comes when Pound effects a transfer of energy from China to America at exactly 1776. The aesthetic question is whether it is more interesting to think about the conceit itself than to reread the 160 pages that allow it.

For the East, as he has done for the West, Pound begins with rite, myth, and prehistoric legends, things that happened, if they happened, long before they were recorded. From the oracular bones of the *I Ching,* the early *Odes,* the *Li Chi (Book of Rites),* and legends of the first emperors, we arrive at the life of Confucius and move through historical times, rapidly across centuries, observing dynasties rise and fall. A didactic pattern appears: When Chinese civilization heeded the teachings of Confucius, it flourished, but under Buddhist and Taoist influences it decayed. As the long history of China draws to a conclusion, there is a "translation," a handing over, as Jesuits bring Western art and science to the East and carry the teachings of Confucius to the

West. The very book Pound was working from bore physical testimony to the exchange: a twelve-volume *Histoire Générale de la Chine . . . Traduit de Tong-Kien-Kang-Mou* by Père Joseph de Mailla (Paris, 1777–1783).

Confucius influenced the French enlightenment and so contributed to events in America. Cantos 62 through 71 present the birth and early years of the Republic, seen through the eyes of Adams, Confucian in spite of himself (he happened to be in Paris as the volumes of de Mailla came from the press). Adams is shown as diplomat, peacemaker, and lawgiver, basing his law on the work of Lord Coke, whom Pound will place in *Thrones*. The snippets from Adams's writings are chosen to display him as a Confucian in action; each of his phrases may be set next to one of the *Analects*. In the first lines of Canto 62, for example, we hear Adams obeying the fundamental Confucian principle of looking into one's own heart, putting order in oneself:

> '*Acquit of evil intention*
> *or inclination to perseverance in error*
> *to correct it with cheerfulness*'

In the passage below from Canto 70, we see Adams combining common sense, knowledge of human nature, and religious inspiration. His credo, *dum spiro amo,* "So long as I live, I shall love," is juxtaposed with the Confucian *chung*[1], balance, the pivot:

I am for balance

and know not how it is but mankind have an aversion
      to any study of government
Thames a mere rivulet in comparison to the Hudson river
73 to Jefferson, to Mr. Burr 73
     DUM SPIRO
nec lupo committere agnum
     so they are against any rational theory.
     DUM SPIRO AMO

Throughout *Cantos LII–LXXI,* Pound continues to remind us that beneath all other voices in the *Cantos* an American voice is speaking. Here, for example, is the beautiful conclusion to the Chinese cantos:

> This princess entered the palace when YONG TCHING was
> > emperor
> as ' a young lady merely of talents
> recited with beautiful voice
> > and had other amiable qualities '
> concubine, and having a son was made queen
> and for forty two years had seen him, this son,
> on the first throne of Asia
> > in the 86th year of her age
> posthumous EMPRESS
> > Hiao Ching Hien Hoang Héou
> and her son as memorial
> > exempted his empire from the land tax
> for a year as indeed he had done before on her birthdays
> when she was 70 and when she reached her eightieth birthday
> and now, in memoriam. And he wrote
> > a poem on the Beauties of Mougden
> and condensed the Ming histories
> > literary kuss, and wuz Emperor
> fer at least 40 years.
> > Perhaps you will look up his verses.

That is Pound at his best, harmonizing effortlessly such levels of diction, and placing the finely chosen "merely" against the record of the empress's long and honored life. I have included these lines, and the final lines of Canto 70 above, to suggest that even in the poetically thinnest stretch of the *Cantos* there are rewards.

When the proofs of the 1940 volume were returned to London, Pound began what he thought would be the final section of the *Cantos.* He was finished, he said, with "money in history," and it was time now for Dante, Cavalcanti, Scotus Erigena, philosophy, the "empyrean." But the war delayed his *Paradiso,* and the final cantos remained thirty years in the future.

◊ ◊

## *from* CANTO 52

THE *Li Chi,* or Records of Ceremonials, one of the Five Classics, is a lengthy anthology compiled from ancient documents in the first century B.C. In Canto 52 Pound has made what Donald Davie calls "an extremely beautiful redaction" of the "Yueh Ling," one of the *Li Chi's* forty-six sections. Legge, the nineteenth-century sinologist whose editions Pound used, translates *Yueh Ling* as "Proceedings of Government in the Different Months." It is a kind of almanac for emperor and nobles, reminding them, each month, of the position of sun and stars and of the proper cere- monial foods and colors and providing animal lore and practical advice for regulating husbandry. Pound has played down the "Yueh Ling's" rituals, in the sense of "routine" or "customs that must be followed," to increase the feeling of a sophisticated world that still retains religious wonder, is aware (the theme of Canto 31) of times and seasons, and has not lost contact with nature.

For Pound, the importance of the Confucian Classics lies in their ethic and sensibility; they provide foundations for dynamic, in- novative action. The *Odes* and the rites of the *Li Chi* provide a balance, a rooting in tradition that prevents discussion from be- coming abstract and innovation from turning into "exaggerations of dogma." Yet he knows that legalist and neo-Confucian com- mentators have given Confucianism a connotation of fussy, re- actionary adherence to custom. A short chapter in *Guide to Kulchur* bears the curious title "Odes:Risks." It recounts a Con- fucian anecdote to the effect that "Confucian pedagogy in the home seems to have consisted in C's asking his son whether he had read a couple of books, one, the Book of Odes, the other the Rites." The second part of this chapter/prose ideo- gram is: "Our general notion of Confucius (Kung) has per- haps failed to include a great sensibility. The Conversations are the record of a great sensibility." The point of the chapter's title is that the emphasis on continual study of the *Odes* and on the observance of *li* or rites, "risks" being misunderstood.

> The Master said, " 'It is according to the rules of propriety,' they say.—'It is according to the rules of propriety,' they say. Are gems and silk all that is meant by propriety? 'It is music,' they say—'It is music,' they say. Are bells and drums all that is meant by music?"

The ideogram for *li* perfectly expresses the desired balance between letter and spirit. One half indicates a ceremonial vessel used in the rites: that is, the specifics, the etiquette, the direction (for example) to eat in a certain autumn month dog meat from a dish of prescribed depth. The other half suggests "prayer" and "spiritual beings": that is, the underlying purpose of the ritual, recognition of a world in which even "The wolf now offers his sacrifice" and ritual offerings are made "to the Lords of the Mountains / To the Lords of great rivers."

Pound has shaped his materials very freely, supplying ambiguities to increase the "Yueh Ling's" aura of a magic world aware of divine immanence, where subtle structures of thought move beneath the apparent rigidity of the almanac instructions. "Sovran" may be noun or adjective, allowing "Lord of the Fire" to be read as one of the emperor's titles or as a spirit in the fire. The Son of Heaven who feeds on roast pork and millet is the emperor, but the Son of Heaven to whom the empress offers cocoons appears to be a divinity. But then, we are in a world where kings still trace their ancestries back to the gods and still mediate between heaven and earth.

When the inspector of dye-works is instructed to "let no false colours exist here," where exactly is "here"? Is it the economic-political kingdom, or does it include also the natural kingdom, the lakes, mountains, rivers, and trees? If the reference is only to the honest operation of the dye-works, the colors, nevertheless, come from nature and are returned to the gods in the emperor's ritual trappings (as the colors of Canto 45, again through ambiguities of language, belong to both nature and art). Why, with

a sudden lift of imperative, is it important to "tie up the stal-
lions"? To recognize that "Orion at sunrise" marks "the month
of ramparts"? Does that dead grass metamorphose into glow-
worms, the way pheasants become oysters, or does the grass merely
offer the glow-worms a shelter for breeding? Is the "concert of
winds" that of nature or of musical instruments? And should
such Western questions even be asked of this world? There are
answers to all of them, mostly in the form of practical advice, in the
"Yueh Ling," but to look them up, or at least to have them in mind
as one reads Canto 52, is to destroy the care with which Pound
has transformed them. One of the *Analects* tells us that:

> Someone said: What does the sacrifice mean? He said: I do not
> know. If one knows enough to tell that, one could govern the
> empire as easily as seeing the palm of one's hand.

As prelude to the Chinese history cantos, the canto drawn from
the "Yueh Ling" reminds us that civilization begins in things
half-remembered, partly comprehensible, partly lost forever. What
truths it reveals, however, are not exclusively Chinese; the constel-
lations are given their familiar Western names, the same as those
by which Hesiod, in Canto 47, counted the seasons and gave almanac advice:

> When the Pleiades go down to their rest,
> Begin thy plowing

The sensibility in which this "folklore" grew is not to be patron-
ized, can not be understood with the eyes of a Diderot, a perfect
example of a mind that, turning from the odes and the rites, tends
to exaggeration of dogma even as it fights dogma:

> We must ride roughshod over all these ancient puerilities, over-
> turn the barriers that reason never erected. . . . We have for
> quite some time needed a reasoning age when men would no
> longer seek the rules in classical authors but in nature.

If we have read modern linguists and anthropologists, a Diderot
sounds almost as quaint as the "Yueh Ling." "Kung is modern in
his interests in folklore," says Pound. "All this Frazer-Frobenius

research is Confucian." The Confucian rites and directives are fetters only if we do not understand the Confucian imperative to "Make it new." The "puerilities" that produce the incomprehensible, unscientific rules governing the *li* of primitive peoples are products of an elaborate reason, if a different reason from ours. "The anthropologists of my generation" Lévi-Strauss writes:

> are disconcerted by Frazer's aversion to the research he had done all his life: "tragic chronicles," he wrote, "of the errors of man: foolish, vain efforts, wasted time, frustrated hopes." We are hardly less surprised to learn from the *Notebooks* how a Lévy-Bruhl considered myths, which, according to him, "no longer have any effect on us . . . strange narratives, not to say incomprehensible . . . it costs us an effort to take an interest in them." . . .
>
> It is to the extent that so-called primitive societies are very different from our own, that we can discover in them those "facts of general functioning" of which Mauss spoke, which stand a chance of being "more universal," and "more real." . . . This observation, privileged by distance, no doubt implies certain differences in nature between those societies and our own. Astronomy requires that the celestial bodies be distant, but also that the passage of time there should have a different rhythm.

Different rhythms are heard in the last five lines of Canto 52, as we leave the "Yueh Ling" and move into Confucian-Mencian ethics:

> Call things by the names. Good sovereign by distribution
> Evil king is known by his imposts.

Then a final Confucian principle, "Begin where you are," carries the poem into the mid-nineteenth century, where Lord Palmerston, who would probably have thought the "Yueh Ling" puerile, nevertheless embodies the true spirit of *li,* and "makes it new" in Ireland.

The long ritual of Canto 52 should be read only for its self-contained suggestions; there are no symbols or codes. If we happen to find things that echo in other cantos, it is because there are signatures in nature. "Strife is between light and darkness" is primarily recorded because the "Proceedings of the Government in the Different Months" has reached the summer solstice; it is merely fortuitous if it reminds us of the strife that informs the entire *Cantos*.

The poem reminds us with great delicacy that our observation of a world beyond history is, as Lévi-Strauss says, privileged by distance:

now sparrows, they say, turn into oysters

"They say" is a twentieth-century voice, a reservation inevitable to the modern mind, not to be found in the "Yueh Ling."

### Page 60

SEVEN / Pound has eliminated most of the Taoist numerology in the "Yueh Ling." Each season has its proper number, as it has a proper color for ceremonial robes, a proper emphasis for sacrifice, and so forth. Seven is the number for summer.

Ming T'ang / A different apartment in the palace ("that house") is appropriate to the emperor's ceremonies in each of the months. Ming T'ang is the apartment for the first month of summer.

*manes* / Latin: "the spirits of the dead."

### Page 62

*chih*[3] / Pound associates the character with making a start on a worthwhile project even if you know you can not see it to completion. "There is no more important technical term in the Confucian philosophy than this *chih*(3) the hitching post, position, place one is in, and works from."

◇    ◇

# CANTO 53

POUND, plugging his way through a tedious digest-with-commentary of the *Nicomachean Ethics,* pauses to note: "Let it stand written that somewhere about III.vii of Aristotle's treatise I was ready to chuck up the job, as a waste of time, and my comment likely to be a waste of the reader's. (This feeling I have had neither with the *Analects* nor the *Chi King*.)" I confess to the same feeling in compiling the chronology and historical notes that follow. They are there for the reader who may find them interesting or useful, and they tell us a good deal about Pound's methods in the Chinese history cantos. Yet the great arc of these cantos makes better reading without an attempt to see much more than is on the page.

My experience in compiling the notes and in checking Pound's sources has, I believe, much to do with his aesthetic. In his prose writings, he never urges us to look into Père de Moyriac de Mailla's *Histoire générale,* as he does insist that we go to so many other books. Yet if de Mailla's history is not an essential book, it deserves honor as an act of translation, a place where two cultures meet. In the pages of the Jesuit de Mailla, as it were,

> Père Henri Jacques still
> speaks with the sennin on Rokku

> (C.88)

The large volumes, with their thick, soft paper and eighteenth-century *s*'s, are as fresh as if printed last month. To touch them is to come closer to the journey itself—that of de Mailla sitting in Peking with ancient documents before him, then that of his manuscript (he died in China) traveling back to Paris, to be published as an act of piety and enlightenment by the suppressed Jesuits. In fact, reading de Mailla is more exciting than reading Pound's Chinese cantos. The eighteenth-century prose suggests a China very different from Pound's, as we can see if we compare "YAO like the sun and rain" with de Mailla's account of the emperor whose *esprit* was

> *éclairé que le soleil dans les plus beaux jours: semblables aux nuages qui fertilissent les campagnes.*

De Mailla's tales of the first mythical emperors surpass Pound's in wonder. They appear, as if from nowhere, to instruct childlike noble savages in the rudiments of civilization, starting with "houses of twigs like birds' nests" (Pound's "Yeou taught men to break branches"). Yet although reading de Mailla is not necessary for reading the *Cantos,* I do not think Pound would wish to separate my afternoons with the *Histoire générale de la Chine* from my experience of his poem. Those afternoons produced an involvement and an awareness that Pound's leaps and obscurities (as so often in the *Cantos*) invite us to complete.

The canto begins beautifully, extending the magical world of Canto 52 for a while, until the emperors become increasingly less a part of nature. It has its moments of excitement, such as the motto on Tching's bathtub, the cry "We are up, Hia is down," and the wry mingling of hope and gloom in Confucius's "I am pro-Tcheou in politics." But surely most readers will find the central pages hard going until the lyrical tribute to Confucius in the final lines.

The verbal play making connections with other cultures and ages is not very effective in this canto. The use of words from Greek, Latin, French, and Italian to suggest parallels with European history is often weak or farfetched. The parallel between Tching and Frobenius is false wit, for the emperor's rainmaking results from penance and prayer, whereas *der im Baluba's* is accidental. At a deeper level, however, the mixture of languages reminds us of Pound's purpose: to create a Frobenian *paideuma* where linguistics and anthropology are as much a part of human activity as is art. (Of this favorite term, Pound says, "Frobenius uses the term Paideuma for the tangle or complex of the inrooted ideas of any period. . . . I shall use Paideuma for the gristly roots of ideas that are in action.") Indeed, in Canto 38 we find Frobenius and Lévy-Bruhl side by side:

> The ragged arab spoke with Frobenius and told him
> The names of 3000 plants.
> Bruhl found some languages full of detail
> Words that half mimic action

Many of the fragments of reported speech and remnants of other languages in the *Cantos* are just that—

> "all them g.d. m.f. generals c.s. all of 'em fascists"
>
> (C.74)

—gestures of the voice, luminous details that are data for linguistic and anthropological research.

Finally, Confucian-Frobenian research contains another dimension, which explains Pound's return to the "Yueh Ling" and the *Shu Ching,* the Confucian *History Classic* (*through* de Mailla's version of it, as in Canto 1 we approached Homer through Andreas Divus). J. P. Sullivan writes:

> The classics, whether Homer's epics or the 'Confucian Odes,' are both the records and the germ of civilization. This view of the classics as *paideuma* (in Frobenius' sense) involves not an *external* apprehension of what they have to say or convey, but rather seeing them as summarizing selectively and intuitively the whole experience of a given age or milieu.

The following notes give only a bare chronology and a rudimentary sense of who is who in this canto. All the names are of emperors unless otherwise stated. The Greek, Latin, Italian, French, and German references are gathered separately at the end of the chronology.

## Chinese and English Words and Phrases

*Page 63* (*72*)

Yeou / Mythical, undated in de Mailla.

Seu Gin / Mythical.

Fou Hi / Legendary. Here de Mailla begins to put dates in his margins.

Chin Nong / Successor of Fou Hi.

Souan yen / A minister to Chin Nong.

Hoang Ti / Still legendary, but dated 2698 B.C.

Ti Ko / Reigned 2366 B.C.

YAO / At this point the *Shu ching*, the *History Classic*, takes up the narrative and runs parallel to de Mailla. Yao's name, and those of Chun and Yu, are capitalized because together they form the trinity of great legendary emperors invoked throughout Chinese history and in all the Confucian writings.

*Page 64 (73–74)*

YU / Here begins the Hia or Hsia dynasty, 2205 B.C.

Yu-chan / The name of the mountain.

Chun / The correct chronology is given below, where the romanized and Chinese characters stand next to each other.

KAO-YAO / A great minister under Chun.

*Page 65 (74–75)*

Chao Kang / Still Hsia dynasty, 2079 B.C. In the lines that follow, the chronology doubles back on itself, repeating three of the pre-Yao emperors, and adding two previously unmentioned.

Chang Ti / Heaven. In de Mailla, *"le Ciel."*

Tching Tang / Began his reign in 1766 B.C., marking the end of the Hsia dynasty and the beginning of the Shun. The four ideograms—*hsin¹/jih⁴/jih⁴/hsin¹*—form the motto that Pound liked so much. In his translation of the *Ta Hio:*

> In letters of gold on T'ang's bathtub:
>
> AS THE SUN MAKES IT NEW
> DAY BY DAY MAKE IT NEW
> YET AGAIN MAKE IT NEW.

The translation here in Canto 53 retains more of the ideogrammic force of the characters. The component on the right in *hsin*[1] is the sixty-ninth radical of the Chinese language, meaning something like "large cutting blade," so, in the context of *hsin*[1], "axe." The component on the left contains (below) the radical for "tree" and (above) what Pound sees as "woodpile." *Jih*[4] is the sun; repeated, it has the sense of "every day." Pound's translation tries to keep as much as possible of the concreteness and active force of the ideograms. Compare Legge: "If you can one day renovate yourself, do so from day to day. Yea, let there be daily renovation"; and de Mailla: *"Souviens-toi de te renouveller chacque jour, plusieurs fois le jour."*

## Page 66 (75–76)

Hia / The same as Hsia, given below next to its ideogram. After Tching Tang's death, one of his ministers is lecturing the grandson (here unnamed) who succeeded him. The minister warns the young emperor not to take his power for granted, that the Hsia flourished while they remained virtuous and that the only reason "we" (the Shang dynasty) are in power is *"le décadence de Hia."*

YIN / The minister talking above; in de Mailla, "Y-yn." Pound's "Yin" is slightly confusing, because Yin is a name for the Shang dynasty itself.

Wen Wang / We are approaching the end of the Shang. Wen Wang was king of Chou, a principality in the West. He was the father of Wu Wang, founder of the great Chou dynasty, and of his brother, the great duke of Chou.

Uncle Ki / The anecdote is meant to show the increasing decadence of the Shang. Bears' paws were a delicacy, a sign of extravagance.

Tan Ki / Sadistic concubine of the last of the Shang emperors, the tyrant Cheou-sin.

Kieou's daughter / Further evidence of the decadence of Shang. Kieou was minister under Cheou-sin. When his daughter protested conditions in the kingdom, Tan Ki had her killed, cooked, and served to her father. The tale forms a subject-rhyme with those in Canto 4.

Y-king / The *I Ching,* or *Book of Changes,* the oldest source of Chinese literature, was said to have been developed by Wen Wang and his son, the duke of Chou. The suggestion is that they are doing something useful while the evil emperor indulges in tyranny.

*Page 67 (76–77)*

Wu Wang / Son of Wen Wang, he led the uprising against Cheou-sin, defeating him in a great battle on the plain of Mou Ye. We have arrived at 1122 b.c., as Wu Wang founds the Chou dynasty, which will last for 900 years. The next three pages supply examples of wise government under the early Chou.

Tcheou Kong / The duke of Chou, a figure revered in Chinese history, perhaps only second to Confucius. On the death of his brother, the duke became regent and held the dynasty together.

*Page 68 (77–78)*

Tching-ouang / The young emperor continues the dynasty's beneficent reign.

Chao Kong / Another uncle of Tching-ouang's. When the latter dies, he takes charge of the funeral arrangements, described below.

*Page 69 (78–79)*

Ouen Ouang / Pound has switched to de Mailla's French version of Wen Wang.

Kang / Son of Tching-ouang, also referred to as Kang-wang and Kang Ouang below.

Confucius / Centuries later, he takes the early Chou emperors as models.

*Page 70 (79–80)*

Grow pear-boughs / From a folksong in the *Odes* (2.2.5). The point is that, for centuries after, the common people remember Chao-Kong.

Tchao-ouang / The dynasty begins to fall from its high standards, so the people are not sad at the emperor's death.

MOU-OUANG / Reigned 1001–947 B.C. Further signs of decadence. The records of him in the *Shu Ching* are moving: He is deeply aware of his own weakness and appeals to his ministers to help him maintain the honor of Chou. A passage in the *Shu* clarifies the words in quotation marks: "The trembling anxiety of my mind makes me feel as if I were treading on a tiger's tail, or walking upon spring ice. I now give you charge to assist me; be as my limbs to me, as my heart and backbone."

*Page 71 (80–81)*

*Chu King* / The *Shu Ching*.

*Lin hing* / A great legal document from the reign of Mou-ouang.

KONG / The rest of the page shows how the Chou, now generations removed from their exemplary ancestors, fall into disorder. Kong-ouang is destructive and moody. In the reign of Y-wang there are bad omens, music and nature turning against him. The memorial spoken for the greedy Li Wang is in sharp contrast to the honors paid his ancestors.

*Page 72 (81)*

Siuen-ouang / Eighth century B.C. We hear of wars with barbarian Tartars, which continue throughout the Chinese cantos. The emperor is praised for appointing the generals Chaoumoukong and Han, but later it is suggested that the people have suffered because he has not observed the rites.

Swift men as if flyers / Here, and in the Latin phrases, Pound turns to the *Odes* describing the reign of Siuen-ouang. This is a description of his army moving against the Tartars. (*Odes* 3.3.10).

RITE is:/ The material is drawn from the first spring month of the "Yueh Ling," the source of Canto 52.

*Page 73 (82)*

He heard the wild geese / Siuen recognizes that the latter part of his reign is a failure, and he has retired to the countryside. His hopes for an orderly succession are ironic, for squabbles among his grandsons hasten the fall of the dynasty.

Lady Pao Sse / Yeou Ouang, Siuen's son, fell under the charm of this evil concubine. In order to give the succession to her own son, she had P'ing, the rightful heir, sent into exile. Later, in a civil war, he was restored to power, but the damage to the dynasty was permanent.

Tçin / Foreshadows the rise of the Ch'in dynasty, about five centuries later.

Ouen Kong / Here the chronicle leaves the Chou dynasty and moves to the state of Lou, where Confucius will be born. Ouen Kong, a good ruler, comes to power in 609 B.C. Evil ministers kill his son, Siang, claiming the death is a hunting accident. Then Lou falls into disorder with a series of "Richards" usurping the throne. We enter the period known as the Warring States, during which the whole of China was in turmoil. Meanwhile, the *Shu* or *History Classic* has ended, about 631 B.C.

*Page 74 (82–83)*

Ling Kong / An irresponsible ruler, as his actions show.

King Kong / Ruler of a neighboring state.

Kungfutseu / Confucius is born (551 B.C.) in Lou. Chung Ni is his "literary" name; the *chung*[1] or the pivot or balance can be seen in one of the characters. The canto now follows his career, beginning with his first job, which Pound describes as "a Douglasite assessment of the productivity of the province set for inspection."

King Wang / The Chou emperor who was in power during the latter part of Confucius's life, called King Ouang on the next page. His economic policies show that the empire is badly ruled.

## Page 75 (83–84)

King Kong / The point is that Confucius found rulers who honored him and his ideas but none who would put his policies into action.

C. T. Mao / At fifty-six, Confucius was made acting chancellor of Lou. He accepted the job on condition that a troublemaker, C. T. Mao, be executed. Pound associates Mao's mentality with that of modern financiers.

LOU rose / That is, during the period when Confucius held office. The neighboring state of Tsi, afraid that Lou will become too powerful, sends a bribe of eighty dancing girls to the prince of Lou. When Confucius sees that the girls distract the officials and that the proper rites are not being observed, he resigns in disgust and enters his long period of exile, seeking a ruler who will adopt his ideas.

Tching / This anecdote and the one that follows (at Tchin) are from the years of wandering.

Yng P / That is, although Yng P was illegitimate, his father offered him the succession to the throne. Yng P, considering himself unworthy, refuses the offer.

Tchin and Tsai / Fearing that Confucius's influence may strengthen a neighboring state, the nobles of Tchin and Tsai isolate him and his disciples in the wilderness, but he is rescued by troops of the Chou (Tcheou) emperor.

cut 3000 odes / According to legend, he edited the *Odes*.

*Page 76 (84–85)*

Min Kong / Ancestor of the Ch'in dynasty, which followed the Chou in 255 B.C. The material that follows shows the chaotic condition of China during the centuries after Confucius's death. During the Ch'in period books and records were burned, and it was not until later, when the Classics and Confucian documents were reassembled, that the influence of Kung was felt in government.

YO-Y / Minister of Yen, about 285 B.C. That he reduces taxes and labor obligations is probably meant to show the underground workings of Confucian thought during the period.

Chou / The honor is given, not to the late Chou period described here, but to the early period Kung had in mind when he described himself as "pro-Tcheou."

## WORDS AND PHRASES IN OTHER LANGUAGES

*Page 64 (73)*

Ammassi / Yu is allowing a hard-pressed province to pay its taxes in goods it has (earth of five colors, pheasant plumes, timber) rather than in specie. Pound sees a connection between Yu's policies and those of the Italian government in the 1930s: "Rossoni, Italian Minister, indicates the policy of *ammassi,* or assemblages of grain with possibilities of a totally different tax system in kind."

μῶλυ / *Moly,* the magic herb Hermes gives Odysseus to protect him from Circe's charms. The suggestion is that this period in China corresponds to the Heroic Age in the West.

que vos vers expriment, etc. / "May your verse express your meaning, and may the music for it conform (to the meaning)." Pound is leaving traces of de Mailla in the poem, reminding us that China first spoke to Europe in French.

## *Page 65 (74)*

der im Baluba / Translated in Canto 38 as "The white man who made the tempest in Baluba." Leo Frobenius, of great importance to Pound, had studied African rain gods. When he made a pioneering expedition to the Babunda (not Baluba) tribe in Africa, a thunderstorm came up, and the Babunda thought the storm was produced by some gestures Frobenius had made. In the Chinese legend, Tching is also a rainmaker. After seven years of drought, he goes to a mountaintop to beg the gods for rain, and a storm comes up at once.

## *Page 72 (81)*

contra barbaros, etc. / He appoints a leader for a war against the barbarians. (All the Latin phrases are from an eighteenth-century translation of the *Odes* by a Jesuit, Lacharme.)

Juxta fluvium, etc. / Without delay, battle positions are drawn up along the river Hoai.

agit considerate / "He acts with caution."

## *Page 73 (82)*

hac loca fluvius alluit / "The river flows by these places."

Campestribus locis / "In places in the fields, or countryside."

## *Page 74 (83)*

μεταθεμένων, etc. / *Metathemenon te ton krumenon.* The phrase, from Aristotle's *Politics,* is repeated four times in the *Cantos.* In context: "Others maintain that coined money is a mere sham, a thing not natural, but conventional only, because *if the users substitute another commodity for it,* it is worthless, and because it is not useful as a means to any of the necessities of life." The point here is that money is a measure, and the task of a good ruler is to keep it from varying.

*Page 76 (85)*

POLLON IDEN / "He saw the cities." Condensation of Homer's *pollon d'anthropōn iden* (of Odysseus): "He saw the cities of many men [and knew their minds]." Tchan-y was a kind of *condottiere*, fighting for whatever state would hire him. By leaving out the *d'anthropōn*, Pound suggests that he saw a lot of cities, but in a dehumanized way.

◊     ◊

## *from* CANTO 62

A SINGLE PAGE of the sixty-one drawn from the writings of John Adams is all that remains in *Selected Cantos*, suggesting that Pound may have had second thoughts about the strategy of this section of the poem. It is the finest of the sixty-one pages.

Pound supplies a table of contents giving, as he saw it, the important moments of Adams's career. The outline is worth looking at, and its final item reinforces the theme of this passage:

JOHN ADAMS
Writs of assistance
Defence of Preston
The congress (Nomination of Washington)
Voyage to France
    (not being diddled by Vergennes or plastered by Dr. Franklin)
Saving the fisheries
Plan of Government
Recognition, loan from the Dutch, treaty with Holland
London
Avoidance of war with France

Adams's apologia is touching and funny (my italics):

Not vindictive *that I can remember*
        though I have often been wroth

His "wont to give his conversation / full impetus of vehement will" is an understatement. The spikey style of the letters makes them hard not to quote from; one can understand Pound's wanting to assemble ten cantos from them.

The passage begins with one of the archetypes of American literature, the apparently innocent American confronting the experience of Europe. We then have glimpses of Adams's humanity and balance, his compassion for "poor dutch Fries" (officially a traitor, but of no real importance), and his contempt for Hamilton (the real traitor, in Pound's view, though seldom recognized as such).

Implicit in this passage is Adams's political courage in pardoning Fries, but especially in opposing his own Federalists, who led the cry for war with France. In 1799 he abruptly dismissed his secretary of state, Timothy Pickering, Hamilton's ally, who was manipulating the country toward war. The theme is pungently restated in Canto 70:

> Vans M/ exhausted all things in enormous bribes ' (ciphered)
> Talleyrand, leaving however reserves for chicanery,
>      and Murray not yet removed from the Hague
>                          about 'peace'
> shortly ago were howling for war with Britain,
>                                peace, war
> aimed at elections. My appointment of Murray
>      has at least laid open characters to me
> ' you are hereby discharged '
>      John Adams, President of the United States
>      to Tim Pickering

This returns in fine, if elliptical, comedy in Canto 114:

> "Pas même Fréron
>      hais personne
>           pas même Fréron,"
> "I hate no-one," said Voltaire
> "not even Fréron."
>      .    .    .    .    .    .
>           "not even Tim Pick"

The fortunate reader will trace this to Adams's letter to Jefferson of 29 May 1818:

> After all, I hope to meet my wife and Friends, Ancestors and Posterity, Sages ancient and modern. I believe I could get over all my Objections to meeting Alec Hamilton and Tim Pick, if I could perceive a Symptom of sincere Penitence in either.

As the editor of his letters tells us, "Adams, with magnificent courage, sacrificed his political career by sending a new peace mission to France, thereby frustrating the demand of the High Federalists for all-out war."

The concluding lines of the canto are particularly fine, descending sharply from the imperial "(my authority, ego scriptor cantilenae)" to the very American, meticulously documented gutter indignation of "Prime snot in ALL American history," then rising again in a marvelously shaped period to the final salute. The line divisions force the voice into gestures of full-throated oratory. Here Pound, as he rarely does in extended passages, uses strongly stressed accents rather than quantitative verse or conversational phrasings:

> But for the clearest head in the congress
>
> > > 1774 and thereafter
>
> > páter pátriae
>
> the man who at certain points
>
> > > máde us
>
> at certain points
>
> > > sáved us
>
> by fáirness, hónesty and stráight móving

Adams, it is fair to say, is the forgotten man among giants of American history. Textbooks recognize his contributions yet never warm to him as they do to Washington, Jefferson, Franklin, and even Hamilton. In his lifetime, too, his sharp tongue and noble Roman independence left him admired but hardly loved. Certainly one of the finest dramatic gestures in the *Cantos* is Pound's compensation for this neglect, reaching for the latin abandon of: ARRIBA ADAMS.

◇   ◇   ◇

## Page 77 (86–87)

Talleyrand / One of the wiliest and most avaricious politicians in history, foreign minister of France during Adams's presidency. During the XYZ affair of 1797, he disclaimed knowledge of the agents who were demanding bribes of American diplomats but secretly expected to share in those bribes.

Murray / Adams thought the appointment of William Van Murray to the Hague one of the important acts of his presidency, for Murray's real mission was to prevent war.

Fries / John Fries led a group of Pennsylvania farmers in a local rebellion against tax collectors in 1799. He was sentenced to hang, but Adams pardoned him.

Hamilton / Having done his best to defeat Adams in the election of 1796, he energetically used his influence with members of Adams's government to destroy the administration and to agitate for war with France.

## Page 78

pater patriae / "Father of his country," the title Rome awarded Cicero after he exposed Cataline's conspiracy.

ARRIBA / "Viva! Hurray for!" (Spanish).

# The Pisan Cantos (1948)

The ancients therefore fabled not absurdly, in
making memory the mother of the muses. For
memory is the world (though not really, yet so
as in a looking glass) in which judgement (the
severer sister) busieth herself in a grave and
rigid examination of all the parts of nature
. . . whereby the fancy, when any work of art
is to be performed, findeth her materials at hand
and prepared for use, and needs no more than a
swift motion over them, that what she wants,
and is there to be had, may not lie too long un-
espied. So that when she seemeth to fly from one
Indies to the other, and from heaven to earth,
and to penetrate into the hardest matter, and
obscurest places, into the future, and into herself,
and all this in a point of time. . . . He therefore that undertakes an heroic poem (which is
to exhibit a venerable and amiable image of
heroic virtue) must not only be the poet, to place
and con, but also the philosopher, to furnish
and square his matter, that is, to make both body
and soul, color and shadow of his poem out of
his own store: which how well you have performed I am now considering.
                          Thomas Hobbes,
                  *Answer* to Davenant's *Gondibert*

THE ELEVEN PISAN CANTOS were written at a time when the poem
including history found itself included within history. In a Washington courtroom in 1946, the court, whose theory of literature did
not take into account the depersonalization of art nor see the poet's

mind as a shred of platinum leaving no trace in the work, allowed a psychiatrist's reading of the manuscript ("incoherent") to be entered as evidence in the trial of the poet.

Before the Pisan sequence, there are two missing cantos, 72 and 73, forming a blank, a white space that is now part of the poem. They mark a time just before, the poem tells us as it resumes, a world came to an end:

> yet say this to the Possum: a bang, not a whimper,
>     with a bang not with a whimper
>
> (C.74)

The poet has become "a man on whom the sun has gone down" (C.74), and what was a mythical prophecy in Canto 1—"Lose all companions"—has become reality. The heroic voyager is

>         As a lone ant from a broken ant-hill
> from the wreckage of Europe, ego scriptor.
>
> (C.76)

The Pisan cantos are about the poet saving himself from the wreckage and rebuilding a new world somewhere beyond the possibility of destruction, building it in the mind.

Pound projects an image of an ideal, indestructible city in which one believes all the more *quia impossibile est,* because it is impossible. It becomes "the city of Dioce whose terraces are the colour of stars" and is invoked in the mysterious cry "Hooo Fasa," for which we need a gloss. Frobenius tells the African myth of Gassire's lute (C.74), in which the spirit of a divinity, Wagadu, is displayed as a splendid city that is built and destroyed four times, as Dierra, Agada, Ganna, and Silla. If Wagadu ever appears again, she will bear the name Fasa.

> Should Wagadu ever be found for the fifth time, then she will live so forcefully in the minds of men that she will never be lost again, so forcefully that vanity, falsehood, greed and dissension will never be able to harm her.
> Hoooh! Dierra, Agada, Ganna, Silla! Hooh! Fasa!

During the war years, Pound's work took two directions, and the conflict between them is a subject of the Pisan cantos. One was "philosophy," preparation for bringing the poem into the empyrean: He continued his study of the Confucian texts and was reading Scotus Erigena and Santayana's *The Realm of Spirit*. The other direction was toward political journalism in Italian and Japanese newspapers; economic pamphlets; and, in frustration that his messages about world order and the Constitution were not heard in an America moving toward what he saw as an unnecessary war, broadcasts in English over Rome Radio. The broadcasts stopped for a few weeks after Pearl Harbor, then resumed.

Scurrilous, uninformed, frenzied, utterly impractical as communication, the broadcasts are probably the worst utterances by a great poet of which there is record. The best one can say for them is that they represent an extreme case of idealism coarsened, driven to a misuse of language by the illusion that one can directly affect world politics. His mistake, from the point of view of the American government, was in broadcasting while American troops were fighting the Axis. His mistake as *he* comes to see it in the Pisan cantos was more serious. In May 1945, when American troops occupied Rapallo, Pound was arrested and transported to the Army's Disciplinary Training Center (DTC) near Pisa.

The cantos he wrote there are filled with memories, some quite private, but it is a mistake to allow unfamiliar allusions to draw our attention from the dramatic and formal movements of the poem. It is not completely self-sufficient, but the only really important reference not repeated from earlier cantos is the myth of Wagadu. To questions such as who are Nancy, Dolores, Amber Rives, Clower, and Upward, the first answer is, people Pound knew and about whom he tells us enough to read the poem. The apparent spontaneity and disorder seem at first held together only loosely by the traditional unities of time, place, and action (mostly subjective action), but they are in fact a play of language over an intricate logic of association.

The passages in *Selected Cantos* do not carry the same weight as when they are read as the conclusion to the Pisan sequence.

(Pound selected Cantos 81 and 84; the American publisher has added the passage from Canto 83.) Pound's choices emphasize the emotional climax of the series, the appearance of the eyes within the tent, which is followed by the passage beginning "What thou lovest well remains" and then by the reestablished Confucian balance of the final pages. He omits the more pathetic and confessional passages as well as most of the American voices and gallows humor of the DTC. It is helpful in reading Cantos 81, 83, and 84 to have a sense of the Pisan sequence as a whole, and this may be given by pointing out the following related themes:

    1. *The DTC.* A man who describes himself as "Old Ez" and "ego scriptor" is in an Army prison within sight of Pisa during the summer and autumn of 1945. He is "an old man (or oldish)," sixty to be exact. No one ever addresses him by name, because he is (like Odysseus in the Cyclops's cave) "noman, my name is noman." When one of his more literate fellow prisoners speaks to him, it is:

> Hey Snag wots in the bibl'?
> wot are the books ov the bible?
> Name 'em, don't bullshit ME.

(C.74)

Sometimes he is in a steel cage among "death cells" open to dust and wind and glaring lights. At other times he is in a tent or hospital scabies ward. In the cage he sleeps on a concrete floor until a kindly black soldier, who embodies the spirit of Kuanon, the Chinese goddess of mercy, brings him a table made from packing crates.

For reading matter he has a Bible, the works of Confucius, and miscellaneous material such as *Time* magazine. Later, just when he feels at the end of his resources, M. E. Speare's 1940 anthology, *The Pocket Book of Verse,* shows up:

> that from the gates of death: Whitman or Lovelace
> found on the jo-house seat at that
> in a cheap edition! [and thanks to Professor Speare]

(C.80)

Snatches from the anthology find their way into a manuscript he is working on. Fragments of the guards' and prisoners' conversation are sharply recorded. Beyond barbed wire he sees the towers of Pisa. An ominous gibbet stands against the sky, and one of his black companions in misery (*comes miseriae*) is hanged from it. He never tells us exactly what has brought him to the death cells, only hinting that history and usury have something to do with it.

2. *The Periplum*. The prisoner recalls, in hundreds of details, the long journey through time, space, art, and politics that has ended in the DTC. He calls it a *periplum* (properly, *periplus*), a voyage made without a neat Dantean map, in which one takes one's bearings from point to point, "as the wind veers." It has been an extraordinary journey, from America, through Spain, Venice, London, Provence, and Paris, to Italy. He has known Henry James, Thomas Hardy, George Santayana; been on intimate terms with Yeats, Joyce, Eliot; and talked with United States Senators. Some of his old friends are dead; he makes up little elegies for them, less in mourning than in celebration of their dreams. This periplum, his own life, looks as if it may end soon, perhaps on the nearby gallows. He wonders, too, about the periplum of civilization:

> and who's dead, and who isn't
> and will the world ever take up its course again?

> very confidentially I ask you: Will it?

> (C.76)

3. *The Examination of Conscience*. Amid the sounds of the DTC and memories of his own life, an examination of conscience takes place. He sees that he has acted stupidly:

> Mr. K. said nothing foolish, the whole month nothing foolish:
> "if we weren't dumb we wouldn't be here"

> (C.74)

Old Ez's stupidity has been in violating the only ethics he truly believes in. He is being punished "for losing the law of Chung Ni [Confucius]." He sees that he has not observed the central Confucian principles, inseparable from each other, of absolute sincerity and the precise verbal definition. Any page of Confucius, or of Pound on Confucius, mocks the broadcasts over Rome Radio. Now the "man with an education" sees that he has talked too much, "thereby making clutter," and the implication is that his art, not political-economic broadcasts and journalism, is where he should have sought the "paraclete or the verbum perfectum: sinceritas." It was a mistake to think that Beauty would come "to a schema":

femina, femina, that wd/ not be dragged into paradise by the hair

(C.74)

He has been "a hard man in some ways," and:

J'ai eu pitié des autres
probablement pas assez, and at moments that suited my own con-
venience

(C.76)

The examination of conscience leads to an effort to sort things out, to restore balance, to find out what he really knows and loves. Action is not entirely futile, and some work of value remains: Duccio, Mozart, Confucius, Cavalcanti, Adams . . . beauty and order are possible: he decides to go on with his poem.

4. *Ceremonies*. Rituals are suggested: There is a preparation before confession, and we hear Villon's cry for absolution. The prisoner passes through Saint John of the Cross's dark night of the soul and undergoes a ritual death and rebirth. A mass for the dead is heard. The prisoner weeps for dead friends, for his sins, for himself, and the tears become waters of purification. After these ceremonies, he is allowed to pass between death and action to "the solitude of Mt. Taishan."

5. *The Pursuit of Beauty*. Images are drawn from memory to evoke beauty under many names and guises: Aphrodite, Isotta, and, at about the time the prisoner was born,

Manet painted the bar at La Cigale or at Les Folies in that year
she did her hair in small ringlets, à la 1880 it might have been,
red, and the dress she wore Drecol or Lanvin
a great goddess, Aeneas knew her forthwith

(C.74)

The divine essence, beauty, love also manifest themselves in phenomenal nature: in the clouds over Pisa, a wasp who builds her nest in a corner of the cage, a dwarf morning glory that twines around a grass blade. Remembering Whitman's "Song of Myself," he sees that it

> will never be more now than at present
> being given a new green katydid of a Sunday
> emerald, paler than emerald,
> > minus its right propeller

(C.74)

The pursuit of beauty is difficult, and when it appears it "gleams and then does not gleam." Paradise

> exists only in fragments unexpected excellent sausage,
> > the smell of mint, for example.

(C.74)

He recalls a story that Yeats told him, which has a parallel with his own situation:

> La beauté, " Beauty is difficult, Yeats " said Aubrey Beardsley
> > when Yeats asked why he drew horrors
> > or at least not Burne-Jones
> > and Beardsley knew he was dying and had to
> > make his hit quickly
>
> hence no more B-J in his product.
>
> So very difficult, Yeats, beauty so difficult.

(C.80)

6. *The Timeless.* The ceremonies and the pursuit of beauty take place in "the timeless air." The meditation where "Time is not" leads to the understanding that everything of true value lives in memory:

> > nothing matters but the quality
> of the affection—
> in the end—that has carved the trace in the mind
> dove sta memoria

(C.76)

But the poem makes it clear that the mental drama is not wholly subjective, that if a rose can be discerned in the magnetized steel dust of memory, it is because the mind is part of a continuum with external reality:

> This liquid is certainly a
>        property of the mind
> nec accidens est   but an element
>        in the mind's make-up
> est agens and functions   dust to a fountain pan otherwise
>        Hast 'ou seen the rose in the steel dust
>               (or swansdown ever?)
> so light is the urging, so ordered the dark petals of iron
> we who have passed over Lethe.

> (C.74)

That the world outside the mind is divine, mysterious, yet capable of being intuited is the point of the prose *Axiomata* written in 1921, and that insight is dramatized and more deeply felt in the meditation at Pisa.

7. *Time.* All of these themes in counterpoint—the timeless meditation in the DTC, the periplum of memory, the ceremonies of purgation, the pursuit of beauty—are set against another time, literally that of *Time* magazine. The first Pisan canto is dated 14 July, and the prisoner tells us that he has been reading *Time* for 25 June. (He does not say if a copy of *Time* for 14 May was still available in the DTC. If it were, he would have found his own picture, captioned "A star is bagged," next to an article saying that "a star Axis propagandist" had been arrested in Italy.) As the world of these cantos is being created out of memory, we hear of another world moving by clock time: Mussolini is killed and hung by the heels; Churchill is voted out of office ("Oh to be in England now that Winston's out"); V-J Day is celebrated:

> [I heard it in the s.h.   a suitable place
> to hear that the war was over]

> (C.77)

The opening of the Atomic Age is announced, and Béla Bartók dies in New York. The final canto is dated 8 October.

◊ ◊ ◊

The manipulation of time in the Pisan cantos provides a formal pattern of great beauty, one that is not applied mechanically but belongs naturally to the poetic universe Pound is creating. There are several "times" running through the sequence, but we must remember that events that define these "times" do not appear chronologically. There are times of eternity, of myth, of history, of nature or "the process," of Pound's own lifetime, reaching from memories of his childhood in Pennsylvania (C.81) to the present moment in the gorilla cage and to the time of the DTC (and of events reported in *Time* during that period), 14 July to 8 October, 1945. The effect within the Pisan sequence is something like that of contrapuntal music, in which each line is distinct, yet the lines sounded together form a single music. A chart of this music would be complex, especially if we were to impose upon it other lines or movements in the poem, such as the vacillations of mood from elation to despair or the variations in levels of diction from "piss-pot" to "Aphrodite." We may also imagine another chart in which these "times" are arranged in concentric circles at the center of which is the poet/prisoner's mind, composed of will, memory, and immediate perceptions. This center is "actual time," the only place where past and future exist. The scheme would be complicated by a final outer circle, created by the mind at the center: the poem itself, which includes everything else.

The pattern allows concentrations of energy and surprise. That is, anything that "happens" in one of these times may be happening in a second, third, or fourth. For example, the first line of Canto 81, "Zeus lies in Ceres' bosom," suggests something that happened in mythic times; was first formulated or recorded as myth during prehistory; represents recurrent processes of love-coition-fertility and day-and-night; presents figures that do not belong to a dead mythology but are "eternal states of mind"; and is a way of saying that it is shortly before dawn at Pisa in the summer of 1945.

◊ ◊ ◊

The Pisan cantos, with their strong autobiographical element, give emotional depth to the *Cantos,* which has been, until this point, a rather bookish poem. They answer, to some extent, Eliot's early charge that Pound's hell is for other people. But the confessional drama is of importance to the poem in another way, for the Pisan sequence enacts a testing, in extreme circumstances, of the fragments for a universe that Pound has been assembling during a lifetime. If his vision has value, it must work now. It is one thing to create an epic of judgment as a man of letters in London, Paris, and Rapallo; another to test one's vision of the Good on the nerves and mind of person and persona.

One measure of the success of the Pisan cantos is the tension they establish between assent to, and denial of, the truth offered by Avicenna in Santayana's *Dialogues in Limbo:*

> Life is not a book to read twice: and you cannot exchange the volume fortune puts in your hand for another on a nobler theme or by another poet.

The Pisan cantos remain part of a longer poem, drawing from earlier cantos and adding to them. To adapt a remark of Eliot's, within the order of the *Cantos* we should "not find it preposterous that the past should be altered by the present as much as the present is directed by the past."

◊  ◊

# CANTO 81

THE CANTO MOVES almost imperceptibly through the early morning hours, as Venus and her stars give way to an "aureate sky" and finally to a light by which we can observe "the green world." Yet one hardly notices the movement of light and time, for the intensity of focus is on the mind within the tent. The shape of the canto dramatizes its own meaning, risking, for the first half, an imitative fallacy to do so. The three major sections (interior monologue, libretto, and final chant) mark a movement from egotism (me, *my* life), through participation in traditions of craft and song, to humility and a sense of the prisoner's true scale within nature.

After a prelude in which a natural world alive with mythological lovers emphasizes the prisoner's isolation (no Althea at his grates), we hear a rambling, prosy interior monologue touching on events of four-and-a-half decades, memories of Wyncote, Madrid, London, Paris, Frankfurt, and Italy. Toward the end, the monologue, which has at least moved from concentration to concentration, becomes deliberately thinned-out and chatty in the lines about George Horace and Beveridge, its discursiveness reflected in the image of the loose rabbit.

Suddenly—with the mysterious cry that forms the refrain of *The Song of Roland*, "AOI!"—he appears to understand what is happening to himself and to his verse: "a leaf in the current." Through the mediation of poetry, and with the help of Speare's *Pocket Book of Verse* discovered in the latrine, the canto makes its "turn." There is a kind of heroic gesture to it, as if by an effort of will (yet the results are artistically effortless) he draws on the deepest resources of his craft to compose a "traditional" lyric in which the history of song in reconstructed. For all his ill fortune, he is still *il miglior fabbro*.

It is this act, this homage to the marriage of words and music, more than the prayers and invocations heard in earlier cantos, that brings the spirits at last. The appearance of the eyes within the tent is the closest thing to a mystical moment in the *Cantos*. The presence of the eyes, an event not willed by the prisoner, then releases the great moral-religious chant with which the canto ends. The chant, like the "libretto," draws on traditional poetic language, imagery, and sentiments (and is marked, as Kenner has noted, by the very iambic pentameter Pound has just boasted of breaking); yet it is unmistakably written in the twentieth century.

The long opening monologue on Spain, custom, politics, and the conservatism of language appears at first to be rambling, but it is not. The spontaneity of association, suggesting the mind's process during long hours of isolation, plays over an intricate substructure of cross-references. Some patterns are clear at first reading: the examples of dialect from Padre José, the black guard, Santayana, and Mussolini; or the line of Iberian references reaching from "Hay aquí" to Santayana.

Other patterns require closer attention. There is, for example, no real break between the classicism of the first three lines and the fussy modernism of the next four. We are meant to remember (from Canto 77) that Padre José had "understood something" about religion; his remark indicates that he is closer to genuine religion as projected in many traditions—Zeus, Cythera, Taishan, and that of his own Church—than to the exclusivist dogma and mechanical exercise of forms in official Catholicism. He understands, too, that kings will disappear because the institution of kingship has been emptied of its content as has institutionalized religion. Padre José, it is implied, would understand a poet who sees a starry dawn and a mountain near Pisa in terms of Zeus, Ceres, Cythera, and Taishan.

Attention might also show that the "table ex packing box" brought by Kuanon/Benin is probably shoddy (under the circumstances it would have to be), which leads to the young Santayana's impression of the "shoddy" quai at Boston, which reminds us that Santayana's journey from Spain to America reverses that of the young Pound from America to Spain.

There are other binding elements, however, that the reader can not see, hidden associations that remain as a magnetism that produced the poem. What, for instance, have Bowers and Beveridge to do with each other? Serendipity reveals that, before he went to Spain, Ambassador Bowers had published a biography of Senator Beveridge. Bowers also wrote on Adams and Jefferson, who appear on the page after him, and all—ambassador, senator, Presidents, and poet—belong to an anti-Hamiltonian opposition to private banking as the basis of national issue. Beveridge sacrificed his political career by opposing Senator Nelson Aldrich's "Plan," which became the Federal Reserve.

One may start at any point in this monologue, and by implication at any point in the *Cantos,* and trace a line that passes through every other point, passes often at several times. Sections of that periplumlike reading of Canto 81 would be:

1. "Zeus lies in Ceres' bosom," rain god and earth mother, the eternal process of copulation-love-fertility. Then Dolores appears as a figure of earth mother (and of Kuanon, who is more visible later in the canto), offering bread (cereal/Ceres) to a young man. There are drum ceremonies, which often have origins in fertility rites, and whereas these ceremonies seem to be authentic "simple village fiesta," we soon hear of other local rituals that have lost contact with their origins, have become uprooted and turned into government-sponsored events, perverted into political demonstrations. Next we find the ironic "Crédit Agricole," in which the sacred process itself has fallen into the hands of an oligarchy (Adams is afraid of "the few"). Then a passing reference to a baker, a cryptic one to cooking, and finally a snapshot of Pound's father hoeing corn in a backyard over which Ceres presides.

2. Or begin again, with Venus attending Zeus and Ceres asleep in each other's arms. The poet remembers his own love, or loves, some who cook and some who don't, who may be at this very moment saying, as Theocritus's lonely girl is saying in Greek, "Bring that man back to my house!" This leads to the lovely irony of Althea, who is both poetic allusion and fact of life in the DTC (Lovelace's "To Althea, from Prison" is in the *Pocket Book of Verse*). The conditions of Lovelace's imprisonment are very different from those of Old Ez:

When Love with unconfined wings
   Hovers within my gates,
And my divine Althea brings
   To whisper at the grates.

The final stanza of Lovelace's song reflects another theme Pound has been writing about in prison and acts as a transition to the next section of the canto:

Stone walls do not a prison make,
   Nor iron bars a cage;
Minds innocent and quiet take
   That for a hermitage;
If I have freedom in my love
   And in my soul am free,
Angels alone that soar above,
   Enjoy such liberty.

The "libretto" that follows, and begins with someone soaring in the air, might almost have been written in Althea's lifetime.

The libretto displays craftsmanship of the highest order, paying homage to the songs for seventeenth-century masques and to Jonson's "Have you seene but a bright Lillie grow." Like many seventeenth-century stanzas, it creates its own pattern as it moves from phrase to phrase. As in the songs for Jonson's masques, we come to expect rhyme, but can not predict where the rhyme will fall, and to expect a measure regular enough to form a tension with the asymmetry of the music. Yet Jonson could depend on composers to provide a variable cadence for his rather strict iambics (in the songs for the masques). Pound knows that no composer is likely to set *his* libretto, so he provides not only the words but the cadence and musical variety as well.

Note the variety of the rhyme scheme (I count *cold* and *should*er as a rhyme, and, indeed, the "er" of "shoulder" may be heard as the first syllable of the anapests in the next line; *"c"* is the off-rhyme *wood/mood*):

      *a a x, b b, c d d, b b, c d e f, e f*

with further variety in that the last two lines appear as "refrain," but form a quatrain with the two lines preceding. The poem begins by hovering between iambic and trochaic tetrameter—iambic if one hears

$$\bar{Y}et \ \acute{e}re \ \bar{the} \ s\acute{e}as\bar{o}n$$

—but this is not the only metrical choice the passage will give us. It becomes firmly trochaic in the second line and from then on leaves tetrameter to the "refrain," as the verse turns to three primarily anapestic beats or breathings, yet with a frequent substitution of iambs. Finally the song "resolves" into iambics in "aright / If Waller sang or Dowland played," as it prepares to join the Chaucerian pentameter of "Your eyen two."

A page earlier, the poet was remembering, from his London days, the heroic breaking of the pentameter. The libretto, moving with quantity and cadence as well as on stress, is a virtuoso demonstration of resources made available by freedom from the dominant iamb. The resources, however, are used not to produce free verse but to add a variable music, as it were, to the text, all of which technical problems Pound was puzzling out in an essay of 1917, "Vers libre and Arnold Dolmetsch." A combined memory of Dolmetsch, Jonson, and Dowland was present at the end of Canto 74:

Hast 'ou seen the rose in the steel dust
(or swansdown ever?)

which echoes Jonson's song from *A Celebration of Charis in Ten Lyrick Peeces,* set to music by Dowland, and published in 1938 by Dolmetsch. That memory persists in the libretto.

The pronouns are decidedly unclear, for some process is happening that "correct" syntax will not contain. It is as if lines from a Jonson masque have lost the speakers to which they were assigned; perhaps if we knew which allegorical character is singing which line, we would know where the pronouns point, but we do not. The "I" in the first stanza may be the poet's spirit released from the cage, or the Muse of Song, or Aphrodite, or all three. The "he" of the second stanza is attached to Dolmetsch, who crafted ancient instruments, yet includes all poets and musicians working within the tradition. The "us" is harder to define, but the "thou" in the third stanza is reciprocally addressed from poet to muse/goddess and from muse to artist/craftsman.

Poetry and music, we observe, arise neither from craft nor from inspiration alone, but from the two combined—with "inspiration" in its root sense, that some spirit beyond the artist has breathed into him. Once again, the artificial and the natural meet in art, as the patient shaping of the wood allows a song "airy" as leaf or cloud.

Finally, the most hidden marvel in this song is "grave" and "acute," which belong equally to language and to music. In fact, music borrowed them from linguistics, precisely for the purpose of reaching toward the voice. Perhaps the highest form of art for Pound is the perfect union of words and music, *motz el son*. The libretto is a homage to, and a summation of, his studies in the techniques of Arnaut Daniel, Chaucer, and Shakespeare—a tradition he loves and of which he is the inheritor. The little clench on "grave" and "acute" gathers together words and music, and if that sounds farfetched, both terms can be found in Dolmetsch's *The Interpretation of Music of the XVIIth and XVIIIth Centuries*, which Pound reviewed for the *Egoist* in 1917.

The tribute to seventeenth-century song is followed by two lines of Chaucer's "Merciles Beaute," two-and-a-half centuries closer to the source of the tradition. Written, Pound says, while England "was still part of Europe," its author uses "the verse art come from the troubadours." The material is utterly conventional; yet nothing diminishes the freshness of these lines (the secret lies in the choice of "may"). Chaucer's "eyen two" form a transition to the mysterious eyes that appear next in the canto. The lyricism comes to an abrupt halt on the flattened rhythm of "And for 180 years almost nothing."

The seventeen lines beginning "Ed ascoltando il leggier mormorio" could only have been written by someone who has immersed himself in the tradition, especially in Dante. Dante is master of a skill in registering, clearly and precisely, states that lie somewhere between presence and absence, between spirit and flesh. Compare, for example, "shone from the unmasked eyes in half-mask's space" or, in Canto 83,

> [Dryas], your eyes are like the clouds over Taishan
> When some of the rain has fallen
> and half remains yet to fall

with Dante's

> Quando a cantar con organi si stea:
> Che si or no s'intendon le parole

or

> E per la viva luce trasparea
> La lucente sustanzia tanto chiara

In these seventeen lines, an intense and delicate miracle is achieved. First, the choice of eyes alone, rather than an attempt to present an entire figure or figures: Eyes are the means through which light becomes "hypostasized" as image and concept, and in a long poetic tradition it is through the eyes that Light passes from a mediating body such as Beatrice's to the eyes of the lover or poet. The eyes within the tent, which seem at times a single pair, at times several, hold the essence of all the goddesses in the *Cantos* (and may include memories of the women Pound has loved), but to name them or even to commit them grammatically to a sex would, at this point, destroy the subtlety of the event.

It is at first not eyes that appear but a "subtlety" of eyes, a perfectly chosen word that includes "penetrating, pervasive," "not easily understood or perceived," and "fine or delicate, to such an extent as to elude observation or analysis." Neither language nor reason is subtle enough to say whether what the poet sees is pure spirit or a hypostasis of spirit and matter. (Duns Scotus is *doctor subtilis* because his subject was fine distinctions among the relations of God, form, and matter.) Then, because Pound can not deal with these eyes as a scholastic, he does what a poet can do, finds an image that gives the moment itself. The bold, very

Dantesque choice of blindfold and carnival mask eliminates any suggestion of a presence beyond the narrow "half-mask's space" and thus intensifies the presence of what is there. The mask image creates an obsessive focus, and then even that is refined with the insistence on the empty space between the eyes, until nothing remains but the color of the staring eyes themselves.

The poet/prisoner seems to have expected anger, but the eyes do not show it, are in fact without emotion, and appear neither to judge nor to communicate with the prisoner as a personality. (And that understanding produces the chant that follows, about seeing one's self in its true scale.) The intensity of their carelessness is such that it almost seems to eliminate *ego scriptor*'s presence. The moment is not static but has duration: It lasts long enough for there to be a need for verbs: *interpass, penetrate, cast, shine*. The subtlety of the event, the question "whether of spirit or hypostasis," is presented in the fine difference between *interpass* and *penetrate*.

*Shade* is surprising and vivid, suggesting that the eyes are so bright that they cast their own shadows within the light of the rising dawn and perhaps of the arc lights of the DTC. It is not an effect of blinding light Pound wants here—rather of something that may be clearly seen, and of something restful and cool. To express what he sees, he abandons all pretense at English syntax (*sky's clear*) and forms an ideogram or, better, a Chinese poem all the finer because it is without a suggestion of chinoiserie. Having drawn on one source of his technique in the libretto, he now draws on another deriving from Imagism and his study of Fenollosa. He brings it just far enough into normal English so that it does not obtrude at a moment when anything too "interesting" would be out of place, but as a Chinese poem it would be (one reads from top to bottom, right to left):

|          |       |
|----------|-------|
| green    | sky   |
| mountain | clear |
| pool     | night |
| shine    | sea   |

This defines through particulars, not concepts. Then with a turn
to the past tense, *shone,* the vision ends; and the potential cliché
about how it "disappeared" or "faded" is avoided.

The chant against vanity springs both from the presence of
the eyes and from the demonstration that the finest poetry is produced through loss of oneself in tradition (though paradoxically,
as Eliot intended, the libretto is a brilliant display of individual
talent). The opening pages of the canto, by contrast, are ingenious
modernism.

For the final page, Pound returns, in a different way, to tradition. We noted in discussing Canto 31 that the "Pull down thy
vanity" passage reflects Ecclesiastes (which was in Speare's *Pocket
Book of Verse*) in language and in the contradictory impulses of
"all is vanity" and "there is nothing better, than that a man should
rejoice in his own works." Ecclesiastes (and Boethius) also informs Chaucer's "Ballade of Good Counsel," the first poem in
Speare's anthology, from which Pound derives "Master thyself,
then others shall thee beare."

The confession of failure and vanity must be read in balance
with "What thou lovest well remains." Some things are worth
doing in spite of the errors and pride that mar human efforts.
The example chosen, something *unquestionable,* is not the no-
toriety of Imagism, nor the invention "of Chinese poetry for our
time," nor the ambitious *Cantos,* nor the energies that went into
economic and political pamphlets, but a visit to a neglected poet
and man of honor one afternoon in 1914. The occasion remains in
the memory, but memory was jogged for the last time in this
canto by Speare's paperback anthology found on the jo-house seat.
For the most idiosyncratic of Speare's selections is surely Wilfred
Scawen Blunt's "To Esther," for which Pound had praised Blunt
in 1912 ("great for reason of his double sonnet"). Here it was,
thirty-three years later, saying much of what Pound has had on
his mind at Pisa, and contributing resonances (time, paradisal
memories, vanity) to the very passage in which Blunt is remembered:

He who has once been happy is for aye
    Out of destruction's reach. His fortune then
Holds nothing secret; and Eternity,
    Which is a mystery to other men,
Has like a woman given him its joy.
    Time is his conquest.

．　．　．　．　．　．

When cities deck their streets for barren wars
    Which have laid waste their youth, and when I keep
Calmly the count of my own life and see
    On what poor stuff my manhood's dreams were fed
Till I too learned what dole of vanity
    Will serve a human soul for daily bread,
—Then I remember that I once was young
And lived with Esther the world's gods among.

The live tradition in Canto 81 was gathered from the air in the cage at Pisa and typed up at night in the prison dispensary.

◊　◊　◊

*Page 79* (*91–92*)

Taishan / A high peak beyond Pisa becomes the sacred mountain of China. It is the home of the Great Emperor of the Eastern Peak, whose daughter, Kuanon, appears later.

Hay aquí, etc. / "A lot of Catholicism here, but not much religion."

Padre José / A young priest who was kind to Pound during the poet's visit to Spain in 1906. They met again in London "about 1917," shortly before Padre José's death.

Dolores / Dolores Carmona, sister of the owner of a pension in Madrid where John Singer Sargent had stayed and where presumably the young Pound stayed in 1906.

Bowers / Claude G. Bowers, American journalist and historian, whose *Jefferson and Hamilton* (1925) influenced Pound's version of American economic history. In 1933 he became ambassador to Spain, where he remained, militantly anti-Fascist, until Franco took power. He wrote extensively of the savagery of the Spanish rebels and points out that the Communists often secretly supported the Fascists in order to create political chaos.

*Page 80 (92)*

Cabranez / Unknown. A Spanish friend of Pound's?

Basil / Basil Bunting, the poet. He lived for a while in the Spanish Canary Islands.

Possum / T. S. Eliot.

Cole / Horace de Vere Cole had a reputation as a practical joker. One of his pranks was "a street demonstration / in Soho for Italy's entry into combat in / 19 was it 15?" (C.80). Pound distinguishes him from the more serious G. D. H. Cole, a writer on economics.

Spire / French-Jewish poet who "preached vers libre with Isaiaic fury" (C.77).

Crédit Agricole / Spire's point is that an economic oligarchy controls the "Agricultural Credit," as it controls French banking through a series of interlocking directorates.

Jo Bard / Hungarian-born journalist, old friend of Pound's.

*Page 81 (92–93)*

"Te cavero le budella" etc. / "I'll slice your guts out!" "And me —your heart!" The exchange between Malatesta and Urbino is quoted in Canto 10. The point is that one can hear the same language in Italy today.

'Ινγξ, etc. / Refrain from Theocritus's second idyll. The speaker is a woman whose lover has stopped coming to see her. Jealous, she spins a magic wheel to cast a spell on him: "Little wheel, get that man back to my house!"

Benin / The face of the American soldier looks like one of the Benin bronzes Pound saw at Frobenius's institute in Frankfurt.

Santayana / Born in Spain, he came to Boston at the age of nine, retired from Harvard in 1912, and returned to Europe. He and Pound exchanged visits in Rome and Rapallo, but Santayana quickly saw that he could not supply the kind of help with "philosophy" that Pound sought from him. Making allowances for Pound's amateur status and Santayana's subtlety, there are profound correspondences in their attitudes toward religion and politics.

George Horace / Lorimer, a neighbor of the Pounds in Wyncote, Pennsylvania; editor of the *Saturday Evening Post*.

Beveridge / Albert J. Beveridge, populist Republican, elected to the Senate from Ohio in 1899.

## Page 82 (93–94)

AOI! / The refrain from *The Song of Roland*.

Althea / Lovelace's "To Althea, From Prison."

*Lawes* / Henry Lawes (1596–1662) had set Waller's "Go, Lovely Rose" (also in Speare's anthology) and Milton's *Comus*. Both poets wrote tributes to Lawes's talent for setting verse to music without distorting the words.

*Jenkins* / John Jenkins (1592–1678), English composer. In a letter of 1937, Pound is trying to obtain copies of music by Lawes and Jenkins for his Rapallo concerts.

*Dolmetsch* / Arnold Dolmetsch was a leader in the revival of seventeenth-century music and ancient instruments. Pound shared his taste in music, wrote about him, and in 1914 bought a Dolmetsch clavichord, which he was still using to compose verse to in his late seventies.

*Page 83 (94-95)*

Your eyen two, etc. / The refrain from a triple rondel, "Merciles Beaute," tenuously ascribed to Chaucer.

Ed ascoltando il leggier mormorio / "And hearing the light murmur." Not from Dante, though it is Dantesque.

hypostasis / As used here, a term belonging to neoplatonic tradition and to theology. It refers to substance and essence, also to person and personality. In the latter sense it is used in discussing the person of Christ, the hypostatic union of divine and human natures.

diastasis / Separation, emphasizing the "stance" between the eyes, with a second connotation that the eyes are wide open, dilated. (The *OED* gives it also as a musical term meaning both "interval" and "dilated.") See also the passage in *Mauberley*: "He had passed, inconscient, full gaze, / The wide-banded irides / And botticellian sprays implied / In their diastasis."

Εἰδὼς / Usually given as "knowing" but, as it also means "having seen," a better English word may be "vision."

*Page 84 (95-96)*

Paquin / The great Parisian couturier.

*Page 85 (96)*

Blunt / An exotic and independent figure, and an outspoken opponent of empire, he was the first Englishman imprisoned for activities in behalf of Irish nationalism. He was living in Sussex, deeply feeling his isolation and neglect, when a group of poets including Pound and Yeats knocked on his door in January 1914 to present him with an alabaster box (carved by Gaudier-Brzeska) containing poems in his honor. Blunt was a controversial figure, and the *Times,* reporting the homage, noted that "a man in the Foreign Office says he will never speak to any of these men again."

◊   ◊

## *from* CANTO 83

IN THESE OPENING PAGES from Canto 83, we find the poet, almost at peace and almost invisible, in a landscape imbued with a moral-religious sense, as the poetry brings together his Confucianism and his neoplatonism. Water (*hudor,* which permeates the canto through references to rain and tears) is hypostasized with light to form a mist or "breath" unifying the landscape. The mist is one of the *plura diafana,* the many translucencies through which the creating Light shines and "divides" itself (the word reflects Scotus Erigena's *De divisione naturae*) to nourish by its "rectitude" as it "fills the nine fields / to heaven"—in phrases drawn from the Confucian scriptures. On the literal level, to borrow Dante's distinction, it is another dawn at the DTC. A hard rain has drenched the tent within the cage, leaving pools of water gleaming in the September sun, which has not yet burned off the bright mist. The scene appears to be afloat in water and light, but lest it become too much like a Chinese painting, the prisoner reminds us where he is, mentioning the cages and presenting, as a sharp brushstroke through the mist, the stockade posts whose bases can be seen firmly anchored in the ground. By the end of the passage, the burning sun stands low in the sky, and later in the canto there is "warmth after chill sunrise."

Although peace and *hilaritas* govern the poet's spirit, he is not without suffering or regret. He is still a "caged panther," and between his thoughts of the grass in Yeats's "Salley Gardens" (with its plangent "and now am full of tears") and nostalgic memories of visits to Siena with a woman he loves, he speaks through the voice of Arnaut Daniel in Purgatory, *consiros,* with sorrow:

"I am Arnaut, and I weep and singing go.
  I think on my past folly and see the stain,
  And view with joy the day I hope to know.

I pray you by that Goodness which doth deign
    To guide you to the summit of this stair
    Bethink you in due season of my pain."

Yet purgatory is a place of gradations, where pain and regret, hope and joy are inextricably mixed, and although Arnaut/Pound will continue to suffer for an indefinite period of time, it is within a "refining" fire.

If we say there is a literal level in Canto 83—the dramatic situation of the caged prisoner during a dawn at Pisa—we should not press too hard for an allegorical level (as Pound reminds us in his story about Yeats at Notre Dame, giving preference to the symbol over the reality). Yet the images have an underlying unity to which a passage in *Guide to Kulchur* provides a key of sorts:

> Two mystic states can be dissociated: the ecstatic-beneficent-and-benevolent, contemplation of the divine love, the divine splendour with goodwill towards others.
>
> And the bestial, namely the fanatical, the man on fire with God and anxious to stick his snotty nose into other men's business or to reprove his neighbor for having a set of tropisms different from that of the fanatic's, or for having the courage to live more greatly or more openly. . . .
>
> The first state is a dynamism. It has, time and again, driven men to great living, it has given them courage to go on for decades in the face of public stupidity. It is paradisical and a reward in itself seeking naught further. . . . The Glory of life exists without further proof for this mystic.

Pound's mysticism, if we may call it that, is his own synthetic version of a neoplatonism approaching pantheism. Scotus Erigena, one of his favorite philosophers, was in fact condemned for pantheism, since his "Nature" includes all reality, both God and created things, though he maintained a distinction between "Nature which creates" and "Nature which is created." Some such distinction is a fair indication of Pound's "philosophy," if we remember that the philosophy takes place, happens, in the poetry, not apart from it. This passage from Canto 83 provides a good example of his temperament or bias among world views.

In the tradition of neoplatonism, the essential intuition of the divine mind or Light, the *nous,* may lead in two directions. One is toward a *contempt* for this world, in which created things are seen as fallen, unsound, second-rate at best and are felt as a separation from the One or from God. Men with this cast of mind want, as Pound puts it in Canto 105, "to bust out of the kosmos." Such a sensibility, for Pound, will not lead to social responsibility, to *jen* or *humanitas,* nor does it have much need for poetry.

The other tradition of thought or feeling within neoplatonism "saves the appearance." From this point of view, if one knows how to look, "In nature are signatures" (C.87), and in Canto 95 we find Saint Hilary reading one of those signatures in an oak-leaf. One may become enraptured by what one sees, rather than thinking of bodies as cages or husks from which the spirit longs to be free. It is this tradition to which Pound belongs, and much in the difficult later cantos will be clear if this distinction is kept in mind. In the later cantos, we hear Plotinus quoted several times to the effect that the body is inside the soul. That is, if one thinks of the soul as inside the body, one may find oneself talking about its "release" from the body, from matter—and perhaps the sooner the better. However, to think of the *nous,* not as at some great remove from nature, but as immanent, present through its *plura diafana,* to see with Erigena that all things that are, are lights, engenders a religious attitude toward nature and a sense of responsibility toward other men. Paradise, the Light, and its attendant beauty, Pound suggests in the first of the Pisan cantos, "will never be more now than at present." Moreover, this unified cosmos, where body inhabits soul, clearly has a need for poetry to multiply and celebrate its splendors.

There are ghosts of philosophers in Canto 83—Thales, Gemistus, Erigena, Grosseteste, Heraclitus, Plato, Confucius—but the canto offers "an expression of philosophy," not "a philosophy," to follow a distinction of Pound's made in a review of Allen Upward, a less visible ghost in these pages. We are not being asked to choose among those who say that the primal element is water (Thales, Gemistus), those who say light (Erigena, Grosseteste), or those who say fire (Heraclitus). These are metaphors; the important thing is the unified vision, that whatever the universe is, *panta rei* or everything flows. A mind in harmony with the Confucian "process," one whose vanity has (as in Canto 81) been brought down to the true scale of man in nature, is aware of this flowing, this continual metamorphosis.

We can see something of Pound's attitude toward "philosophy" in the chapters "Sophists" and "Neo-Platonics Etc." in *Guide to Kulchur*:

> Mechanism, how it works, teleology, what it's aimed at, the soul of the world, the fire of the gods, remembering of course that the "history of philosophy", when dealing with the greek start, now flickers about among fragments, and that every word is used, defined, left undefined, wangled and wrangled according to the taste of the wrangler, his temperament, his own bias. . . .
>
> And they say Gemisto found no one to talk to, or more generally he did the talking. He was not a proper polytheist, in this sense: His gods come from Neptune, so that there is a single source of being, aquatic (udor, Thales etc. as you like, or what is the difference).

Yes, what is the difference, if one reads, as Pound does, Heraclitus or Thales or Anaximeses (who said everything is air) not as early scientists, nor as philosophers in the modern sense, but as poets of a sort, expressing an intuition of a "single source of being," of unity in difference. For Pound, the best vocabulary for discussing such matters is always myth, though perhaps we should extend "myth" to include the fragments of philosophy he is interested in. Myth (and religion if rightly understood) unifies, is not exclusive:

> When you don't understand it, let it alone. This is the copy-book maxim whereagainst sin prose philosophers, though it is explicit in Kung on spirits.
>
> The mythological exposition permits this. It permits an expression of intuition without denting the edges or shaving off the nose and ears of a verity.

Pound is attracted to neoplatonism in its broadest sense and can make it harmonize with Confucius because it is hospitable to his need for myths. He is less interested in the technicalities of any philosophy than in what it produces. Gemistus's philosophy, Pound liked to think, produced the bas reliefs in the 'Tempio, where carved gods float amid images of water; they may not be what Gemistus had in mind; yet they are an indirect result of his "conversation," as Pound looks back at him through a remark of Yeats's.

The prisoner, to whatever extent he is now a sage, greets the day with quiet and *hilaritas,* a term that Pound has made peculiarly his own. He approaches Erigena more familiarly than that philosopher has been approached for centuries, but the "hilarity" moves beyond jocularity into an awareness of the joyful speed and exhilaration of the spirit. The word comes to Pound via two sources. The first is a comic story about Erigena (see below) recounted by his editor, "the prete," who adds that Scotus had a reputation for piety and hilarity. As a divine virtue, however, it derives from an unexpected second source, an Italian schoolbook, which "It is unlikely that the 'advanced' will look into." The two passages Pound quotes from the schoolbook add resonance to Canto 83. First:

> *O God, in whom we live and move and are, concede a restoring rain, so that we, aided sufficiently in our earthly needs, may reach up with great trust to eternal things. So be it.*

That is not a prayer for those who want to "bust out of the kosmos." The second is "A prayer for serenity (that is fair weather)":

> *We implore, omnipotent God, thy clemency, so that thou having made to cease the flooding rain, shalt show to us through the calm sky the hilarity of thy face.*

Pound comments: "Hilarity. The italian is just that: *l'ilarità del Tuo Volto.*"

As the passage proceeds, Greek and Christian references gradually make way for a Confucian vocabulary. "The sage / delighteth in water / the humane man has amity with the hills," derives from the copy of Confucius from which the poet is translating in the DTC but is also remembered from a book by Allen

Upward. With "this breath wholly covers the mountains," Confucian terms come to dominate: *rectitude, equity, the process.*

In the last line of the passage, observed nature, Confucian wisdom, and Erigena's and Grosseteste's light are brought together in a single image. Looking at Legge's translation of *Analects* 16.10, Pound reads: "In regard to the use of his eyes, he is anxious to see clearly." Looking at the Chinese characters, he sees

示見

("to see, observe") and next to it

明

("the total light process"). In the first ideogram, the radical for "eye" is at the upper right, beneath it the "running legs" that indicate action or motion, while on the left there is something like rays coming down (it is the sign for "spirits"). In the second ideogram, *ming²*, the "sun" on the left resembles the "eye." Pound's translation of the passage will neoplatonize Confucius as:

> in seeing, that he see with intelligence or with his intelligence,
> *definite pictogram of moving eye and light from above, very strong*
> *and very inclusive phrase.*

For Canto 83, in which what the prisoner sees—weather and landscape—becomes the occasion of an active serenity based on mutual intelligence between man and the cosmos, Pound's study of the Chinese characters produces:

the sun as a golden eye

The Confucian solemnity of the final lines is counterpointed by the lighter tone of the passing reference to the death of Socrates ("have I perchance a debt"), reinforcing the canto's combination of piety and *hilaritas*. Socrates has achieved a mood of serenity and cheerfulness: "Crito, I owe a cock to Asclepius; will you remember to pay the debt?" Like Pound, at least on this Septem-

ber morning, he has stopped arguing: "I cannot make Crito believe that I am the same Socrates who have been talking and
conducting the argument. . . ."

◊ ◊ ◊

**Page 86**

HUDOR / The Greek word for "water" just above.

Pax / Canto 82 abounds in echoes of the Mass, so this peace
reaches back to the *pax vobiscum* at the end of the ceremony as
well as forward to the Confucian peace and to the "Dryad, thy
peace is like water" on the following pages.

Gemisto / See the glossary note to the next-to-last line of
Canto 9.

lux enim / The first words of a quotation from Robert de
Grosseteste (1175?-1253), which Pound includes in his essay "Medi-
evalism": "For light of its very nature diffuses itself."

ignis est accidens / "Fire is an accident" (of light). The thought
is a continuation of Grosseteste's, although the words are not.

the prete / The abbé Migne, editor of the *Patrologia*, in which
Pound read Scotus Erigena.

Scotus / John Scotus Erigena (ca. 810–ca. 877), the first Scholastic philosopher and probably the best Greek scholar in Europe
during an age when Greek was little known beyond a few Irish
monasteries. Little is known of his life, and much of what Pound
says about it is fanciful. About 850, Charles the Bald (Charles le
Chauve) brought him to Paris, where he wrote philosophy, made
important translations from the Greek, and became an intimate of
the royal household. His poems, mostly in honor of the king, do
have many Greek tags in them.

Hilaritas / Scotus and the king were seated across from each
other at dinner. The king makes a joke: *"Quid distat inter Scot-
tum et Sottum?"* [What separates a Scot from a sot?] Solemnly
the philosopher answers: *"Tabula tantum."* [This table.] The

editor then comments on Erigena's reputation for *pietate et hilaritate*. For Pound, who uses the word frequently in later cantos, *hilaritas* takes on a connotation something like "the joy or exhilaration that accompanies speed of thought."

Paris / Suggesting that all poets at one time or another wind up in Paris? The words seems to turn the king into a *café concert* performer for a moment.

omnia, quae sunt, lumina sunt / One of two key quotations that attract Pound to Erigena: "All things that are, are lights."

De Montfort / Simon de Montfort led the Albigensian Crusade in the early thirteenth century. The Albigenses, a Provençal sect, were condemned as heretics and slaughtered in great numbers. Pound likes to think that Erigena belonged to the "conspiracy of intelligence" or underground tradition within the Church, which maintained its roots in paganism and informed the troubadours, Cavalcanti, and the brighter manifestations of medieval Christianity. He then imagines that during the Albigensian Crusade the body of Erigena was dug up and burned as that of a heretic. It is not literally the case, yet it is true in spirit: Erigena's works were important to the Albigenses, and the body of a later philosopher who held similar views was in fact dug up and desecrated. Erigena, who is still to some theologians a heretic or near-heretic for his "pantheism," was several times condemned by the Church during his lifetime; in 1225, three-and-a-half centuries after his death, all copies of his *De divisione naturae,* were ordered sent to Rome to be "solemnly burned."

Le Paradis, etc. / "Paradise is not artificial." Baudelaire's *Les paradis artificiels* is about hallucinogenic drugs.

Uncle William / Yeats.

## Page 87

St Etienne / Twelfth-century church in Périgueux.

Dei Miracoli / Pietro Lombardo (see Canto 45) and his son Tullio carved mermaids for the interior of the Venetian church Pound calls "the jewel box" (C.76), Santa Maria dei Miracoli.

as the grass grows / From Yeats's "Down By The Salley Gardens":

> She bid me take love easy, as the grass grows on the weirs;
> But I was young and foolish, and now am full of tears.

*consiros* / "With sorrow." From Arnaut Daniel's speech in *Purgatorio* 26.

"Cane e Gatto" / "Dog and Cat," a place in Siena. The following lines are made up of private memories of visits to Siena.

soll deine Liebe sein / "Shall be thy love." Probably remembered from a concert of lieder heard at Siena.

Palio / See Canto 43. The *palio* is run at Siena in the summer, when the grass would be high, but it is September in the DTC, so the grass would now be higher.

Olim de Malatestis / "Formerly the Malatestas'." A phrase used throughout the Pisan cantos as an elegy for things passing away. It first appears in Canto 11, describing a palace: "OLIM *de Malatestis.*"

Maria / Pound's daughter.

## Page 88

πάντα ῾ρει / *Panta rei*. Heraclitus's "Everything flows."

as he was standing / In *Analects* 13.21, Confucius and a disciple are conversing "below the rain altars."

Δρυάς / Dryas, a dryad, wood nymph.

## Page 89

Chocorua / A mountain in New Hampshire.

Plura diafana / A phrase from Grosseteste, for whom one of the three ways the Light transmits itself is "through many transparent things."

*Page 90*

Clower / Probably Clowes, the printer who set the privately printed edition of Pound's *Lustra* in 1916, but only after infuriating the poet by censoring it.

◊   ◊

## CANTO 84

THE LAST OF THE PISAN CANTOS is dominated by

*chung*[1]. To Pound's eyes, the character does not present a static balance, but is in motion on its "unwobbling pivot." Emotions move quickly from warmth to weariness, from hope to disappointment, from irritation to detachment, the changes registered by tones of voice and by prosody.

At places where there is a warmth of emotion, the verse is denser, with a high proportion of long or stressed syllables; the sardonic passages, where the poet is commenting on an incorrigible world, are marked by conversational rhythms with a preponderance of light or rushed syllables. The two kinds of verse are clearly heard in Pound's recorded reading; the former, for example, in the elegy for Angold and in the passages beginning "snow-white" and "Under white clouds"; the latter in the fifteen lines beginning "this day October the whateverth." In the five lines where the prisoner gives his blessing to soldiers leaving the DTC ("and Demattia is checking out"), forty-eight syllables receive twenty-eight stresses; in the five lines in which he expresses a tired exasperation with politicians ("you can, said Stef"), fifty-two syllables are given only thirteen strong stresses, as in:

d̄o̅ n̄o̅t̄h̄īn̄g̅ w̄īt̄h̄ r̄ēv̄ōlūt̄īōn̄ār̄īēs̄

ūnt̄īl̄ t̄h̄ēȳ ār̄ē āt̄ t̄h̄ē ́ēn̄d̄ ōf̄ t̄h̄ēīr̄ t̄ét̄h̄ēr̄

Tones of voice change dramatically: Angold (chanted mourning); Bankhead (fury); Borah (puzzlement); Richardson (skepticism); the departing prisoners (affection); Mr. Beard (parody of
the academic lecturer or *TLS* reviewer, with his "admirable");
the old dynasty's music (lyric); my great aunt (anecdotal-cracker-
barrel); *cielo di Pisa* (exaltation); our norm of spirit (pride and
determination). One shift of tone is particularly quick and delightful: "O moon . . . ," which appears about to reach for an *o
altitudo*, but becomes "my pin-up," then moves easily back to the
elevation of *humanitas* and *jen*.

The salute, *Xaire*, more farewell than greeting, brings us directly, for the first time in *Selected Cantos*, to Pound's admiration
for Mussolini. There is not much to say about it, or perhaps there
is too much to say about it, because it will be a long time before
these lines can be read as dispassionately as we read about Guelph
and Ghibelline, puritan and cavalier. Pound's version of Mussolini
is sincere, but selectively and naïvely perceived, and bears little
relation to the "real" Mussolini. From the perspective of three
decades, Pound's credence in Mussolini's public statements and his
hope to convert the Duce to Douglas's economics, appear blind to
reality. His admiration for Mussolini is directly in a line with
Carlyle's hero worship and corresponds to the curiously persistent
theme of the search for a leader that marks even poets of the Left
in the thirties. Pound is interested in what he sees as intelligent
men of action, and we can find him praising within a single
sentence Mussolini, Jefferson, and Lenin.

Behind the salute to the dead Fascists and collaborators lies a
personal appeal for justice, a hope that his own judges will recognize "gradations." The men he hails were, like himself, on the
losing side yet were, he is saying, all different, driven by different
motives. They have all been summarily executed, often after trials
that, whatever the ultimate justice, were hardly models of legal
procedure. Europe in 1945 was not the place for accused traitors

to seek to be judged by the gradations and distinctions of Dante's purgatorial "stair." However misguided, *Il Capo* and his companions were patriots; the collaborationists like Laval and Petain claimed that their nations fared better under compromise than they would have under Nazi occupation; and Pound sees his own motive as having wanted to prevent the war and save the Constitution. He had made a quixotic trip to Washington in 1939 to do just that; the results are reported on the first page of the canto. He had not been able to meet the President, who was "stubborn az a mule, sah," but he had talked with a Cabinet member, Senators, and Representatives, to no result.

The question Pound is asking here is did these men including himself, now indiscriminately grouped as "fascists," display a sensibility *more* to be censured than that of the financiers behind Imperial Chemicals or the managers of I. G. Farbenindustrie, whose giant headquarters (it is noted in Canto 74) remained untouched in a city otherwise leveled by Allied bombs? This is the appeal Pound is making, but he also presents himself as an Old Testament prophet who knows that perfect peace, justice, and mercy may only be sought in some apocalyptic future. The cities of men, we hear if we follow out Micah's "Each in the name of . . . ," are places where there are "yet the treasures of wickedness in the house of the wicked," and as for justice, "Shall I count them pure with the wicked balances, and with the bag of deceitful weights?"

By this time the reader of the Pisan cantos knows that the city of Dioce, the "hidden" city, is to be sought in the mind and heart. In Micah it will appear in "the last days," and only then will mercy and compassion replace iniquity:

> and they shall beat their swords into plowshares, and their spears into pruning hooks: nation shall not lift up the sword against nation, neither shall they learn war any more. . . . For all people will walk every one in the name of his god.

In "there is our norm of spirit," the verb has the force of "should be," for the two examples given are modified by ironic actualities. John Adams, in a letter Pound often quotes from ("every bank of discount . . . is downright corruption") had

thoughts similar to the balance of appeal and confession in the
Pisan cantos:

> Have I not been employed in mischief all my days? Did not the
> American Revolution produce the French Revolution? And did not
> the French Revolution produce all the calamities and desolations to
> the human race and the whole globe ever since? I meant well,
> however. My conscience was clear as a crystal glass, without a
> scruple or a doubt. I was borne along by an irresistible sense of
> duty. God proposed our labors; and awful, dreadful, and deplor-
> able as the consequences have been, I cannot but hope that the
> good of the world, of the human race, and of our beloved country,
> is intended and will be accomplished by it.

As for the second norm of spirit, the work of the brothers Adam,
the question of have they "bitched the Adelphi" is ironically
juxtaposed with "and the Farben works still intact" (C.74).

The wisdom that balances the ideal city of Dioce against the
injustices of earthly cities is reflected in the two references to
China earlier in the canto, both of which are new versions of material in Canto 53. The first reminds us of a folksong honoring a
legendary golden age; the second, of a depraved emperor who
burned a town. The abandonment of hope that the hidden city will
become political reality produces such sardonic observations as
that the Nobel laureate, Sinclair Lewis, has not mentioned the
"basis of issue" and that leaders like Stalin and Vandenberg make
no effort to understand each other or John Adams.

There are two fine dramatic touches against which these
thoughts assemble. The first is the scene in which other men
leave the Disciplinary Training Camp as Old Ez remains alone
in his tent, suspended in time. The final prayer, too, with its
nursery-rhyme beat, is beautifully balanced between thanks that
one kind of night is over and a question about when the figurative
night will end.

One more dramatic gesture has been carefully held in reserve
for the last page of the Pisan cantos. The dialogue between the
prisoner and the little Italian girl, "through the barbed wire," ends
with the balance of *uguale,* the same. The conversation appears

realistic yet is delicately classicized by a sound heard throughout the *Divine Comedy, ed ella, ed io.* In the entire Pisan sequence, the words in this dialogue are the first the prisoner has spoken aloud. He has done almost everything else—talked to himself, prayed, made up songs and poems, recalled old conversations, recorded language heard in the DTC, been talked to by others, anthologized the history of lyric poetry from Sappho to Yeats—but this is the only time he talks to another human being.

◊   ◊   ◊

*Page 91 (97)*

Si tuit li dolh elh plor, etc. / "If all the grief, the tears, the worth, the good." From Bertrans de Born's lament on the death of "the young English King." In 1909, before Angold was born, Pound had published his translation, which begins:

If all the grief and woe and bitterness,
All dolour, ill and every evil chance
That ever came upon this grieving world
Were set together they would seem but light
Against the death of the young English King.

Angold / J. P. Angold, a young poet Pound admired, who joined the Royal Air Force in 1939 and was killed in action in 1943.

τέθνηκε / *Tethnéké,* "he is dead."

Bankhead / Senator from Alabama, speaking of FDR.

Borah / Senator from Idaho, Pound's native state.

Richardson / Officer in charge of prisoner training. The names that follow are of officers, guards, and fellow prisoners.

*Page 92 (97–98)*

Mr. Coxey / "General" Coxey led an army of unemployed on Washington in 1894; among his demands was that the government issue non-interest-paying bonds. He continued as a populist leader, running for President in 1932. *Time* (1 October) reported a recent speech: "The Government takes 20% out of your salary to pay you interest on the 10% you have deducted from your salary to buy bonds. . . . Then they have to tax the people so the Government can pay interest to the banks, so the banks will support Government bonds upon which the money is issued."

Bartók / *Time* (8 October) reported the death of Béla Bartók in New York. Sinclair Lewis was the "cover story."

Mr Beard / Pound admired Beard's work on the economic history of the United States but found in the Armed Services Edition of his textbook only one sentence on the currency: "If any government keeps control over its currency, it will, in practice, more or less manage its economy."

Carrara / The quarries at Carrara, near Pisa, had supplied sculptors and architects with fine white marble for centuries.

## Page 93 (98–99)

Κύθηρα δεινά / Aphrodite as "the dread goddess."

Natalie / Natalie Clifford Barney, wealthy expatriate writer, had been a friend of Pound's since 1913. Here, remembering his great aunt Frank's zest for life, he recalls a sentence from Miss Barney's *Lettres d'une amazone:* "Having got out of life, oh having got out of it perhaps more than it contained."

Wei, Chi and Pi-kan / In *Analects* 18.1, Confucius states that during the decadence of the Yin dynasty there were, as Pound translates it, "three men (with a capital M)." Under tyrannical rule, one had refused to accept office, one had gone mad, and the other had his heart torn out.

## Page 94 (99–100)

Xaire / "Hail!"

il Capo / Mussolini, *Capo* (Head) *del governo Italiano,* after the fall of his Salò Republic in the spring of 1945, was captured and shot by Partisans, as were his colleagues, Alessandro Pavolini and Fernando Mezzasoma, who were with him.

Pierre / Pierre Laval, prime minister of Petain's Vichy regime in unoccupied France, was executed 15 October 1945.

Vidkun / Vidkun Quisling, who headed the collaborationist government in Norway, was executed on 24 October.

Henriot / Philippe Henriot, right-wing French deputy, became Petain's minister of propaganda, making frequent radio broadcasts. In June 1944, he was assassinated by members of the French Resistance.

quand vos venetz al som de l'escalina / "When you come to the summit of this stair." Pound either misremembers or reshapes the line from Arnaut Daniel's speech in *Purgatorio* 26. (See *consiros,* Canto 83).

ἠθος / *Ethos.* Custom, usage, habit. The plural, "character," makes better sense here.

ming² / The ideogram combines the characters for sun and moon. Pound's definition displays the connection he makes between Confucius and neoplatonism: "The sun and moon, the total light process, the radiation, reception and reflection of light; hence, the intelligence. Bright, brightness, shining. Refer to Scotus Erigena, Grosseteste and the notes on light in my Cavalcanti."

the Brothers Adam / Robert and James Adam, eighteenth-century architects and designers, noted for meticulous craftsmanship and graceful adaptation of classical models.


*Page 95 (100–101)*

Kumrad Koba / Stalin. *Time* (27 August) reported that, at the Potsdam Conference, Stalin refused to believe Churchill but was willing to accept the word of Truman.

δῖα ὑφορβα: / *dia huphorba,* "a goddess tending swine." The Homeric epithet connects the girl to Circe. (The Greek words are not included in all editions.)

e poi io dissi, etc. / "And then I said to the sister of the shepherdess tending her swine, 'And these Americans? Do they behave well?' And she: 'Not too well. Not too well.' And I: 'Worse than the Germans?' And she: 'The same.' "

Vandenberg / Senator Arthur Vandenberg had assumed power over American foreign policy as the leading Republican sponsor of "bipartisanship."

◇

# Section: Rock-Drill (1955)

◇

MUCH OF WHAT NORTHROP FRYE has to say about Blake's difficult
later poems holds true for Pound's later cantos: "If we read *Milton*
and *Jerusalem* as Blake intended them to be read, we are not
reading them in any conventional sense at all: we are staring at a
sequence of plates, most of them with designs. . . . The artist
demonstrates a certain way of life: his aim is not to be appreciated
or admired, but to transfer to others the imaginative habit and
energy of his mind." In place of Blake's designs, we have Pound's
expressive typography cum Chinese ideograms and Egyptian hiero-
glyphs. The later cantos are presented to an ideal reader who is
willing to say, as Pound says of his relation to the universe (C.95):

Responsus:
    Not stasis/
    at least not in our immediate vicinage.

Pound (like Blake, Joyce, and Elliott Carter in their different
ways) asks us to participate in his creation to an extraordinary
degree. The demand raises questions about our attitude toward
such "difficult" art. To say that one takes delight in *Rock-Drill* and
*Thrones* is not to deny that it is perfectly reasonable for others to
find them a preposterously arrogant gesture, a *reductio ad ab-
surdum* of one of Pound's favorite sayings from Remy de Gourmont, "Sincerely to write what one thinks—the only pleasure of a
writer." The absurdity may be seen in a list of books to be looked
into by what Donald Davie calls "students, I'm afraid, rather than
simple readers of the poem." A partial list would include: Couvreur's edition of the *Shu Ching;* Senator Thomas Hart Benton's
*Thirty Years' View;* Coke's *Institutes;* John Heydon's *Holy Guide*
(which Pound had Yeats's widow send him from Ireland); as-

sorted works by Alexander Del Mar and Louis Agassiz; Philostratus's *Life of Apollonius of Tyana;* Charles de Rémusat's *Anselme de Cantorbéry;* and Baller's textbook edition of a salt commissioner's popular version of the emperor Yong Tching's expansion of his father's cryptic *Sacred Edict*. Moreover, it is possible to do your homework today but forget it when you take the examination.

Some of these works arrive at the poem with a certain logic, even an inevitability. Others are "found objects" like the bicycle handlebars or toy automobile that Picasso's alchemy transforms into animals' heads. Some have a poetry inherent in them, as do the text and photographs of John Rock's *The Ancient Na-Khi Kingdom of South West China,* whereas others, like Baller's edition of the *Sacred Edict,* have almost no interest apart from whatever Poundian magnetism attracts them. Moreover, even if the reader/student takes the trouble to obtain the works he needs, he remains faced with poetry in which they are connected to each other by secret passageways of allusion and etymology.

It is perhaps too easy, after one has assembled (with pleasure and instruction) a set of notes on these cantos, to suggest what another reader might see just by reading and rereading with innocence and attention. Clearly, however, examples of beneficent rulers and other "paradisal" elements begin to predominate, although they continue to be set against the poet's irritations and denunciations, even as in the fifth heaven of Dante's *Paradiso* we hear the great complaint against Florence—and Dante continues muttering about his city's injustice and insanity even when he reaches the Empyrean. Unmistakable, too, is Pound's own delight in what he has seen and his wit and skill in recording it:

> from brown leaf and twig
> The GREAT CRYSTAL
> doubling the pine, and to cloud.
> pensar di lieis m'es ripaus
> Miss Tudor moved them with galleons
> from deep eye, versus armada
> from the green deep
> he saw it,

in the green deep of an eye:
    Crystal waves weaving together toward the gt/
                healing

                        (C.91)

Above prana, the light,
        past light, the crystal.
Above crystal, the jade!
The clover enduring,
        basalt crumbled with time.
"Are they the same leaves?"
    that was an intelligent question.

                        (C.94)

There are few places in the later cantos where the dazzling changes of rhythm and voice do not move forward on the poet's pleasure and impatience to strike the next spark, to reach toward a simultaneous presentation that, indeed, strains the resources of the medium. Yet there are Rock-Drill cantos in which, as Davie says, "it may be thought that the writing of *The Cantos* is at its most daring, assured, and splendid."

The forbidding title, *Rock-Drill,* disguises wit and affection. It appears to say that with repeated bursts of energy the poet is going to hammer his message into our heads. There is a good deal of repetition, but the governing principle is organic, not mechanical: "pine seed splitting cliff's edge" (C.87). *Rock-Drill* is also personal nostalgia, the title Pound's old comrade, Wyndham Lewis, gave to his review of Pound's *Letters* in 1951; and almost forty years before, it was the name of a handsome bronze by Jacob Epstein, one of the monuments of the London Vortex. Throughout the later cantos, Pound includes references to his early life, as if he is trying to discover an organic unity in his own career.

*Rock-Drill* and *Thrones* represent a personal triumph over the conditions under which they were written at a federal institution for the insane, Saint Elizabeths Hospital in Washington. Yet having dramatized his own situation at Pisa, Pound now displays the finest artistry in refusing to exploit the personal drama of Saint Elizabeths. Only rarely does he suggest where he is:

Passed that day drawing a grasshopper
"Loans from Tibet" said old Gallagher,
Patrick, and died in this bughouse?

(C.105)

There is no comparison with the severity of conditions in the
DTC; yet the verve it took to transcend the surroundings at Saint
Elizabeths is felt in the poem.

Strangely enough, the appeal Pound makes in Canto 84 for
gradations and distinctions was granted. Flown to Washington in
late 1945, he was judged incompetent to stand trial, as he was at
that time, then allowed to remain for thirteen years in a legal limbo.
After a difficult initial period in a ward he called the hell-hole,
Pound was given a room in a relatively livable ward, where he
could keep papers, books, and a typewriter. His wife took a small
basement apartment nearby and visited daily. The famous, many
of them old friends, came to call: Eliot, Williams, Cummings,
Marianne Moore, H. L. Mencken, Edith Hamilton, Juan Ramon
Jiménez. There were great numbers of younger people, from
naïve disciples (some with unfortunate political interests) to
serious artists and scholars. In good weather the conversations took
place under the trees; in bad weather in a corridor crowded with
the insane. The strange parody of the porches of Athens or of the
walk by the dynastic temple has been described by many visitors
but most memorably in Elizabeth Bishop's fine poem, "Visits to
St. Elizabeths."

There was an incredible outburst of energy during the years in
Washington: literally hundreds of publications, thousands of letters,
involvement in projects for which Pound organized his young
admirers. In 1946 the Pisan cantos began to appear, to be published
as a volume in 1948. Awarded the Bollingen Prize, it became the
subject of an acrimonious controversy. 1947: new translations of
the Confucian *Pivot* and *Great Digest*. 1948: first collected edition
of the *Cantos* (1–84). 1951: the Confucian *Analects*. 1954: translation of the Confucian *Odes*. 1955: *Section: Rock-Drill, 85–95 de los
cantares*. 1956: translation of Sophocles' *Women of Trachis*. 1959:

(mostly written at Saint Elizabeths) *Thrones, 96–109 de los cantares.*

These are major new works. Other works long out of print or never collected include: *Selected Poems* (1949); *Letters, 1907–1940* (1950); *The Translations of Ezra Pound,* with an introduction by Hugh Kenner (1953); *Literary Essays,* edited by T. S. Eliot (1954); *Pavannes and Divigations,* lighter essays (1958); and *Diptych Rome-London,* which displayed *Mauberley* and *Propertius* in a new light. Pound was now a world figure, and his work was being translated into at least twenty languages from Arabic to Yiddish.

Moreover, from about 1950 on, his work began to receive the full academic scholarly-critical treatment. In 1951, Kenner published a full-length study, *The Poetry of Ezra Pound.* There was a *Pound Newsletter* at Berkeley, an *Analyst* at Northwestern; an *Annotated Index,* also at Berkeley; and a number of excellent books on the *Cantos* and earlier poems.

I have specified all this activity by Pound and his critics to make a point about the later cantos: Their obscurities are not those of a man talking to himself. On the contrary, the poem changes, in part at least, because of the poet's new sense of an audience; among the forces shaping the cantos of the 1950s, not the least was the economics of American academic life. In *Rock-Drill* and *Thrones,* Pound writes with the confidence of a man who knows that, if he uses snatches of a Na Khi ceremony, someone will annotate it; that if he writes "stimulate anagogico," someone will discuss its source in a footnote to Charles de Rémusat's book on Saint Anselm (*vide infra*). At Saint Elizabeths, Pound was in many ways less isolated than at Rapallo; he could obtain almost any book or research he wanted, and he could use them as he wished, in the knowledge that a scholarly-critical industry had grown up about his poem even before it was completed. It was clear that the fame of the *Cantos* was now independent of his own energies and those of a few friends. The methods of the later cantos are an extension of methods Pound has been using from the start, but an extension that makes a quantum leap.

Pound writes for an audience willing to share the intuition behind these later cantos, that of a "Confucian universe . . . of interacting strains and tensions," and the poetry has the merit of not attempting to make that intuition less complex than it is. Yet to say that *Rock-Drill* and *Thrones* provide an image of, or an equation for, Pound's "Confucian universe" leaves us with an unwieldy truth, one that begs more questions than it answers.

A few years before "Imagism" was invented, Pound was struggling with an analogy that is useful in thinking about the later cantos. He took it from Blake on "line" in painting and redefined it for poetry as the "perfect cadence" that joins with the "perfect word." So far, nothing exceptional, but then:

> In painting, the colour is always finite. It may match the colour of the infinite spheres, but it is in a way confined within the same frame and its appearance is modified by the colours about it. The line is unbounded, it marks the passage of a force, it continues beyond the frame.
>
> Rodin's belief that energy is beauty holds thus far, namely, that all our ideas of beauty of line are in some way connected with our ideas of swiftness or easy power of motion.

He is trying to resolve a classic problem, how can art be one thing and life another, without having to admit some fatal separation between them. On the one hand, how can one avoid putting "ideas" into poetry and so turning it into what Sidney calls "a medicine of cherries," and on the other hand, how can poetry be more than a game of words receding into an infinite distance of irony?

In the later cantos especially, there is a "frame" of form in which each word modifies each other, and there is also a universe of energies beyond, which enter and leave the frame. Pound's analogy to Blake and Rodin brings us to the "swiftness" of these cantos, a swiftness he has come to think of as *hilaritas*. This may help to explain what often looks like an arbitrary choice and arrangement of materials: The line must be definite or it is nothing, yet it is drawn from the infinite possibilities of the Idea of Line. It could not be so arbitrary nor use such an apparent miscellany of materials if its subject were something that can be *named:* Social Credit, or the history of China, or life in a hospital for the insane. The subject can only be named by reading each word in the poem: *Nomina sunt consequentia rerum.*

If the "frame," then, is not an impassable barrier, if it allows the passage of a force that extends beyond it, perfection of form may be less important, for even an imperfect poem may be a diaphan for the universe of energy:

> i.e. it coheres all right
> > even if my notes do not cohere.

> > > (C.116)

If one accepts such an aesthetic, if the poet intuits a coherent universe, if his meditation is deep enough, and if his *techne* (art or skill) is fine enough, then, as Eva Hesse says,

> Oddly enough, the inductive process of the *Cantos* is set in operation in the reader's mind irrespective of whether he broadly accepts or rejects the inferences that the poet wishes to be drawn from his juxtaposition of facts and fiction, sense impressions, snatches of conversation, literary quotations, multiple allusions and recorded events. In other words, they continue to "make Cosmos" in the reader's head.

There is a great deal more one can say about the later cantos: their metrics; their "cipher technique"; the way in which a single word is, as Pound said it could be, "almost an ideogram" or in which the poet "ventures into pre-formed worlds, submerges into ancient rivers of language." Clearly, this is difficult poetry to discuss, and critics often find themselves reaching for metaphors or writing their own poems in the attempt.

It is as if these later cantos were an enormous silk tapestry, as large as the ceiling of the Sistine Chapel. There is an overall design, but there is no single point from which we can see it evenly; we must walk around, move back and forth. Moreover, in *Selected Cantos* we have only small sections of that tapestry. Some of the important figures, such as Apollonius of Tyana, are not here at all; and others, such as Benton and Agassiz, are suggested by only a few words. We must limit ourselves to what we have in the selection, for it is impossible to discuss in detail the whole of *Rock-Drill* and *Thrones,* sections of the *Cantos* that, more than ever, as Davie says, "defeat exegesis by inviting it so inexhaustibly."

◇   ◇

*from* CANTO 85

THIS FIRST PAGE OF *Rock-Drill* is a good example of a relatively separable Poundian ideogram, more a prelude to all eleven cantos than a part of Canto 85 proper, which moves into a detailed study of the *Shu Ching,* the *History Classic.*

The great LING², which will be repeated in later cantos, is only partly or temporarily defined by "sensibility" in the next line. The statement connecting sensibility and government is followed by examples of rulers who exemplify the sensibility that is invoked throughout *Rock-Drill* and *Thrones:* Wellington's moderation, Cleopatra's attention to the question of money, Elizabeth's transla- tions (with everything that "translation" and "Ovid" have come to stand for), the great minister Y Yin's wisdom and awareness of the Process, and implicitly those of later dynasties who remember Y Yin and take him for a guide. (Pound refers to him both as I Yin and Y Yin.) These become points that define a periphery and suggest a richness of sensibility possible in government. The de- fined sensibility becomes *chih*³, something we can fasten to, a place to begin. The forms of these rulers, moving within the records that tell of their accomplishments, are "shadows" from which we may derive knowledge. Hence, obscurantism—any suppression or scattering of the records of sensibility—is counter to the active and sincere intelligence necessary for civilization. As an example, we have come to think of Galileo as a scientist, but he was a complete humanist; an author of verse, satires, and literary criticism (some of which would have fit into the pages of *ABC of Reading*); and a stylist whose principal "scientific" work, a dialogue among philosophers, is a masterpiece of Renaissance prose. The last line on the page implies a definition of *politics* opposite to that held by most "politicians."

From the Chinese characters on the page, we may form a perfectly good five-character line of poetry

$$ling^2$$
$$Y$$
$$Yin$$
$$chih^3$$
$$hsien^2$$

that, like each line in the Confucian *Odes,* can become the occasion for extensive commentary, comparison, and definition but that may be translated as "the spiritual forces registered by Y Yin provide a point of reference for sincere and intelligent action."

Beyond that, our gloss on this page/ideogram/Confucian ode takes us into the "pre-formed worlds" and submerged "ancient rivers of language" noted on the original dust jacket of *Rock-Drill*.

1. *Ling²*. The complete story behind this character would require an essay of some length. We may put together a brief version of that story with only a little, and delightful, trouble, just as Pound did. Chinese characters present the Westerner with a mystique more formidable than need be, unless he has looked into the Confucian books. If you have a transliteration of the signs (which is why Pound presents so many of them), you may look them up in Mathews's dictionary, where they are listed alphabetically. Karlgren's dictionary is harder to use, but with some diligence you may find them there, with notes on their early forms and underlying meanings. If you have Legge's editions (most of which are easily obtained in paperback), there is an index listing each occurrence of a character in the Confucian books, which leads you to a series of contexts and to Legge's helpful commentaries. The only problem is finding them in the index, for they are listed under their "radicals," and that takes some searching. Yet some such process has produced the first four lines of *Rock-Drill*—carried out, of course, by

the luminous eye. If we follow such a process, we will see that Pound's way of defining a term like *ling*² is essentially the Chinese way.

The character derives from the one hundred seventy-third radical, "rain." The three "squares" in the center are enlarged raindrops but look to Pound very much like the thirtieth radical, "mouth." The strokes beneath show a ceremony or ceremonial dance. Thus the ideogram suggests transfers of energy between heaven and earth, and an awareness (of the Process) necessary for good government.

The difficulty in supplying a Western definition for *ling*² may be seen in Couvreur, Mathews, and Legge. It is not a common character, not to be found in the *Unwobbling Pivot,* the *Great Digest,* nor in the *Analects;* it occurs only three or four times in the *Shu* and once in Mencius (where it is a quotation from the *Odes*). We discover it in only 4 of the 305 odes, used quite differently each time, though always with a generally favorable connotation. For those four appearances in the *Odes,* Couvreur's glossary definition is either desperation or a kind of buckshot ideogram: "*Esprit, merveille, merveilleux, puissant, grand, majestueux, bon, favorable.*" Mathews gives (4071): "Spirit of a being which acts upon others. Spirit; spiritual; divine. Supernatural. Efficacious." At one point, Legge gives up: "The *ling*²," he says, after facing the complexities of *Ode* 3.1.8, "may be variously translated."

It must have been when he was translating that same ode at Saint Elizabeths that Pound was struck by its extraordinary uses of *ling*²; it is unlikely that he would especially have noticed it in the *Shu.* (We might expect, by the way, to find in the *Shu* a statement something like "Our dynasty came in because of *ling*²," but we do not.) In the ode, it undergoes a wonderful metamorphosis as it is used to describe first a marvelous tower, then a park, then a pond, all built by Wan, the great ancestor of the house of Tchou.

Legge decides to translate it in all cases as a simple adjective, "marvelous." But Pound, putting together everything he knows about the character—a rejected reading from Legge's notes, Karlgren's analysis, Couvreur's translation, all other appearances of *ling*$^2$ in the Confucian canon, and what he sees by just looking at it—decides that the character attracts to itself the meaning of the entire ode, a lyrical presentation of a Tory paradise in which king, people, nature, and music are in constructive harmony and where pond-park-tower appear not to be a "real" place but to be a symbol of a civilization informed by the spirits of the ancestors, or by "Heaven." When he translates the ode, he includes as much of this as possible, with "spirit tower," "Park Divine," and "haunted pool."

*Ling*$^2$ combined with "Our dynasty came in because of a great sensibility" captures the spirit of what ministers and emperors say throughout the *Shu Ching,* from Y Yin's own lecture to the young emperor (which we have heard in Canto 53) through the later dynasties that take Y Yin as a guide to the spiritual-natural-social harmony that is an ideal for wise rulers. At each appearance in *Rock-Drill* and *Thrones,* the character brings with it a new context that modifies or extends the definition. The entire group of cantos explores the implications of *ling*$^2$ in the lives of people like Queen Elizabeth, Galileo, Senator Benton, and Desmond Fitzgerald, whose sense of responsibility is "rooted" in an ample awareness of the natural order.

2. *Gnomon.* An English word is no more a closed system than is the ideogram for *ling*$^2$. Fenollosa's essay reminds us that a word is not an ideogram (there remains an all-important distinction, the picture or action that remains in the brushstroke), yet that if we assemble its roots and cognates it can be, as Pound says, "almost" an ideogram. In *Guide to Kulchur,* Pound decides that a word can be "aperient"—and immediately demonstrates what he means by inventing a definition for "aperient" that is not in any English dictionary, that opens up to root meanings from *aperio,* to uncover, make something accessible. This *aperient* occurs in the discussion of a word from Aristotle that Pound decides can not be translated by "any ready made current English," because Aristotle's term

"lets in" not only its own roots and pre-Aristotelean history but also "all the Arabian commentators" and all related aspects of medieval theology. This is not quite Humpty Dumpty's concept that a word means what he wants it to mean, but it implies that the meaning attracts to it anything we consider a legitimate application or extension.

No word can be more aperient in that sense than *gnomon* as it is used on this page of Canto 85. Its roots are in the Greek for *perceive, know.* It becomes the pointer on the sundial, through whose shadow we know time and the position of the sun. By extension it is any scientific instrument (like the many devised by Galileo) that acts as an indicator. The page on which it occurs also exemplifies another meaning of *gnomon* as "a saying, rule, canon of belief or action." Each line is a gnomon, a shadow or indicator of whole systems of light/wisdom/history and of a habit of Chinese thought that lasted for centuries and formed the basis for preserving old records. (In a note at the end of Canto 85, Pound records that Confucius, who is supposed to have gathered the documents that form the *Shu,* "said he had added nothing." That is, the roots of his teachings were all there in the gnomes attributed to legendary figures such as Y Yin.)

A more arcane use of *gnomon* in the later cantos is the myth of the "world tree," which has roots in the earth and its topmost branches in heaven, representing a harmonious society as well as an image of the spiritualized "science" of men like Galileo, Frobenius, and Agassiz. "All these requirements of the specialized sciences," Frobenius writes, "have been set aside. We see the earth in its entirety. . . . The whole of it one huge tree, the tree of heaven, Ygdrasil." The tree, which stands symbolically at the center of the earth—and which Pound associates with the *chung,* "the pivot perceived by Y Yin"—is also a "gnomon."

This *gnomon* is casting a long shadow, but there is one more meaning we may be aware of, for Pound is interested (as we see in Cantos 95 and 105) in the ways in which "grammar" expresses "reality." If one were to translate the Confucian records into classical Greek, presumably it would require the use of the "gnomic

aorist," a tense used to "express what once happened and has
thereby established a precedent for all time." We do not have that
tense in English, but the feeling of the gnomic aorist is behind
much of the *Cantos.*

3. *Science.* In addition to the etymology and history of *gnomon,*
we must be aware, in the next line, that *science* operates in its
contemporary sense and in its root sense, "knowledge," and that
*shadow,* through that great gnomic work the *OED,* brings in
"comparative darkness caused by the interception of light," "shades
of the dead," "the faint appearance of something seen through an
obscuring medium," and "a symbol, type."

Galileo's knowledge of the universe came literally from the
watching of shadows. That is, he had worked out his speculations,
but they remained necessarily intuitive until the moment when,
as Giorgio de Santillana says, "the circle of proof was concluded
in his mind." That was the moment when he first looked through
his telescope and observed that the Moon was not, as the Aristote-
lians claimed it must be, made of some smoother, lighter, purer
substance than the Earth. What he saw, as he tells us, were
shadows:

> I wished by means of more accurate observations to go on to find
> other details, not only in the actual classic and very large spots,
> visible to the naked eye, but in the small shadows (*piccole adom-
> brazioni*) dependent on the heights and cavities . . . visible and
> observable only through the telescope.

Each issue of *Scientific American* reports on extensions of Galileo's
techniques in which the most dazzling precisions of, say, radio
astronomy or nuclear physics are calculated from the shadows of
events that will never be observed directly. We are also reminded
by modern scientists that, after a period of hubris, science has made
what Santayana called a "progress in modesty" and is content to
work with shadows and without hope of attaining ultimate knowledge of the universe. Thus "Our science is from the watching of
shadows" embraces Plato's epistemology (the shadows in the cave),
Galileo's telescope, and this morning's discovery at MIT.

4. *Hsien²*. In Mathews (2617) this *hsien²* is "virtuous, worthy, good." By now, Pound has presumably trained us not to accept *that*. We can at least see the balance or pivot in the upper corner. Combined with the strokes just beneath it, the sign for "heart," it becomes an ideogram common in the Confucian writings, meaning something like "good faith" or "sincere action from the heart." The component at the bottom is the "luminous eye" (eye with running legs beneath), which we discussed in relation to "the sun as a golden eye" in Canto 83, where it suggests a mutual perception of intelligence between person and universe. So this particular "virtue" contains much of its own definition, something like "faithful action proceeding from a heart/eye (sensibility) aware of the Process." Certainly one possessing it would not scatter records nor opportunistically jump to the winning side.

The cantos that follow explore in hundreds of particulars the ideogram formed by the words on this page: *ling²*, sensibility, roots, peace, science, translation, money, *hsien²*. They gather scattered records of "top flights of the mind," of sensibilities that are not "split." In Canto 89, for example, Galileo is associated with Mencius (in Pound's eyes, also a scientist), two men whose interest in natural phenomena is not divorced from a sense of public responsibility. Galileo moves naturally from his scientific discoveries to the same moral insight that lies at the heart of Pound's economics. He sees people disappointed to hear that heavenly bodies are imperfect and mutable. On the contrary, he writes, the universe is noble and admirable if, like the Earth, it allows "generation":

> I say the same concerning the Moon, Jupiter, and all the other globes of the universe. . . . What greater folly can be imagined than to call gems, silver and gold noble, and earth and dirt base? It is scarcity and plenty that make things esteemed by the vulgar, who will say that here is a most beautiful diamond, for it resembles a clear water, and yet would not part with it for ten tons of water. . . . These people deserve to meet with a Medusa's head that would transform them into statues of diamond and jade, that so they might become more perfect than they are.

*Page 96 (105)*

LING² / The superscript means that this *ling* is pronounced on
the second tone; *ling* on another tone would be a different character.

I Yin / The characters to the right form his name, which is
transliterated as Y Yin in other editions and in other parts of the
poem. He plays an important part in the documents collected as
*Shu Ching,* from which Canto 85 is taken, joining legendary figures such as Yao, Chun, and Yu in the definition of "wise ruler."

Galileo / Earlier cantos (48–49) remind us that, although he was
a "heretic," the Jesuits introduced his thought to China during the
seventeenth century.

Wellington / After Napoleon's defeat, Wellington headed the
occupation of France, acting as a moderating influence against
those who demanded overly harsh reparations, avoiding conditions
that might have led to another war.

*chih*³ / As with *ling*² this character is defined by the totality of
its appearances in the *Cantos.* We saw it at the end of Canto 52
as a "hitching post, position, place one is in and works from." In
its common dictionary definition as "stop" it suggests something
like "take action to bring to an end undesirable conditions." It
makes a final appearance in Canto 110, where it is juxtaposed with
"root," the organic process celebrated in the Eleusinian rites (much
like that pictured in *ling*²) and the warning "not with jet planes."
Here, it also suggests visually the gnomon casting its shadow.

Queen Bess / As far as I can determine, Elizabeth did not translate Ovid, but Pound is essentially correct, for she knew Greek and
Latin and translated Boethius, Horace, Seneca, and Plutarch.

◊    ◊

## *from* CANTO 88

THE TECHNIQUE OF THE LATER CANTOS, based on what the jacket copy for *Rock-Drill* calls "small units of mathematical composition," makes them difficult to excerpt, as we can see from Pound's somewhat arbitrary though representative cuttings from Cantos 88, 105, and 108. The counterpoint is so quick, the lines so short, the voices so many, that this music less resembles a Bach fugue than the effects of Webern or the last works of Stravinsky. Yet the concentration of these fragments is so great that commentary has a tendency to expand, as it has for *ling²* and for *gnomon*.

Cantos 85 and 86, drawn from the Chinese *History Classic,* retrace the ground of Cantos 52 through 61 but emphasize the philosophic principles discoverable in Chinese history rather than chronicle. Canto 87, to extend the loose musical analogy, is a fantasia on dozens of subjects. Cantos 88 and 89 concentrate on the dramatic struggle for economic democracy in the administrations of Jackson and Van Buren. The dominant figure is Thomas Hart Benton, whose *Thirty Years' View* supplies most of the information as well as the diction and rhythms of the documentary passages.

The theme of this page from Canto 88 might be summed up in the ironic epic announcement (C.86), "Bellum cano perenne" [Perpetual war I sing], that is, the economic war and its inevitable extension to imperialism and bloodshed. The contrast between dreams of brotherhood and the realities of history is clear from the references to China and Japan. Mr. Tcheou's remark (is the name chosen to rhyme with the great Tchou dynasty?) must be understood as applying to a relatively few scholars reading the classics. We remember that Pound's introduction to Chinese poetry came by way of Fenollosa's work with Japanese, not Chinese, masters. In the twentieth century, too, many important Chinese texts survived only in Japan. Unfortunately, for all the common roots of Chinese and Japanese cultures, Mr. Tcheou's words must be read with the emphasis on "should," for when Perry "opened" Japan, he also opened it to its Western-style military and economic aggressions, attacks on China, annexation of Korea, and Pearl Harbor.

The Negro dialect in the following lines is a way of saying, as Adams and Douglas said in their different ways, that political democracy without economic democracy leaves us slaves to masters against whom we appear reluctant to rebel. One attack on that slavery—of one people to another, and of the common man everywhere to those who (C.38) "faire passer ces affaires / avant ceux de la nation" is Anatole France's *Penguin Island,* which exposes the financial oligarchy's control of foreign affairs, leading to economic-military imperialism.

Although the tone is different, Pound's history of the United States is much like the history of Penguin Island. The main outline of that history was suggested in Cantos 31 and 62: Just as in the Bible, the Fall comes early in the story, when Hamilton, clever and attractive as Satan was to Eve, persuades the nation to hand over its sovereignty in coinage to the private Bank of the United States. Unlike Original Sin, however, the bank had a limited charter. Pound's heroes are Jackson, Benton, the President's leading supporter in the Senate, and Van Buren. The villains include the unscrupulous head of the bank, Nicholas Biddle, and the bank's bought spokesman, Daniel Webster, who fought to have the charter renewed. (Henry Clay, also in the bank's pay for years, was another of its supporters.) Benton, who represented Missouri from 1820 to 1850, was a man who refused to "jump to the winning side" (C.85) and was a master at arousing public opinion. When the bank's charter was renewed by Congress, Jackson vetoed it, and there were not enough votes to override. Jackson and Benton defeated the bank, and by 1834, for the first time in American history, there was no national debt.

Cantos 88 and 89 draw up a bill of particulars against the bank from fragments of Benton's writings and speeches (he could, and did, talk for four days if necessary). We hear Benton declaring that our financial system is contrary to the Constitution, that the bank's powerful officials are not elected by the people, that it is a private monopoly on public resources. In Canto 89, answering the claim that the bank is beneficial to the nation, Benton asks, "If beneficial, why not several?" The lines we have before us from Canto 88, beginning "Use of foreign coin until 1819," are a synecdoche for the entire question.

It is quite simple, though as usual Pound avoids a clear exposition. To Benton, Section 8, Article 5 of the Constitution was plain. The Congress shall have the power:

> To coin money, regulate the value thereof, and of foreign coin, and fix the standard of weights and measures.

When the nation began, large sums of foreign specie were in circulation. Its relative values regulated by Congress, this foreign coin was legal tender and served every legitimate function of money. Moreover, it was money on which the nation was paying no interest. In 1819, the bank got Congress to declare that foreign coin was no longer legal tender, but for some reason Spanish milled dollars were excluded from the change in policy. In effect, the nation was now required to use the bank's paper, created "out of nothing," and to pay the bank interest on it. Clearly, the profits were enormous. Benton could see no reason, other than corruption, why the foreign coin was removed from circulation.

In addition to profiting from its own paper, the bank and other speculators bought up the devalued foreign coins and sold them abroad at a profit. Since Pound wants us to turn to page 446 of Benton's memoirs, we should do so:

> An exception was continued, and still remains, in favor of Spanish milled dollars and parts of dollars; but all other foreign coins . . . have ceased to be legal tender, and have lost their character of current money within the United States. Their value is degraded to the mint price of bullion; and thus the constitutional currency becomes an article of merchandise and exportation. Even the Spanish milled dollar, though continued as legal tender, is valued not as money, but for the pure silver in it, and is therefore undervalued three or four percent. and becomes an article of merchandise. The Bank of the United States has collected and sold 4,450,000 of them.

It was on another issue that Benton finally lost his seat in the Senate, although he was not helped by having the financial interests and their controlled press against him. During the 1840s he became increasingly opposed to slavery, and his position on the Missouri Compromise ran counter to that of his constituents. As Pound sees American history, the defeat of the bank in Jackson's administration was temporary. The financial interests reasserted their power, and the bank, a mask of Geryon, reappeared in subtler shape, or at least more difficult to understand, as the Federal Reserve System.

◊   ◊   ◊

*Page 97 (106)*

Marse Adams / The reader has heard what Adams "done tol' 'em" in earlier cantos, so only a shorthand reminder is given in this passage.

Our whole banking system I ever abhorred. . . . A national bank of deposit I believe to be wise, just, prudent, economical, and necessary. But every bank of discount, every bank by which interest is to be paid or profit of any kind made by the deponent, is downright corruption. It is taxing the public for the benefit and profit of individuals; it is worse than old tenor, continental currency, or any other paper money. Now, Sir, if I should talk in this strain, after I am dead, you know the people of America would pronounce that I died mad. (To Benjamin Rush, 28 August 1811)

The Major / The remark below, "To the consumer," is shorthand for Douglas's $A + B$ Theorem quoted in Canto 38.

First Folio / Whoever it was who had the copy of Shakespeare locked up provides an example of the state of mind opposed by Adams, Douglas, and Benton.

◊   ◊

## CANTO 95

THE FINAL CANTO OF *Rock-Drill* is so open and allusive that an attempt at complete explication would be unreadably diffuse. It seems better to provide as much comment and continuity as possible in the page-by-page notes that follow. The technical problem Pound sets for himself is suggested by the first two lines:

> LOVE, gone as lightning,
> enduring 5000 years.

The canto is a meditation on the interaction between the individual mind or soul and the enduring Light (5000 years = forever), which includes an abundant, unceasingly creative Love; the Divine Mind; Paradise; Santayana's "Something *there*"; and the Elder Lightfoot's "design in the process." The poet's mind intuits the persistence of this force within the universe yet cannot maintain a steady contemplation of it; it comes in lightning flashes, in quickly shifting fragments of memory and allusion. The situation is dramatized in a passage from Canto 92, where we find two figures from Canto 95, Saint Hilary and (through a most hidden allusion to his *The Improvisatore*) Beddoes:

> Le Paradis n'est pas artificiel
>                     but is jagged,
>        For a flash,
>                 for an hour.
>        Then agony,
>                 then an hour,
>                         then agony,
>        Hilary stumbles, but the Divine Mind is abundant
>                 unceasing
>                 *improvisatore*

Pound tells us that "the major theme as the *Cantos* move into their third and final phase" is "the domination of benevolence" and that one expression of the theme is the quotation from Richard of Saint Victor that stands (in Latin) as epigraph to Canto 90. He translates it as:

> The human soul is not love, but love flowing from it . . . it cannot, ergo, delight in itself, but only in the love flowing from it.

Yet the mind or soul remains, at the end of *Rock-Drill*, an imperfect conductor of that "Something *there*," of that love that is not itself.

There is an amazing unity to Pound's career, and in later cantos he is often rewriting the poems of his youth, poems he could not then realize because of outworn literary convention and cautious assumptions about the relations of poet and audience. His "modernism" is in a sense an interruption, or perhaps a long discovery of a means to an end. A poem published in 1909 prefigures in technique and content the work of almost half a century later:

> Aye, I am wistful for my kin of the spirit
> And have none about me save in the shadows
> When come *they*, surging of power, "DAEMON,"
> "Quasi KALOUN." S.T. says, Beauty is most that, a
> "calling to the soul."
> Well then, so call they, the swirlers out of the mist
> of my soul,
> They that come mewards bearing the old magic.

What has been gained in fifty years is only superficially the abandonment of inversions and words like "mewards." Rather, it is a greater *hilaritas* and a love for the particular word and detail, which no longer need depend on conventional means of "elevation."

The references to "S.T." and "Quasi KALOUN" lead to Coleridge's "On the Principles of Genial Criticism": "Hence the Greeks called a beautiful object *kalón* quasi *kaloun*, i.e. *calling on* the soul, which receives instantly, and welcomes it as something connatural." Coleridge's essay and his related essay "On Poesy or Art" have much to tell us about the aesthetics and "vision" (they are not separate) of Pound's later cantos. Without exploring thoroughly Pound's relation to Coleridge, we may excerpt a few sentences that suggest Coleridge's peculiar Platonism and the demands it places on poetry. My italics emphasize phrases that may throw some light on the difficulty and complexity of the later cantos:

> The sense of beauty subsists in *simultaneous* intuition of the relation of parts, each to each, and of all to a whole.
>
> Beauty does not arise from association, as the agreeable does, but sometimes lies in the *rupture of association*.
>
> Man's mind is the very focus of all the rays of intellect which are scattered throughout the images of nature. Now so to place these images totalized . . . to superinduce upon the forms themselves the moral reflexions to which they approximate . . . is the mystery of genius in the Fine Arts.
>
> The poet may learn nature's unspoken *language in its main radicals.* . . . Yes, not to acquire cold notions—lifeless technical rules —but living and life-producing certainty that they are essentially *one with the germinal causes in nature,*—his consciousness being the focus and mirror of both.

The last is particularly interesting, as Coleridge brings together metaphors of etymology and of organic growth—themselves joined in *radix*/root—just as Pound does throughout *Rock-Drill* and *Thrones*. At the center of "On the Principles of Genial Criticism" is a passage from Plotinus similar to that from Richard of Saint Victor that Pound says expresses the theme of these cantos:

> When the mind perceives the form intertwining itself through the concrete, and conquering the material reality opposed to it: then, after perceiving the dominating form, visibly emerging, the mind—collecting together the diverse materials into a harmonized union—bestows this form it has perceived back upon the object— a form quite in keeping with the character of the inner principle [actually there] in the object.

When this "communicative intelligence in nature and man," as Coleridge describes it (we have seen it in action in Canto 83) becomes both the subject and the governing principle of verse, it may produce those ruptures of association and a reaching for a simultaneity of effect that make Canto 95 so difficult.

The canto, which catches up all the themes previously stated in

*Rock-Drill,* seeks to create a poetic world in which the delight of the soul in the love that is not itself but which flows from it, seems natural. One tactic is to reinvigorate language itself, to shake us from the complacency with which we accept impoverished meanings for certain words. So the Latin fragments from Bede on the first page allow an opportunity to place *anima* above *animal* for inspection, reminding us that "spirit" and "soul" inform "animal," though we often forget that, when we use phrases like the one examined below: "Man is a political animal." The citizen, the *compagnevole animale,* has been reduced to:

> reproducteur,
> contribuable. Paradis peint

He reproduces, he pays his taxes, he accepts a painted paradise on his church wall—and he hands over civic affairs to politicians in the narrowest sense of the word. Both Pound and Remy de Gourmont, whom he is quoting, are ironically using *reproducteur* and *contribuable* in their most reductive senses, leaving it to us to infer the abandoned possibilities.

The voices in the sacred oak-wood, the oracles—Dante, Benton, Adams, Hilary, Santayana—speak with a larger vision, or in Coleridge's words, "one with the germinal causes in nature." The voices lead to the exultation of:

That the crystal wave mount to flood surge

chin⁴

hu¹

jên²

The light there almost solid.

The Chinese characters force us to slow down, to look, to wonder. "There" refers to the context they come from, Chapter 20 of the *Unwobbling Pivot.* In sections 8 through 11 of that chapter, visibly arising from "radicals" of unity and organic nature, in Legge's words, "there is brought before us the character of the 'men' . . . on whom depends the flourishing of *'government,'* which government is exhibited in paragraphs 12–15." The same sequence is roughly that of the later cantos, in which an emphasis on individual sensibility in *Rock-Drill* gives way to a stricter examination of law, economics, and government in *Thrones*.

What are we to make of an allusion such as this to three characters from the Confucian *Pivot?* We will never recognize it as we recognize "Our revels now are ended" or "April is the cruelest month." Are we to interrupt our reading to hunt for the characters in Confucius so that the context will allow us to read with sufficient weight the word "men" in "And damn it there were men even in my time"? Pound wants us, I believe, to read past such allusions if we must, to see whatever is to be seen (and by now the reader should have a fair sense of Pound's Confucianism); but better, he would like us to know the *Paradiso* and the *Unwobbling Pivot* so well that their atmospheres, their moral sensibilities, are immediately available to us. It may remain for the occasion when we are studying, not reading, the canto, to discover the exact context and to consider all its implications.

Finally, to take an even more difficult passage, how are we to read:

"O World!"
        said Mr Beddoes.
"Something *there.*"
        sd/ Santayana.

Pound has just protested what he calls the "Indian Circe of negation and dissolution," by crying his own "O world!" as he invokes one of his sacred places, Lake Garda. Then the idea is reinforced as Beddoes addresses the world with an exclamation point and as Santayana insists in italics that there is something *there.* Beyond that, we must trace hidden passageways.

Beddoes can hardly be said to have a "philosophy," but he expresses a kind of Romantic Platonism that Pound brings out in his tribute, "Beddoesque" (1908), which ends, "The whole great liquid jewel of God's truth." But Beddoes was much concerned with death, and his Platonism led him not to responsible action but to the cynical despair of *Death's Jest Book* and to a longing to dissolve the oppressing self, to merge with the universe in a way that Pound associates with the way in which "Hindoos / lust after vacuity." To hear Beddoes' "O world!" in context is to hear at once a cry of loss and of mockery. It is from a speech by a "zany," Mandrake, and Pound quoted it in a 1917 essay on Beddoes:

> The dry rot of prudence hath eaten the ship of fools to dust; she is no more seaworthy. . . . O world, world! The gods and fairies left thee, for thou wert too wise, and now, thou Socratic star, thy demon, the Great Pan, Folly, is parting from thee. The oracles still talked in their sleep, shall our grand-children say, till Master Merriman's kingdom was broken up: now is every man his own fool, and the world's sign is taken down.

Beddoes led a rootless life, making sporadic attempts to do something useful but never bringing much to completion; he killed himself, after a leg had been amputated, leaving a note: "I am food for *what I am good for*—worms. . . . I ought to have been among other things a good poet; Life was too great a bore on one peg & that a bad one.—"

For the man of vision, there is a thin partition between hope and despair. "It is difficult to write a paradiso," Pound said in 1962, "when all the superficial indications are that you ought to write an apocalypse." The springing exultation and light of *Rock-Drill* play constantly against shadows of "it might have been," and there is throughout these cantos a fine dark thread of references to madness, suicide, and despair:

> The wrong way about it: despair.
>     (I think that is in Benton)

(C.89)

In contrast to the failed poet Beddoes's despair, George Santayana's last volume, *Dominations and Powers* (1951), on the philosophy of government, and his posthumous *Letters* (both of which Pound read), show a man decidedly not bored, working, responsible to the whole people, almost to the day of his death at eighty-nine. In his last letter, he writes that, as he is now almost blind, all he can do is write poetry; he hopes to complete a twenty-three stanza poem in *ottava rima*. His "Something *there*" points to the tenor of his lifelong battle against idealism and solipsism, but Pound is remembering a specific passage from *Dominations and Powers* in which "vacuum" and "fool's paradise" reflect the Hindu "vacuity" of Canto 95, as well as Beddoes's dying world where "now is every man his own fool." The passage, which may serve as a gloss on *Rock-Drill*, is the second below, but we need the first as introduction and for a larger sense of why Santayana is in this canto:

> I assume that here are the sun and stars set far above us, and the earth beneath, with the sea a little beyond, and all the sea-routes leading to islanded nations scattered about the globe. I assume that these lands have been inhabited by many peoples now extinct or unrecognisable, regarding some of whom we have historical records; so that their moral experience was the beginning of ours, is intelligible to us, and often, when pondered, renders our own experience intelligible. . . .
>
> The literary philosophy and the psychological novels which have been dominant in modern times assume, if they do not teach, that thought is something substantial and self-developing; that it has no origin or milieu except in other thoughts; and even sometimes that the evolution of this ideation in a vacuum is itself guided by dialectic. Nothing could be better calculated to keep politics in a fool's paradise of verbal reasoning.

Santayana's sonnet beginning "O world" (which was in the indispensable *Pocket Book of Verse* at Pisa) ponders some of the concerns in Beddoes' "O world!" passage from *Death's Jest Book*, though it comes to a conclusion more in harmony with Canto 95:

> O world, thou choosest not the better part!
> It is not wisdom to be only wise . . .
> .   .   .   .   .   .   .   .
> Bid, then, the tender light of faith to shine
> By which alone the mortal heart is led
> Unto the thinking of the thought divine.

There are indeed "many sounds in that oak-wood," and we must listen with extraordinary attention, even making excursions far from the poem itself, before we will fully understand them.

*Page 98 (107)*

"Consonantium demonstratrix" / "Demonstrator of harmonies." In the Venerable Bede (673–735) it refers to music, but placed next to the "great stars," it suggests the music of the spheres. (The Latin, miscopied, should be *consonantiarum*.) Pound has assembled eight phrases from assorted works by Bede to form, as it were, his own Latin hymn.

ἔφατ᾽ / *Ephat'*, "said."

Baeda / Misprint for "Beda," Bede.

Deus est anima mundi / "God is the spirit (or soul) of the world."

animal optimum et sempiternum / (God is) "the best of beings and everlasting."

Tempus est ubique, non motus / "Time is everywhere, not motion."

in vesperibus orbis / A puzzle, for Pound has either miscopied or consciously changed Bede's *vepribus* (thornbush), arriving at a Latin that does not quite make sense. He may want a suggestion of Vesper, the evening star, and its association with Venus/Love.

Expergesci thalamis / "To be awakened in an inner chamber" (or bedroom–marriage chamber).

gravat serpella nimbus / Translated in the following line. In Bede it is an evening mist. One can only guess at what Pound has in mind; perhaps, "God is everywhere in nature, morning and evening."

Delcroix / Carlo Delcroix, a friend mentioned several times in the *Cantos*. The juxtaposition suggests that, like Adams, Delcroix had a sense of responsibility to "the whole people." "They repeat" is a shorthand reference to Delcroix's belief that one must repeat ideas often, before they go into people's heads—the "rock-drill."

Van Buren / In earlier cantos (see Canto 62), Talleyrand is presented unfavorably, mostly because Pound is following Adams, but in later cantos he receives a revisionist treatment. Pound seems to have decided that Talleyrand's intelligence served France and Europe. Van Buren met the aged Frenchman in London in 1832. He reports a speech by the duke of Wellington that "went far to remove from my own mind unfavorable impressions in regard to Prince Talleyrand's sincerity and good faith in which I had participated in common with a large portion of the world."

Adams to Rush / See the gloss note to "Marse Adams," Canto 88.

Byzantium / A foreshadowing of the material in the Byzantine Eparch's Book, to be developed in *Thrones*. The idea may be that supervised guilds represent a more "companionable" social order than an irresponsible free enterprise system that ignores (one of the themes of the canto) the "family" of man.

Dante / Continuing the theme of a universe infused by "the Love that moves the sun and other stars," Pound corrects or extends Aristotle's "Man is by nature a political animal" by quoting Dante's version (*Convivio* 4.4) : *"E però dice lo Filosofo che l'uomo naturalmente è compagnevole animale"* [And so the Philosopher says that man is naturally a companionable (sociable) animal.] The intention is clear in a passage from Canto 93:

> That love is the "form" of philosophy,
> is its shape (è forma di Filosofia)
> and that men are naturally friendly
> at any rate from his (Dant's) point of view

πόλις, πολιτική / The passage continues to redefine or reinvigorate "political" by using, as Pound does throughout the later cantos, what Curtius, in *European Literature and the Latin Middle Ages,* calls "etymology as a category of thought." *Polis,* one's city or state, leads to *politike,* policy or politics, then to πολεύω (*poleuo*), a related word with connotations of "city" and "nature": (1) to move about in, that is, to live in one's city, and (2) to turn up the soil with a plow. The etymologizing rejects a Machiavellian sense of "political," to suggest a natural, organic basis for society.

Paradis peint / The "painted paradise." See Canto 45.

πολύγλωσσος / Polyglossos, "many-tongued," an epithet of the Dodonian oaks (see below). This final transformation is playful: polyglossos merely stands next in the dictionary to the cognates of polis. It leads to the "many sounds" in the (polyglot) oak-wood.


*Page 99 (107–108)*

that oak-wood / The sacred grove of the oldest of the Greek oracles at Dodona, where the oak-leaves spoke the oracular statements. On the last page of the canto, an oak-leaf speaks in a different way (through its *forma*) to St. Hilary.

Benton / See Canto 88.

Alexander / The point is that coinage should be the exclusive right of sovereignty, a right Benton, Adams, and Van Buren thought their country had given away. On one of his expeditions, when his troops demanded to be paid, Alexander took the booty from the campaign, melted it down, and coined it on the spot.

stemma / The degli Uberti coat of arms, but the word is also used to describe a family tree drawn as root, trunk, and branches.

"degli Uberti" / The quotation marks bring out the literal meaning, an individual of the Uberti family. Ubaldo degli Uberti, a retired naval officer and writer when Pound met him in 1934, was probably Pound's closest Italian friend. In Vicenza, in 1943, he discovered the carving of the Uberti crest on what turned out to be the tomb of Lapo degli Uberti, who had died a Ghibbelline exile six hundred years before. (Lapo was a descendant of the great Florentine leader, Farinata, who is in the *Inferno*.) The admiral wrote to his son, "Who knows if I too will not die, a Ghibbelline exile in Vicenza, from some *vento di siepe?*" (Literally "a wind from the hedge," but with the sense of "a shot from ambush.")

Mistaken for a Partisan, he was killed in Vicenza in April 1945. Toward the end of the Fascist Era, Pound came increasingly to see that Mussolini had surrounded himself with inferior men lacking the *jen* that is a subject of the canto, but he notes some exceptions, including Delcroix and Admiral degli Uberti.

Κάδμου θυγάτηρ / *Kadmou thugater*, "daughter of Cadmus," the sea nymph Leucothea, who appears later in the canto. Note the continued theme of family.

λευκὸς Λευκόθοε / *leukos Leucothoe*, "white Leucothoe." Pound is aware that they are two different nymphs. He brings about a fusing or interlacing of their stories, a practice common in the classical tradition. Both suffered greatly before they received the mercy of divine metamorphosis, and the prayer "Queen of Heaven bring her repose" includes Leucothea and Leucothoe, even as it extends to Florence as synecdoche for an embattled civilization. Leucothoe was beloved of Apollo, but a jealous rival had her buried under earth. Apollo's rays ("light *per diafana*") transformed her into a fragrant "shrub of frankincense."

Nicoletti / An Italian official whose sense of tradition is established in Cantos 74 and 76.

Ramperti / Marco Ramperti, Italian journalist.

Desmond Fitzgerald / An example of a politician with "jên²," he was a figure of heroic stature, poet, theologian, revolutionary, and for many years a minister of the Irish Government. One of Pound's first friends in London, he introduced the poet to the circle that became the Imagists.

chin⁴, hu¹, jên² / "Near to benevolence." "Confucius said: Love of study is near to knowledge; energy is near to benevolence."

YAO / "YAO like the sun and rain" (C.53) is almost synonomous with *jên²* in the Confucian writings.

i¹·⁵·, jên² / The first = one; the second = man. In the *Shu,* emperors refer to themselves as "I, the One Man," implying responsibility for the welfare and for the tone of behavior of the whole people.

*Page 100 (108–109)*

Windsor / Given as an example of what One Man can do—
though few historians would agree that Edward VIII delayed the
war. Pound believed the real reason for his abdication was the
British Government's fear that the king would refuse to sign the
mobilization orders for the war. This sounded a bit cracked when
Pound published these cantos; yet he had reasonable sources of
information, and in light of evidence since published, the point
must be considered.

Saint Bertrand / Village in southern France, mentioned in
Canto 48, which Pound associates with a destroyed civilization and
with the suppression of "the light of Provence" during the Albigensian Crusade.

Elder Lightfoot / The Elder Lightfoot Micheaux broadcast his
sermons over a Washington radio station.

Miss Ida / A cryptic reference to a touching story of ends and
beginnings, and of a "design in the Process." On his trip to Spain
in 1906, Pound met two American tourists, the Misses Ida and
Adah Lee Mapel. During the first weeks in Washington, Pound
was confined in a jail cell, and the two ladies, who lived in George-
town, came to visit ("from Madrid more than 40 years earlier").
Charles Olson reports: "The two old ladies, one 80, who came and
sewed a patch for the shoulder of his jacket. And he worries over
them coming, something about their car, and senses that they can't
do much."

"de Nantes," etc. / "At Nantes there is a prisoner." As so often
in these cantos, Pound recalls a point along the "periplum" of his
life. (He had written a poem to Desmond Fitzgerald, and one
about the baroness von Freytag, who appears on the next page.)
In 1912, never suspecting he would become a prisoner himself, he
had translated this seventeenth-century song, which had been collected by Yvette Guilbert.

"Bret" / Remembering the original of Hemingway's heroine.

the jap girl / A light reminder of the theme of the meeting of East and West.

"daughters of Memory" / Again, "real" women become goddesses. That the muses are the daughters of Memory has been repeated since Hesiod.

Pirandello / This is not an attack on Pirandello, rather on those who want to read Pirandello's art as "psychology." It is also witty, because what Pound is doing on this page is somewhat Pirandellian. "Pirandello was *concerned,* while Cocteau was writing Oedipe, for Cocteau's danger of tackling that subject without a plop into Freud . . . but it ended with the Italian's shrug: 'NO, on the whole, no, he won't fall into the Freudian mess. Il est trop bon poète.' "

And if I see her not / From a poem by Bernart de Ventadorn quoted in Provençal in Canto 20.

*Page 101* (*109–110*)

Kassandra / The baroness Elsa von Freytag Loringhoven was an eccentric figure in the literary scene of the 1920s. Williams gives a brilliant sketch of her in his *Autobiography.* Her writings move on the borders between indulgence and insight, madness and modernism.

Dinklage / Unidentified, as is "what's his name."

Gardasee / Lake Garda in Northern Italy. Why would anyone "lust after vacuity" in a world that contains such splendor? Garda has associations with Catullus and with Pound's early (1911) "Blandula, Tenulla, Vagula," in which the poet rejects an abstract or transcendent paradise in favor of a paradise formed from the landscape around Lake Garda.

hand without face cards / That is, we are ruled by forces not responsible, because they remain anonymous; with perhaps a suggestion that the universe is not impersonal.

*Page 102 (110–111)*

*dicto millesimo* / "I repeat for the thousandth time."

St. Hilary / The next lines provide a complex series of multiple references and scholarly jokes. Hilary, a fourth-century convert to Christianity, did much to transmit Greek thought to the West. As bishop of Poitiers, he becomes associated, for Pound, with the "light" and "sanity" of Provence. He was exiled during the Arian schism for refusing to sign the condemnation of Athanasius (Saint Dionysius was condemned by the same decree). Socially, he had the "sensibility" and "responsibility" we have seen exemplified throughout *Rock-Drill,* for he was a peacemaker, attempting to bring together the warring factions in Church and empire.

vine-leaf? / A passing joke, inasmuch as Dionysus is the god of wine. Pound abhorred the "Calvinistic" Eighteenth Amendment.

Saint Denys / Denys is a form of Dionysus-Dionisio, etc. There are several figures collapsed within this name: (1) The Saint Dionysius who, as anti-Arian bishop of Milan, was banished with Saint Hilary. (2) Saint Dionysius or Denys (Denis), Patron Saint of France, legendary first bishop of Paris (ca. 258), who established Christian worship on an island in the Seine (thus, "en l'Isle"). He was beheaded with his companion, Eleutherio, and walked carrying his head in his hand, from Montmartre (whence its name, the hill of martyrs) to the present Saint Denis. In the seventh century, the great Abbey of Saint Denys was built above the martyrs' tombs. (3) In the ninth century, Hilduin, abbot of Saint Denys, in good medieval fashion, identified the abbey's patron saint with Dionysius the Areopagite, who was converted by Saint Paul. (4) Hilduin went on to identify both of these figures with the Pseudo-Dionysius, whose writings were translated a few years later in Paris by Scotus Erigena and became the main source through which Christianity absorbed paganism and the neoplatonic tradition. Hilduin's identification was accepted for centuries: The combined Pseudo-Dionysius/Areopagite appears in the tenth canto of the *Paradiso.*

Eleutherio / With this name, Pound can close the circle of the tradition deriving from the Greek mysteries, continuing through the "conspiracy of intelligence" of which the Pseudo-Dionysius, Hilary, and Scotus were a part, and arriving through etymological metamorphosis at this canto. Eleuthereus (suggesting "freedom" and "the-god-as-liberator") is a name of the pagan god, Dionysus (also Iacchos-Bacchus), who was worshipped in the Eleusinian mysteries.

Calvin / Finally, Pound announces that the tradition, though often forgotten or suppressed, is never wholly lost, for everything the name "Calvin" represents has not been able to black out the "light from Eleusis."

νόστου γαίης Φαιήκων / Nostou gaies Phaikon, "the (homeward) journey to the land of the Phaeacians." The waves crashing at Poseidon's command, the raft tossing like a thistle in the winds (Notus, Boreas), Odysseus about to drown, and Leucothea arriving to say, "My bikini is worth yr/ raft" (page 100) are from Odyssey 5. As Ino, daughter of Cadmus, her mortal life had been miserable; she was afflicted with madness for having sheltered the infant Dionysus. When she leaped into the sea to kill herself, Dionysus transformed her into the sea nymph, Leucothea. She tells the drowning Odysseus to "get rid of parapernalia" (C.91) and to trust in her divine bikini. He arrives on shore and, with additional help from the gods, continues his journey to the land of the Phaeacians.

◇

# *Thrones* (1959)

◇

*Thrones* CONTAINS SOME PAGES of great lyric beauty, especially in Canto 106 and in many short passages, at times only a line or two, in which Pound is at his best:

> With the sun and moon on her shoulders,
>     the star-discs sewn on her coat
>
> (C.101)

(This is inspired by a not-very-interesting posed photograph in the *National Geographic* showing a Na Khi girl in a bulky costume.) There are lines that catch the attention and stir curiosity even when we don't know what they mean, an occasional sharp aside ("Ike driven to the edge, almost, of a thought," C.97), and a remark by a fellow inmate at Saint Elizabeths that is a solvent for a great deal of literary theory:

> Said Yo-Yo:
>     "What part ob yu iz deh poEM??"
>
> (C.104)

However, the *Thrones* cantos are largely ineffective as poetry, and no amount of extracurricular reading will help. The problem is not obscurity—if we have come this far we are accustomed to that—but the ruling subject itself, Justice, as Pound chooses to present it. His method takes him into periods of history with which he is not familiar, into data on ancient coinage and interest rates, and into the growth of English law. Too often, he sounds like a teacher who is suddenly aware that the end of term is in sight and that he has only covered half the syllabus. Moreover, this professor is only one step ahead of the class in his reading. He sends us away from the poem to investigate a variety of subjects—

exciting investigations to be sure, of Agassiz, of von Humboldt, of Coke—and we are to bring back reports. If the students complain, he answers (and who can argue?):

> *If we never write anything save what is already*
> *understood, the field of understanding will never be*
> *extended. One demands the right, now and again,*
> *to write for a few people with special interests*
> *and whose curiosity reaches into greater detail.*

(C. 96)

For poetry, the method is fatal: Pound has not lived long enough with his materials to have developed a sure feeling for them (although he is convinced they are important), and his talent for selection of "luminous detail" often fails him. What carries us through these pages is their energy, wit, and nobility of spirit.

History is seen as a confused landscape, the darkling plain, governed by the Moon, by chance and change:

> all under the Moon is under Fortuna

(C.96)

> above the Moon there is order,
> beneath the Moon, forsitan [perhaps]

(C.97)

Shapes of order and civilization appear and quickly pass from sight, as *sophia* (wisdom) and *panurgia* (knavery) contend forever. Slowly, the tradition of English law arises, from the jury trial at the end of the *Oresteia*, through Justinian's Code, to Magna Charta, the equivalent for our civilization of the Confucian *Pivot*. The constitutional principle established in Magna Charta and later developed by Coke—that the gains of one generation may remain for the next without being subject to arbitrary change—appears to be relatively permanent; yet in Canto 97 we hear that *panurgia* is "now at the top." Against the cry of "Agada, Ganna, Faasa," the invocation of the ideal city beyond time, we are reminded to "Make it new" and that it is "our job to build light."

Pound stated his intentions in an interview with Donald Hall in 1960:

I have made the division between people dominated by emotion, people struggling upwards, and those who have some part in the divine vision. The thrones in Dante's *Paradiso* are for the spirits of the people who have been responsible for good government. The thrones in the *Cantos* are an attempt to move out from egoism and to establish some definition of an order possible or at any rate conceivable on earth. One is held up by the low percentage of reason which seems to operate in human affairs. *Thrones* concerns the states of mind of people responsible for something more than their personal conduct.

"There *are* epic subjects," he insisted in the same interview. "The struggle for individual rights is an epic subject, consecutive from jury trial in Athens to Anselm versus William Rufus, to the murder of Becket and to Coke and through John Adams."

There are many heroes for the epic subject of these cantos, perhaps too many, and it may be that Pound, in an attempt to "move out from egoism," has been too willing to efface the human features and the dramatic gestures of Justinian, Anselm, Agassiz, Del Mar, and Coke. We hear of the results of their struggles toward the "conceivable" order, but too often they are merely names, or

> sages standing in God's holy fire
> As in the gold mosaic of a wall

The hundreds of fragments Pound has arranged for his paradisal mosaic in praise of Justice are often witty, interesting, dazzling— but seldom moving. Aristotle (*Poetics* 3.1) warned epic poets against choosing "an action which, though one, is composed of too many parts." In *Thrones,* Pound has not discovered a structure suitable for his epic subject.

◇  ◇

## *from* CANTO 99

CANTOS 57 AND 58 chronicle the decline of morals and public order in China during the late Ming dynasty. In the mid-seventeenth century, we hear of a people from Manchuria conquering China and establishing its last dynasty, the Manchu. These new emperors are civilized, men of letters, and devoted to the teachings of Confucius. They become, as H. G. Creel says, "more Chinese than the Chinese," and a kind of fundamentalist Confucianism forms the basis of their policy. The *Sacred Edict,* which Pound translates and paraphrases in Cantos 98 and 99, is a palimpsest that begins not long after the Manchus forced the Great Wall and established themselves in Peking. It has, as it comes to us in Canto 99, five stages:

1. *1670.* The second Manchu emperor, Kang Hi (or K'ang Hsi), published the original *Sacred Edict,* consisting of sixteen maxims, each of seven characters, in a high "literary" style. They sound platitudinous, however, as Baller translates them: "Elucidate Courteousness, with a view to improving Manners and Customs."

2. *1724.* Kang's son, Yong Tching, turned his father's maxims into chapters of a short book. He supplies the original maxims, then says, "The meaning of the Emperor is," and adds explanations and examples. Yong Tching writes in a simpler style than his father, but one which is still available only to an educated class.

3. *Shortly thereafter.* A salt commissioner, Wang, rewrote Yong Tching's version in "colloquial language." Wang "took it down to the people," who "speak in quotations; think in quotations" (C.98).

4. *1892.* H. W. Baller, an American missionary in China, turned Wang's version of the *Sacred Edict* into a textbook for the China Inland Mission. Baller has little use for it other than as a reader for beginning students of Chinese, for its "mere morality" has left the people of China "enveloped in a darkness which may be felt."

In the middle of Chapter 7, as the *Sacred Edict* praises scholars "because they study the books of the Sages, know the rights of things, are pure minded, and are examples to the people in word and deed," Baller can no longer contain himself. "Beautiful in theory," he exclaims, "but not in agreement with facts." His translation does not make good reading, for whatever the *Sacred Edict* sounds like in Chinese, in Baller it is pure missionary: "Won't this be splendid! All you soldiers and people obey and conform to these words, and all will be well."

5. *Mid-1950s.* At Saint Elizabeths, Pound, who had written about Kang Hi and Yong Tching in cantos of the 1930s, working from all four versions of the *Sacred Edict,* finds an opportunity to repeat the Confucian theme first stated in Canto 13 and to employ metaphors of seed, root, branch, and society-as-a-single-body, corresponding to governing metaphors of *Rock-Drill* and *Thrones.* In 1958 he wrote a note for the first publication of Canto 98:

> Canto 98 will be judged "more poetic," but the two Cantos [98 and 99], at least the writer hopes so, indicate that the poem has a structure. That is: ten cantos on the Emperors of Cathay, the Middle Kingdom, 51–61, continuing the theme of 13 (Confucian motif), leading to 98–99, which are a summary of the Confucian ethic, put into law and practice by the amazing Manchu administration, as the teaching of the State. *Si monumentum requiris.*

The *Sacred Edict* attacks Buddhism, Taoism, and the Catholicism that was growing under Jesuit influence. ("The Papacy has had its agents in China since the 13th century," says Baller darkly, not seeing himself as an "agent.") With their emphasis on magic, the Invisible, chanting, these sects emphasize personal salvation, a spiritual "covetousness." The *Edict* then instructs the people in its simplified version of Confucian orthodoxy: Be duteous, understand clan relationships, practice thrift, attend to your obligations, respect each other, avoid strife and pride.

Pound retains some of the homiletic coloring of the original, but he is most selective; he works imaginatively with the ideograms, and above all he finds a voice with more variety and compassion than the monotony of Wang's (or Baller's) spiritually complacent,

228 ◇ *Thrones* (1959)

know-it-all paternal figure. In the canto, instruction rises from the speaker's meditation on, and continuing moral involvement with, the dream of a filial society in the largest sense of the word, within a universe in which we are truly at home, in which everything is affiliated. The voice in Canto 99 may scold, play the cracker-barrel philosopher, display sardonic modernism, perform etymological stunts; but there is always a root, a tone, a great bass beneath it, dissolving egoism:

> This is not a work of fiction
> nor yet of one man
> . . . . . . . .
> The whole tribe is from one man's body,
> what other way can you think of it?

There is genuine humility: "All I want is a generous spirit in customs," as if to say, "That's what this long, troubled, clever poem is all about." The filial relationship of reciprocity and benevolence is explored broadly, from parents and children, to rulers and people, and beyond to an archetypal Tory vision in which the individual ego is paradoxically diminished and augmented within a semimystical feeling for continuity.

Unlike most of *Thrones,* this canto is based on material (not the *Sacred Edict,* that is, but the Confucian ethos) with which the poet has lived closely and within which his imagination and emotions are free. Moreover, after years spent translating the *Odes,* Pound—to make a paradoxical distinction—approaches Confucian texts as no Chinese can but as any Confucian does. In the last two lines of Canto 99 and in many passages in the later *Drafts and Fragments,* it is pointless to ask where "translation" ends and "original composition" begins, as pointless as to ask, "What part ob yu iz deh poEM? ?" The metric, too, is profoundly influenced by the discipline of translating the *Odes.* A word is often separately displayed, pronounced on its own "tone." The concessions to English syntax, such as "the" and "and" in the last two lines of Canto 99, are necessary for the limpidity of the verse, for to omit them would create a distracting chinoiserie ("fu jen receives heaven, earth, middle / grows"). And yet, they are almost not there.

Yong Tching's text that stands behind these last two lines has been translated by a scholar as "And after this, man can accept the cosmos and his formative relationship with it." Is Pound's version more literal or more free?

> The fu jen receives heaven, earth, middle
> and grows.

The word *grows* is left open, growing, as it were, by the abrupt break in rhythm, and it has gathered to it, from its context in the later cantos, associations that place it as far beyond ordinary lexicography as *jên²*, *chung¹*, *chih³*, and *ling²*. The "fu jen" (briefly, happy, or blessed man) produces "receives heaven, earth, middle" by the following process. *Jên²* is the radical for "man" (see the second page of Canto 95). *Fu²·⁵* (the ideogram included in the lines from Canto 61 below) is harder to translate. The dictionary meaning (Mathews 1978) is "happiness, good fortune, prosperity," but none of these will do unless we understand them as indicating a state of being blessed/wise/in harmony with the Process. The components show the rays of spirits descending (on the left), the earth or "sacred field" (lower right), and mouth / word in the "middle" between earth and heaven. It is, then, a kind of spiritual prosperity, but without the spiritual "covetousness" warned against in the *Sacred Edict*, which radiates between the individual and the cosmos. The difficulty in defining it can be seen in Canto 61, where Yong Tching, in whose version of the *Sacred Edict* the ideogram is found, says:

> ' A man's happiness depends on himself,
> not on his Emperor
> If you think that I think that I can make any man happy
> you have misunderstood the FU

(the Happiness ideogram) that I sent you.

*Page 103 (115)*

And if your kids don't study / A front porch version of the *Sacred Edict* 11: "Hence, if people's youngsters don't follow the right, it is all the fault of you elders."

*Page 104*

Born of the blue sky / "Repress the violence of your temper." Pound sees the character for "passion" (Mathews 4959) for which the Mathews dictionary gives related meanings of "blue sky," "tiger," and "rain."

Yao / Here the *Sacred Edict* alludes to a story in the *Shu.* Yao's worry, we were told in Canto 95, was to find a successor. Shun, a man of "the lower people" is recommended:

> The sovereign said, "Yes, I have heard of him. What have you to say about him?"
> The Chief said, "He is the son of a blind man. His father was obstinately unprincipled; his stepson was insincere; his half brother Hsiang was arrogant. Shun has been able, however, by his filial piety to live in harmony with them and to lead them gradually to self-government, so that they no longer proceed to great wickedness."
> The sovereign said, "I will try him; I will wive him and thereby see his behavior with my two daughters."

Hsiang i hsiang / "Think it over." (M. 2564.1)

tsou[4] / "To report to the emperor." (M. 6808)

k'ao ch'eng / Translated below: "tax as a share of something produced." The system, explained in Mencius, contrasts with the modern economic system, which (according to Poundian-Douglasite analysis) taxes people for things not actually produced.

Thiers / Pound is interested in the writings of the Rémusat family, one of whom, Paul de Rémusat, published (1889) a biography of the French statesman and historian, Thiers. Throughout, Rémusat presents Thiers in a way that makes it possible to see him as a Confucian.

PANURGIA / "Knavery, viciousness."

SOPHIA / "Wisdom."

XIV / Chapter 14 of the *Sacred Edict* is "Payment of Taxes" and is related to *k'ao ch'eng* above, and to "taxes in kind" below.

liang² / "Grain, food ration, taxes in kind." (M. 3944)


*Page 105*

INCORPORATE / The *Sacred Edict* is based on organic metaphors in which society grows from an "Ancestral spring" and works together "in one body" politic.

Yong (2. 2. 3) / The numbers refer to Yong Tching's version.

Ancestral spring / We have seen the importance in the Confucian tradition of continual interaction with spirits of ancestors, who (visibly in such characters as *ling²*) send natural and spiritual rain. In the later cantos, Pound returns often to his own "ancestral spring," his early career. Elkin Mathews (Pound is reminded of him because he is using a dictionary by another Mathews) was his early publisher, thus an "ancestor," who took a risk on the unknown young American poet. In one of the first important reviews, Pound received (23 April 1909), W. L. Courtney used the following metaphor to praise *Personae:* " 'Most can grow the flower now, for all have got the seed,' said the late Laureate. Mr. Pound is of the few who have gone forth into life and found something of a new seed, and his 'flower' is one that is unquestionably beautiful." The conversation suggests the young poet glowing with this praise and the older publisher telling him not to take it too seriously, that reviewers just write for their guinea an inch.

Chou rite / The early Chou dynasty, which formed the Confucian point of reference for later dynasties.

*Page 106*

*manesco* / "Quarrelsome, troublemaking."

Small birds / Pound sees the radical for "bird" in the character for "harmony."

chao[1] / "Bright, brilliant," with a connotation of "intelligence." (M. 236)

CHÊN / "I, the Emperor." That is, Kang Hi, who first promulgated the *Sacred Edict*.

*Yo el rey* / "I, the King" (Spanish).


*Page 107*

logistica / Contains "getting provisions to where they are needed" and "logic, reasoning." The root is *logos,* word.

nung sang / *Nung,* "to farm, cultivate"; *sang* "mulberry tree." Together they mean "agriculture" and "cultivation of silkworms." (M. 4768.20)

From of old / *Sacred Edict,* Chapter 4: "In springtime the Emperor went plowing in person; our Lady the Empress set herself to rearing silkworms."

chao[4] / The word for "labor" contains the radical "fire," thus "the heat of labor." The fire radical also leads to *chao*[4], which shows a tortoise shell cracked in the fire, the cracks to be read as omens. (M. 247 and Karlgren 1182)

The plan / The plan is the Confucian Process, with "a must at the root of it." Here, the plan is also the immediate plans of the emperor for agriculture, education, and all aspects of society.

Thru high-low, etc. / *Sacred Edict* 4: "But the soil of the south differs from that of the north: the one is high and arid, the other is low-lying and swampy. The former should be cultivated with different varieties of rice. It is still farming, though the yield is different."

wu² mu, etc. / *Sacred Edict* 3: "Don't seek extraordinary gains, double profit (or interest). . . . Take for instance the case of a poor villager. I ought to assist him, and if I give him a loan, must not take more than 36 per cent interest: or in a debt of many years' standing that cannot be repaid, the thing to do is let him off on generous terms, and not exact compound interest, or exceed the current rate." Pound's only quarrel with the *Sacred Edict* is its concept of 36 percent as a fair interest rate, thus "Byzance did better" under its lower rates.

*Page 108*

Michelet / Pound may have in mind a passage from Michelet's *History of Rome* concerning the violation of the familial society urged by the *Sacred Edict:* "As priests, the politicians exercised other vexations over the people. . . . Under pretext of sacrifice, they took the first ram, the best bull, from the plebeian."

Ambrose / Fourth-century bishop of Milan, whom Pound admires as a scourge of usurers and relates to Confucius and Mencius. He is thinking here of yet another text about the perversion of the filial:

"We accuse borrowers of acting imprudently," says St. Ambrose in *De Tobia,* "but there is nothing dirtier than the lenders of money. . . . They go after new heirs . . . and simulate paternal and avuncular friendship. . . ." St. Ambrose says that a fish swallows the hook without seeing it, but you (the borrower) see it and swallow it. "I have seen sons sold," he says, "for their fathers' debts."

a mistranslation / Looking at the character for "timid," Pound sees components that suggest to him "rain" and "phallus." As on page 109 ("no, that is not textual"), he is playing with critics who find his translations inaccurate.

anagogico / Pound, taking the word from Saint Anselm, uses it here to mean "contemplation."

en¹ / "Grace, kindness, mercy." (M. 1743)

*Page 109*

TUAN / The four "corners" of the universe; the four fundamental principles of Confucianism: *jên* (love), *i* (duty), *li* (propriety), *chih* (wisdom).

sane curricula / That is, the phrase translates a character for
"learning," and Pound recognizes that "sane curricula" is stretch-
ing a point.

◊　◊

*from* CANTO 105

IF WE HAD THE WHOLE OF *Thrones* in mind, we would be aware
that some phrases, references, and attitudes on these two pages are
more fully developed elsewhere; yet even as we recognize our dis-
advantage in looking at a short passage, the failure of communication seems evident. The surface obscurity may be partly inherent
in the complexity of Pound's enterprise: simultaneously to bear
witness to a profound intuition of "the intimate essence of the
universe," to obtain knowledge of it by observing the shadows of
history, and to derive a personal and social ethos from that knowledge. The mind is "leaping like dolphins" (C.116), as new discoveries and enthusiasms flash from the sea of tradition. Yet in
pages such as these, the poem remains perilously close to the notes
that assemble around the basic intuition. That Pound knows this
(and his knowing it immediately becomes part of the poem, which
is being written as we look on) is seen in the apology with which
the passage begins, "You cannot leave these things out," and the
disarming remark that poet and reader are in it together and "shall
have to learn a little Greek to keep up with this."

The essential action is again the encounter between theology and
government. By now we are familiar with Pound's enthusiasm for
figures who combine responsible rule with intellectual and artistic
achievement. Such a figure is Saint Anselm (ca 1033–1109), who is
seen in his role as earthly shepherd to his flock, refusing to submit

to the lawlessness of King William Rufus, and in his role as writer, registering "by sheer grammar" his perceptions of the mysteries. Pound's own grammar points to the underlying meaning of the passage, as the Greek rendered "They want to bust out of the cosmos" is followed by "but from at least here [that is, the struggle between Anselm and William] is the Charta Magna." Once a man has perceptions such as Anselm's (which are given more fully earlier in the canto), in which the universe is not something to bust out of but is seen as a sacred place of encounter between man and Divine Love, the moral imperative is upon him to build earthly justice as a reflection of the divine. The point is made by Dante in *Paradiso* 6, as Justinian, who is also among Pound's *Thrones,* explains the connection between his religion and his monumental codification of law, which prefigures Magna Charta:

> Caesar was I, and am Justinian,
>   Who by the will of Primal Love possessed
>   Pruned from the laws the unneeded and the vain.

Before undertaking the Code, he explains, he floundered in heresy, but Pope Agapetus "taught me the pure faith to espouse." Then:

> So soon as with the Church I moved my feet,
>   It pleased God of his grace to inspire me for
>   The high task, and I gave me whole to it.

In Canto 105, the two themes, intelligence of love and struggle for civic order, unite in the figure of Anselm.

History is presented as a jumbled chronicle, though to what extent the jumble is intended is not clear. We hear of individual rulers making gestures of justice through tax exemptions, of respect for local custom, of peace offerings between warriors, of the establishment of civilized institutions such as "hundreds" and guilds. Yet the ground of history, against which some rise of civilization is discerned, remains "savages against maniacs," and the good impulses of selected rulers are intermixed with tales of the murders of Kenelm and Erigena and with the superstition of "Gerbert at the astrolabe." Anselm takes his place in this chronicle: He is born during the reign of Canute and dies just a century before Runnymede; his struggle with William Rufus is directly in line with events leading to Magna Charta. The chronicle leaps somewhat ambiguously to our own day, for although Magna Charta and the common law have been achieved, the "swine" with their *panurgia* seem undiminished in strength and are ineffectively counterbalanced by "a Crommelyn" and "a del Valle." The choice of these obscure retired military men, about whom Pound seems to know little, certainly not enough to place such weight on their names, mars the passage and seems careless of the epic subject attempted.

Moving against linear history, and providing the countertheme of the canto, is the timeless awareness flashing beyond the reach of savages and maniacs. Here Anselm also finds his place together with Ambrose, Erigena, Charles of the Suevi, Cavalcanti, and Villon. Pound is always sure of his feelings when dealing with his version of neoplatonic tradition, but we must not expect him to approach Anselm (nor any of the others in that tradition, such as Erigena and Richard of St. Victor) as would a historian of philosophy. He likes the tenor of Anselm's writings, and he snatches words and phrases from them without much regard to the scholastic arguments and distinctions involved. In fact, he approaches Anselm's *Monologion* and *Proslogion* more as poems than as technical philosophy, as in this passage earlier in the canto:

> Guido C. had read "Monologion"
> vera imago
> and via mind is the nearest you'll get to it,
> "rationalem"
> said Anselm.
> Guido: "intenzione".
> Ratio,
> luna,
> speculum non est imago,
> mirrour, not image;
> Sapor, the flavour,
> pulchritudo
> ne divisibilis intellectu
> not to be split by syllogization
> to the blessed isles (insulis fortunatis)

All this has little to do with Anselm as philosophers see him, nor with the "ontological proof" for which he is best known. Rather, Pound is delighted to find him speaking of the flavor and beauty of the universe and of the undivided intellect (which might be something like Eliot's "sensibility" before it succumbed to "dissociation").

The last two lines of the passage convey a quiet enthusiasm with a sense of loss. We do not know if Cavalcanti (whom Pound refers to familiarly, "Guido") had read Anselm, but it is not farfetched to suppose that he had, for his friend, Dante, placed Anselm among the great doctors of the Church in the *Paradiso,* and Pound detects, in Guido's canzone translated in Canto 36, traces of Anselm's influence. There is less reason for claiming that Villon had read Anselm, except that "presumably" as master of arts from the University of Paris, he would have done so. All three—Anselm, Cavalcanti, and Villon—share an awareness of that "radiant world" that, Pound said, writing of Cavalcanti in 1928, "we appear to have lost." The late cantos attempt a sustained, if not wholly articulate, celebration of that radiant world; their ultimate didacticism is intended to revive it in the reader's mind.

◊   ◊   ◊

*Page 110 (116)*

οὐ θέλει ἔην εἰς κόσμον / *Ou thelei eēn eis ḳosmon.* Whatever the source (Plotinus?), the Greek is miscopied and cannot be translated, if that is what Pound intends, by "They want to bust out of the universe."

accensio / "Striking a light, kindling a fire." Cognates of *accendere* are frequent in the *Paradiso,* with meanings of "ablaze," "shine," "inflame desire."

Anselm / In 1093 he succeeded his master, Lanfranc, as archbishop of Canterbury but soon went into exile as a result of a dispute over civil and ecclesiastical authority with King William Rufus. Thirteen years later, he returned to Canterbury. Karl

Jaspers writes that "he showed equal greatness as a monk by his piety, as archbishop by his courageous defense of Church rights, and as a thinker by his originality, depth, and clarity."

"Ugly? a bore" / Paraphrase of two lines from "Song of Contempt for This World" attributed (spuriously) to Anselm, expressing a conventional monastic antifeminism: "If a man has an ugly wife, he loathes her; if she is pretty, he has to fear adultery."

digestion weak / A light reference to an anecdote from the *Life* of Anselm, recounted earlier in the canto: The saint becomes sick and cannot eat ordinary food but says, ". . . eh . . . / I might eat a partridge."

grammar / On the surface, Pound is implying that, if Anselm is antifeminist in his (unimportant) poem, he is not in his theology, where he uses the feminine gender to express his sense of the Trinity and of the universe. Beyond that, one of Anselm's works is a *De grammatico,* an exploration of language and logic and the problems they create in discussing subjects such as the Trinity. In the *Monologion* and other works, Anselm expresses both the mystery of the Trinity and his "clear line" on it through grammar, that is, by employing paradoxes of grammar itself, such as "which by itself are one." That "correct" syntax will not always contain "reality" is a Fenollosa-Pound idea that has been explored and employed throughout the *Cantos*. Examples can be found easily in Anselm.

Ambrose / See Canto 99. This quotation is from "De moribus Brachmanorum," which Pound finds suspiciously labeled apocryphal in Migne's *Patrologia*. Ambrose is placed here because (1) he stands chronologically just before the historical roll call that follows, and (2) like Anselm, he stoutly defended the rights of the Church against tyrannical civil authority (in the person of the Valentinian mentioned below).

Franks / The next twenty-one lines are snatched from the first two books of William of Malmesbury's *History of the Kings of England*. It is hard to make sense of the passage without reconstructing William's chronicle, in which a history of France runs parallel to a history of England. After describing the death of Bede in 735, the history goes back four centuries to the origins of the kings of the Franks. Valentinian, troubled by marauding Alani, seeks the aid of a ferocious Germanic people, the Franks. The Franks strike a bargain: They will come to his aid in ten years' time if in the meantime they are released from tax obligations. "It is incredible," remarks William, "how this once meager people grew in strength because of this ten-year freedom from taxation." They drive out the Alani, take over "all Gaul," and become kings of, and give their name to, what will become France.

Faramond / First king of the Franks, A.D. 425.

Pepin / Faramond's Merovingian line continues until 752, when it gives way to Pepin, father of Charlemagne. Pepin is crowned at the church of Saint Dionysus (*apud Sanctum Dionysium*), the same church of Saint Denys we encountered in Canto 95. Pound moves from the Christian saint to his pagan namesake, who is also Zagreus.

Ethelbald / William's history returns to England, where he chronicles a long period of chaos in which a precarious Christianity thinly covers barbarism. Ethelbald comes to the throne in 716 and maintains an orderly forty-two year reign during which, as penance for a sinful life, he issues a charter that exempts churches and monasteries from public taxes during his lifetime. This charter is part of the long prehistory of Magna Charta. Ethelbald's reign ends with his murder.

Charles to Offa / Offa's reign begins in 757. After a period of enmity, during which trading ceases between France and England, Charlemagne bids for peace. Among the exchanged gifts listed in the peace treaty are the sword and belt. In a despotic reign, Offa began the encroachment on rights that culminated in the struggle between Anselm and Rufus. In the *Institutes,* Coke will cite Offa as an example of why Magna Charta was necessary.

Quendrida / An example of the kind of barbarism English civilization is rising from as it approaches Magna Charta. The chronicle has now reached 821, as King Kenulf dies leaving a seven-year-old heir, Kenelm. He is murdered by his sister, Quendrida, and with this the line of Mercian kings effectively comes to an end.

Egbert / At this point, William turns to the history of the West Saxon kings and the unification of the kingdoms of Britain under Egbert, who rules from 800 to 839. The unification takes place by force, but once any people has been subdued, Egbert is wise enough not to destroy their local customs.

## Page 111 (116–117)

Charles of the Suevi / William interrupts the history of England to return to France, where he traces the line of rule after Charlemagne. Charles, king of the Suevi, assumes rule over the Franks and Romans in 885. Here William transcribes a wonderful story he finds in another chronicle, Hariulf's. Charles falls asleep and has a vision in which a "guide" appears, holding a globe of brilliant light. The light sends out a thread, which Charles ties to his finger; then, accompanied by his guide, he leaves his body and goes on a journey remarkably like a miniature *Divine Comedy*. In the infernal regions, he is threatened by dragons, but his guide loops the thread of light over Charles's shoulder and pulls him to safety.

Alfred / His reign begins 872. William portrays him working toward order and culture against great odds. He establishes the "hundred," a geographical subdivision, but really a social unit to which each Englishman must belong and within which he receives legal protection. The hundred is a move away from tribal, arbitrary, or confusingly conflicting claims against the individual. Alfred is shown as a writer and is praised for his efforts to increase learning in England. As part of his cultural program, he brings Scotus Erigena from France to England. (The story is without foundation in fact.)

Erigena / Erigena's English students stab him to death with their pens, for making them think too much.

Athelstan / Alfred's grandson, reigned 924–940, presented as a great king. "Gon yilden rere" is from Layamon's *Brut:* "began to set up guilds."

Ethelfled / Alfred's daughter, one of the remarkable women of English history. Coruler with her husband, she continued to rule and to contribute to the development of English law after his death and passed on the traditions of Alfred to the young Athelstan.

Canute / The chronicle observes him invade England and take power, then develop from a semicivilized figure into a model prince, lawgiver, and supporter of the Church. The reference here is to a pilgrimage he makes to Rome. Discovering that his people, pilgrims and traders, are not allowed to pass freely through Europe but are subject to oppressive local tolls and taxes, he successfully negotiates an end to such practices. Canute dies 1035, and the chronicle has arrived at the lifetime of Anselm.

Gerbert / The first French pope, Sylvester II, one of the most learned men of his time. Why Pound moves backward in time at this point is hard to discover. William presents Gerbert in his legendary role as a sorcerer, remarking in passing that he outdid Ptolemy at the astrolabe. Pound appears to be creating a contrast between Gerbert as a superstitious, reactionary figure, playing at astrology, and the English kings moving toward the light of law and reason.

tenth tithe, etc. / A sample of the sanity and precision arrived at through the heritage of Magna Charta.

Crommelyn . . . del Valle / Admiral John Crommelin and Marine Corps Lieutenant General Pedro A. del Valle were combat veterans of World War II with whom Pound had some indirect contact. In letters, he refers to them as heroes. They were retired from military duty and were involved in conservative politics.

Proslogion / A particularly fine work by Anselm: technical theology expressed as a fervent address to God.

◊   ◊

## *from* CANTO 108

SIR EDWARD COKE (1552–1634) began his long public career as a lawyer and member of Parliament. He became speaker of the house, Queen Elizabeth's devoted attorney general, and, as Lord Coke, chief justice of the Common Pleas under James I. He was also, as the inscription on his tomb reads, *"Duodecem Liberorum, Tredecim Librorum Pater,"* [the father of twelve children and thirteen books]. His *Reports,* issued from 1600 to 1616, and his four *Institutes* are among the most influential books written in England; it is amazing that a busy public man could find time for the immense industry they represent. As his biographer, Catherine Drinker Bowen, says:

> No law reports had hitherto been half so comprehensive; Coke must have lived and walked and sat and talked with notebook in hand. At once the books became—as Blackstone indicated in 1765 —an intrinsic authority in the courts of justice. For two centuries and more, a citation from "the Lord Coke" was to be the final word.

His labors were rooted in a passionate devotion to the common law, whose growth he traces (as Pound has been tracing it in preceding cantos) from the early kings of England.

As conflict arose between king and Parliament, Coke, now almost seventy, found himself in opposition to the Crown he had served faithfully all his life. If he was forced to side with the king or with Parliament and the common law, there was no choice:

> The privileges of this House is the nurse and life of all our laws, the subject's best inheritance. If my sovereign will not allow me my inheritance, I must fly to Magna Charta and entreat explanation of his Majesty. Magna Charta is called . . . The Charter of Liberty because it maketh freemen. When the King says he cannot allow our liberties of right, he strikes at the root. We serve here for thousands and ten thousands.

Coke was stripped of his offices, accused of treason, and confined in the Tower for, as he recorded it with characteristic precision, "twenty-six weekes and five days." In 1628, sitting in his last Parliament, Coke proposed the great Petition of Right that King Charles reluctantly approved. The first part of the *Institutes,* which became famous as "Coke upon Littleton," was published in 1628. The manuscripts for the last three *Institutes* were suppressed by Charles, who feared (as well he might) Coke's interpretation of Magna Charta. They were published posthumously by order of the House of Commons in 1642 and 1644. Coke's reading of the common law was to play an important role in the American Revolution, as his arguments against James and Charles became the central theoretical argument in the bill of particulars presented to King George as the Declaration of Independence.

Pound, of course, knew of Coke if from nothing other than his reading of Adams and Jefferson. He did not, however, look into Coke's writings until October 1957. His friend, David Gordon, remembers the day when the poet

> finally got the volumes of Edward Coke. That day he was as ex-
> cited as I had seen him in some time. It was a cold bleak late after-
> noon in late autumn and Mrs. Pound and I had sat out on the
> lawn with him for a short time. We knocked at the ward door and
> were waiting for the attendant to let us in. EP waited too. . . .
> He was standing there puffing through his lips and I knew he
> was cold and was struck by his patience at the long wait. . . .
> It was then that he muttered unsmilingly to me, "Coke. As good
> as Confucius." At first I thought his endurance had collapsed
> but then I realized that the meditative intensity of his expression
> was due to Coke not to the weather.

As good as Confucius! It is easy to understand Gordon wondering if for a moment Pound had lost his balance. The enthusiasm for Coke, however, continued through Pound's last years. It was a travesty of education, he thought, that he had to wait until he was seventy and in his "second kindergarten" to discover the *Insti-tutes.* The "obstructors of knowledge" he placed in the hell of

Canto 14, he suggests, may have been at work in their unceasing effort (C.107):

> to drive truth out of curricula.
> Coke's quotes might have told something.

And Coke was by no means merely for "lawyers engaged in technicalities." Pound discovered in Coke a mind that in many ways resembles his own. ("On these crowded pages," Bowen says, "Coke flung, it would seem, everything that he knew from books and from life, pell-mell and helter-skelter—his only fear being that he might leave something out. . . . Coke's etymologies, like certain of his historical facts, went very far off the mark.") Coke thought of the ancient documents from which he worked, as Pound thought of those from which he had been wresting poetry in the *Cantos,* not as records of a dead past, but as "the witness of times, the light and life of truth." The law, for Coke, is more than technicalities; it is the soul of civilization itself.

Cantos 107 through 109, drawn from the *Institutes,* seem to betray some frustration on Pound's part in trying to convey an experience that can only be had by spending hours with the actual volumes into which Coke transcribed a lifetime's passionate industry. To say that Coke codified the common law and the statutes that sprang from it hardly suggests the flavor of the active, inquiring, inspired mind that discerns a living form in scattered acts of Parliament and in ancient charters. As Bowen says, "In his head the English law lay outlined, a vast and intricate map. . . . The proofs and cases seem to come alive on the page." Beneath the assembled facts and citations there is a lively colloquial voice seeking "to delight . . . the Reader." Coke will interrupt a complex argument about the king's prerogative in coinage for the lyrical outburst from which Pound has drawn the opening and closing lines of his selection from Canto 108:

> Queen Elizabeth (Angliae amor) finding in the beginning of her reign some Copper money, and all too much, and against law allayed, amongst many others, reformed the same, as upon her

Tomb in Westminster it appeareth, *Religio reformata, pax fundata, moneta ad suum valorem reducta, classis instructissima apparata, gloria navalis restituta, rebellio extincta, Anglia totos 40. annos prudentissime administrata, ditata, & munita, Scotia a Gallis liberata, Gallia sublevata, Belgia sustentata, Hispania coercita, Hibernia pacata, orbisque terrarum semel atque iterum circumvagatus.*

No more than Pound can he resist the poetry he finds in documents.

◊ ◊ ◊

But now, as Coke says at the end of the proeme to the second part of the *Institutes,* "let us peruse the Text it self." Canto 108 is much like Canto 31, where we find one poem on the surface, in the flavor of Adams's and Jefferson's prose and in a sampling of their wide-ranging interests, and another poem available after we have done the research Pound wants us to do. The surface suggests Coke's learning and passion for detail, his concern for tradition and for the precise definition. There are suggestions that the law is rooted in an understanding of natural process (the distinction between "grosbois" and "acorns" and the definition of "day"); is aware of the weaknesses of human nature; is against fraud, the decay of learning, and the introduction of "damnable customs"; and manifests constructive tendencies ("Who for bridges / reparando"). The *"amor"* that acts as parentheses for the selection reminds us that the impulse behind the minds of men such as Coke and those who achieved the common law against the forces of "savages and maniacs" was inspired by an awareness of the Love that moves the sun and other stars and is the foundation of civilization, as the later cantos have so often insisted.

One of Pound's translations from Richard of St. Victor reads, "The plentitude of law is charity." The cantos drawn from the great ingathering of charters and fundamental statutes in Coke's second *Institute* are meant to demonstrate that in Coke's mind thousands of minute "legal" perceptions come together within a larger awareness. Coke, who personifies the common law, which in turn embodies a collective struggle toward the Light, is given a place of honor in Pound's *Paradiso,* among "the masters of those who know." Thus we find, in Canto 107, Elizabeth's attorney general in the company of a Chinese philosopher, a medieval theologian, and a Swiss-American naturalist, all conductors of the divine energy that transcends centuries, cultures, and professions:

> this light
>> as a river
> in Kung; in Ocellus, Coke, Agassiz
>> ῥεῖ, the flowing
>> this persistent awareness

◊   ◊   ◊

*Page 112* (*118*)

Angliae amor / "England's love."

ad valorem reducta / From the Queen's epitaph: *"Moneta ad suum valorem reducta"* [(she) returned the coinage to its true value]. The slight change in the Latin also allows the reading, "Elizabeth's true value was as England's love."

non extat memoria / In discussing "the case of the mines," Coke cites a document from the reign of Edward I in which one Henry de Whiteby and his wife, Joan, sue for certain forestry rights. At issue is the sovereignty of the monarch, which has existed *"a tempore quo non extat memoria"* [time out of mind], over the mining of silver and gold, the only metals that may be used for money. The Crown's right to cut down trees is related to its control of precious metals, for the wood is needed *ardendam, fundendam,* for burning in melting down the ore. Pound takes every opportunity to emphasize the importance of a nation's control of its currency.

souls of the dead defrauded / From this line through Coke's acerbic marginalia about "damnable customs intoduc of new in

Roma," Pound is quoting from a commentary on a statute from the thirty-fifth year of the reign of Edward I "concerning the removal of religious things," generally regulating the activities of foreign clergy and the export of wealth in their control. Coke says that "it appeareth . . . that the Clergy (whereof Priors aliens [*alienigenae superiores*] were part) had a third part of the possessions of the Realm." Many of the foreign clergy were appointed by Rome to English sinecures, as was Cardinal Paragots, who drained above 10,000 marks a year from the English economy. The intention of the statute is not to intrude on the spiritual affairs of the Church (thus, "alien abbots may visit"), only to stop the export of the nation's wealth. To that end, a prior, who might be foreign, may not have exclusive control of an abbey's seal but must share the custody with the four most worthy (*dignioribus*) men in the house. Among the evils following upon ecclesiastical greed and corruption are the diminution of worship, the reduction of alms available for the poor and the sick, and the defrauding of the souls of the dead, who had left their property to the Church for worthy causes, not to fill the coffers of a Cardinal Paragots. Simony brings other evils. Coke remarks that

> the Broakers of the sinful City of Rome for money promote many Caitifes, being altogether unlearned, and unworthy, to a thousand Marks Livings yearly, where the learned and worthy can hardly obtain twenty Marks, whereby Learning decayeth.

Rot., parl / The Rolls of Parliament.

grosbois / These lines are from a discussion of what sorts of wood are excluded from certain tithing obligations. The distinction is between "grosbois" (large trees) and "underwood": "Here it is to be demanded, To what kinde of wood grosse boys do extend? And the answer is, that Oke, Ash, and Elm, are included within these words; and so is Beech, Horsbeche, and Hornbeam, because they serve for building. . . . So for the bark of Okes, being Timber trees, no Tithes shall be paid, because it is parcell of the tree, and renueth not de anno in annum, But for Acorns Tithe shall be paid, because they renue yeerly."

nel Tirolo / Pound observes that a tax mentioned in Coke is similar to one still paid in the Tirol in Italy.

*Page 113* (*118–119*)

dies solaris / Defining the word *day* in laws governing markets and fairs: "The sale must not be in the night, but between the rising of the Sun, and the going down of the same . . . where (dies) is taken for dies solaris; for if it should be taken for dies naturalis, then might the sale be made at midnight."

ut pena ad paucos, etc. / "So that the punishment of the few should send fear into the many." (*Pena* should be *poena*.)

Phil, Mar / Among the laws cited are statutes from the reign of Philip and Mary, as the legal records refer to the period beginning 1554. It is curious to note that elsewhere Coke refers to Philip (later Philip II of Spain) as king of England.

HORSFAIRE / Most of this page is drawn from Coke's "Exposition of the Statute of 31 *Eliz. Cap.* 12. concerning Sellers of Horses in Fairs and Markets, &c." The "&c.," as usual in Coke, means that what looks to be merely a codification of antiquated practices opens into a discussion with broad implications for law and government. Pound is asking us to "Make it new" in ways more serious than suggested by the parallel between horse theft in the age of Elizabeth and car theft in the age of Eisenhower. The complex of law here attempts to reduce illicit traffic by providing for public trading "in a place that is overt and open, not in a back room, ware-house, etc." As a means of controlling horse theft, the keeper of each fair or market in the Queen's dominions (to be fined forty shillings if he fails to do so) is to make a written record of buyers and sellers "and the colour, with one special mark at the least of every such horse." Moreover, he is to conduct a spring horse fair at which all horses sold during the past year must be publicly displayed so that the owner of a stolen horse may claim it. But "because horse-stealers may flee farre off in a short space," the "old rule, Caveat emptor, doth hold herein: and when two rights come together, the ancient right is to be preferred."

Iong Ching / The Yong Tching of the *Sacred Edict* (C.99), "responsible," like Coke and Justinian, for having codified the law.

par cretance del ewe / "By increase of waters." Under "An Exposition upon the Statute of 22. H.8. *Cap.* 5. concerning the repairing of decayed Bridges in Highwaies, and by whom," Coke codifies laws stipulating who is responsible for keeping every sort of bridge repaired, the quality of the repairs, the amount of adjacent highway included, etc. This was more complicated than one might think, in an age in which lines of civil authority, and among civil, private, and semiprivate obligations were less clear than they are today. If any individual or institution failed to fulfill the obligation, a *writ de ponte reparando* could be issued.

For every new cottage / The act declares that "No person shall within this Realme of England," build a cottage "unlesse the same person do assigne and lay to the same Cottage or Building foure acres of ground at the least." Commonsense exceptions are made for places where this would be impossible, but in his discussion Coke (and this is what interests Pound) shows an awareness of the relation between economics and housing conditions and of how slums and crowded conditions affect poverty and young people raised in such conditions.


◊ ◊


*from* CANTO 109


MOST OF CANTO 109 is made up of further excerpts from Coke's *Institutes.* The lines Pound has selected here are the conclusion to the canto and the conclusion to *Thrones,* a coda in which themes from the entire volume are recapitulated. The first four lines—with "wing," "foot-grip," "sunlight," and "snow slope"—suggest the "more rapid" ascent into a brighter, more rarefied region. The chill of the snow on these upper slopes is counter-balanced by the warmth of the sunlight and by the bloom of the azaleas. The last line of the canto, translating Dante's warning to his readers at the beginning of the *Paradiso,* announces a riskier, more dangerous stage in the voyage that began so long ago with "And then went down to the ship." Yet this journey in Canto 109, beginning with a steep climb into rarefied heights and leading to an embarkation in a small boat, is different in tone from the journey of Canto 1. The solemnity of "that swart ship" has changed to the *hilaritas* of "dinghy"; and the heavy stresses of the first line of Canto 1 are exchanged for the quicker, lighter beat of the Italian diminutive, *piccioletta.*

The paradisal suggestions of the first four lines are interrupted by the "hellish" desire on the part of the forces of darkness to "get rid of" the king who (as one of the *responsabili*) prevents the war they want; and the lyrical rhythms of the opening lines turn to flat, colloquial speech.

With "Jury trial was in Athens" (a refrain throughout *Thrones,* referring to the trial at the end of the *Oresteia*), the poem returns to its celebration of law. The springing rhythms of

    Who for bridges
        reparando

and the important reminder that Elizabeth was not only England's queen but its "Love" lead to new material from Coke, displaying paradisal understanding of the proper source of the value of gold. (The sovereign's prerogative forms a subject-rhyme with King Edward VIII's authority to sign or not to sign the orders for mobilization.)

The "unnatural" implications of "false stone" and the reminder that there are forces other than the sovereign who would like to control the privilege "to put value / and to make price of the quantity" are set against the natural order suggested by the al-lusions to Agassiz, "wing, colour of feldspar" and "phyllotaxis."

The presence of the sacred oak and the wicket gate, both pre-sided over by divinities, evoke the mysteries and a mysterious passage. We are next reminded of the "conspiracy of intelligence" in the special neoplatonic tradition Pound has assembled for his poem, as both the poem and the members of that tradition "fight" their way toward the light, Helios, the sun. There is an aspiring movement in the mention of a trinity of beautiful romanesque churches, then suddenly a downward movement both in diction and in the quality of (now Usura's) architecture, as manifested at Saint Peter's. As the last line tells us, we still have a way to go. This passage is especially successful in turning scattered allusions and fragments into verse. The suspension, the forward movement, is largely produced by the many spondees that fall at the ends of lines or before sharp caesuras (a rhythm Kenner calls Pound's "personal signature"). The concentration of spondees gives the passage a unity it needs to hold together its sharp disjunctions, varying line lengths, and centrifugal references and levels of diction. The spondees of the *Cantos* began on the first page of Canto 1 (and are heard clearly in Pound's recorded readings):

We set up mast and sail on that swárt shíp,

Bore sheep abóard hér, and our bodies álsó

Heavy with wéepíng, and winds from stérnwárd

Bore us out onward with bellying cánvás,

Circe's this craft, the trim-coifed góddéss.

In this passage from Canto 109, the spondees are heard in the opening lines (and the awkward transition from *p* to *f* forces a caesura between *foot-grip* and *firm*):

Wing like féldspár

        and the fóot-gríp firm to hold bálánce

Green yellow the súnlíght, more rápíd,

Azaleas by snów slópe.

252 ◇ *Thrones* (1959)

They continue (not to list them all) through *Athens, bridges, reparando, true gold, phyllotaxis,* to *astern there.*

The conclusion to the sequence (really to *Rock-Drill* and *Thrones* together) ends with a rhyme, *Pierre/there.* The last end rhyme of this sort we have heard in the *Cantos* was at the conclusion to the Pisan sequence, 234 pages earlier, the almost-Shakesperean:

> If the hoar frost grip thy tent
> Thou wilt give thanks when night is spent.

Here, the rhyme is less definite, partly because our attention is drawn from it by the change from French to English, partly because one half of the rhyme (Pi*erre*) is preceded by a light syllable; the other half (astern *there*), by a stressed one. It is appropriate that such a rhyme should end this canto in which something is concluded but (as the last line reminds us) not *quite* concluded.

◇    ◇    ◇

*Page 114 (120)*

Monroe / An English journalist. (For the "three years' peace we owe Windsor," see Canto 99.)

Who for bridges, etc. / Repeated from Canto 108.

And false stone not to be set, etc. / These lines, through "leopard," are from Coke's discussion of the king's prerogative over all matters relating to silver and gold: "Counterfeit stones should not be set in gold, to the end that the subject should not be deceived thereby."

to the king only, etc. / "Here is offered just the occasion to speak what prerogative the King hath in silver and gold, and first and principally in making of money currant within the Realme. It is said by those that were of Counsel with the King in the case of the Mines, That it doth pertain to the King only to put a value to the coine, and to make the price of the quantity, and to put a

print to it; which being done, the coine is currant for so much as
the King hath limited."

auxy soit signe teste leopard / "Also that it be (stamped with)
the head (of a) leopard." The leopard, part of the blazonry of
English monarchs, was the name of a coin. Coke is here discussing
an ancient amendment to the charters, that no silversmith may offer an article of silver for sale before it has been inspected by *les
gardeins du misterie,* "the guardians of the mystery" (the king's
assayers), and officially stamped with the leopard's head.

Taormina / Remembering a paradisal moment in Sicily.

form is cut in the lute's neck / Recalls the "libretto" of Canto 81,
where musical instruments are associated with nature and the gods:

> Has he tempered the viol's wood
> To enforce   both the grave   and the acute?
> Has he curved us the bowl of the lute?

Oak boughs alone over Selloi / The spirits of the grove at Dodona. See Canto 95: "many sounds in that oak-wood."

phyllotaxis / The only trace in *Selected Cantos* of Louis Agassiz
(1807–1873), of great importance to Pound for his insistence on an
active intelligence in nature. "Phyllotaxis" is the title of a section,
which Pound had reprinted in 1953, from Agassiz's *Journey to
Brazil.* He is observing Brazilian palm trees: "Their differences
seem to me to be determined in great measure by the peculiar arrangement of their leaves; indeed, palms, with their colossal leaves,
few in number, may be considered as ornamental diagrams of the
primary laws according to which the leaves of all plants throughout
the vegetable kingdom are arranged; laws now recognized by the
most advanced botanists of the day, and designated by them as
Phyllotaxis. . . . this law, by which leaves, however crowded, are
so arranged around the stem as to divide the space with mathematical precision, thus giving to each leaf its fair share of room
for growth." We may recall that the "Stat. de 31 Eliz." relating to
cottages (see Canto 108) is concerned with giving people a "fair
share of room for growth."

Over wicket gate / A wicket gate is a small door set into a
larger door or gate. The narrow gate or wicket is an archetypal
metaphor for a moral or spiritual passage, as in the many "gates"
in the Bible: of heaven, of death, of righteousness, of the "city"
of the Apocalypse, and so forth.

Ino Kadmeia / The daughter of Cadmus, before her metamorphosis into Leucothea. See Canto 95.

*Page 115 (120–121)*

Herbert / Lord Herbert of Cherbury (1583–1648), poet, statesman, and philosopher. In Canto 100, his *De veritate* is mentioned
(Anselm also wrote a *De veritate,* and Charles de Rémusat wrote
books on both Anselm and Herbert). The same progression, the
conspiracy of a certain kind of intelligence passing through the
centuries, is noted near the reference to Herbert in Canto 100.

Καλλἴαστράγαλος / *Kalliastragalos.* In the *Odyssey,* Ino-Leu-
cothea is given the epithet "of the beautiful ankles."

San Domenico, etc. / The progression from the three earlier
churches (which Pound said belonged to his "line") to Saint
Peter's marks the decline of architecture, accompanied by the
growth of usury.

le chapeau melon / "The derby hat." The colloquial French is
the ultimate insult to the dome of Saint Peter's.

You in the dinghy / Toward the beginning of his *Paradiso*
(Canto 2) Dante warns readers who have been following him in
their "little barks" that they may lose their bearings if they follow him into the uncharted seas ahead. Yet "you other few," who
long for more of the "angels' bread" of sacred knowledge, may
more confidently continue the voyage.

◊

# Drafts and Fragments
# of Cantos (1969)

◊

DURING THE 1950s, Pound's friends—among them Frost, Eliot, and MacLeish—as well as Dag Hammerskjold, the secretary general of the United Nations, and some members of Congress, had been working for his release from Saint Elizabeths Hospital. In April 1958, with the approval of President Eisenhower, the Justice Department agreed to drop the charge of treason. Pound appeared before the judge who had committed him to Saint Elizabeths thirteen years before and heard the indictment dismissed. He spent some weeks with friends in Washington, visited Richmond, Virginia, and the house where he had spent his boyhood in Wyncote, Pennsylvania, then returned to Italy in early July.

He lived for a while with his daughter and her family at Brunnenburg Castle in the Tirol and, from time to time, at Rapallo and Rome. His last years were spent in Venice with Olga Rudge, to whom he dedicates *Selected Cantos, 'Tempus loquendi.'* In his seventies, he was now an international literary celebrity, interviewed, invited as an honored guest to assorted celebrations. He traveled about Italy, made a first visit to Greece, and returned briefly to the cities where the first cantos were written, London and Paris. (The trip to London was for the memorial service for Eliot in Westminster Abbey. "Who is there now for me to share a joke with?") Physically vigorous, with a keen, though tired, mind, he settled increasingly into long silences. In 1969, he made his last trip to the United States, to receive an honorary degree from Hamilton College. Honored, discontented with his own work, he died at eighty-seven in Venice, where he had paid for the publication of *A Lume Spento* sixty-four years earlier.

He had brought with him to Italy cantos and notes prepared at Saint Elizabeths, and he completed the manuscript for *Thrones*. He immediately began to assemble notes for the continuation of the poem but told Donald Hall in 1960:

> It is difficult to write a paradiso when all the superficial indications are that you ought to write an apocalypse. . . . Okay, I am stuck. . . . An epic is a poem containing history. The modern mind contains heteroclite elements. The past epos has succeeded when all or a great many of the answers were assumed, at least between author and audience, or a great mass of audience. The attempt in an experimental age is therefore rash.

He found it difficult now to concentrate on the poem. In August 1960 he wrote to his friend Harry Meacham, "the plain fact is that my head just doesn't WORK." When a young visitor asked if he was doing any writing, Pound answered, "Five minutes a day." He continued to revise, rearrange, and add short passages to the manuscripts written during the first year or so after he left Washington. During the 1960s, they began to appear in small magazines, usually with titles saying they were "From" or "Notes for" a canto.

As Pound passed his eightieth birthday, it was clear to him that the long poem would have to be brought to an end, if not to a conclusion, its final section presenting an image of a life coming to an end. With help from his publisher, he selected from what manuscripts he had, arranged them for the last time, and published them in 1969 as *Drafts and Fragments of Cantos,* which ends with two of the finest passages Pound had ever written. They appear under the title "Notes for Canto CXVII et seq." *Et sequens:* The only way the poem could reach a conclusion was to incorporate its own recognition that there was none.

The much-publicized conversations in which he spoke of his profound sense of failure, of a "growing consciousness of error," and of "bad intentions—the preoccupation with irrelevant and stupid things" seem as much a continuation of a lifetime's effort to "Make it new" as they are the expression of an old man's failing powers. Michael Reck reports a conversation between Pound and

Allen Ginsberg, who was paying tribute to Pound's influence on younger poets. Ginsberg paused to ask, "Am I making sense?"

> "Yes," said Pound, and after a moment mumbled, "but my poems don't make sense." Ginsberg and I assured him that they made sense to us. "A lot of double talk," said Pound. . . . "Basil Bunting told me that the *Cantos* refer, but they do not present."

In a conversation in 1966, Daniel Cory began to speculate on the aesthetics of the *Cantos:*

> But Ezra scotched all these fashionable hypotheses with one short devastating sentence.
> "It's a botch," he said firmly.
> "Do you mean it didn't come off?" I asked rather artlessly.
> "Of course it didn't," Ezra mumbled.

He had not known enough, he went on, to which Cory replied, "But you can't know everything."

> He was not satisfied.
> "Ain't it better to know something about a few things if you're going to do a work like the Cantos?"
> Again, I was at a loss for words. After a long hesitation, Ezra resorted to a rather striking illustration. He mentioned a shop-window full of various objects.
> "I picked out this and that thing that interested me, and then jumbled them into a bag. But that's not the way to make"— and he paused for a moment—"a *work of art.*"

Remarks such as these, however, do not demand that we read *Drafts and Fragments* largely as "confessional" poetry. It would be as naïve to accept the self-critical passages as a rejection of the *Cantos* as it would be to accept unqualified the apparent premise of *The Education of Henry Adams.* Yet the lines in which Pound's dissatisfaction have been transformed into poetry have drawn the most attention.

M'amour, m'amour
>            what do I love and
>                  where are you?

That I lost my center
      fighting the world.
The dreams clash
     and are shattered—
and that I tried to make a paradiso
            terrestre.
                     (C.117 et seq.)

Attention is due these lines as much for their artistry as for the comment they make on the poem. Few poets could have conceived the "what" that interrupts the intimacy of the opening line and then becomes absorbed into "you." The intimate voice is all the more remarkable because it addresses some thing or some one absent and unknown. The break at the end of the second line transforms the aspiring "what do I love" into a question more conversational and more intense, containing an awareness that it will not be answered.

*Drafts and Fragments* is among Pound's greatest successes. The frankness of its *"et seq."* and of its fragmentary form—

From time's wreckage shored,
    these fragments shored against ruin
                     (C.110)

—becomes a component in an achieved ideogram, an image of the poet's spirit, with all its imbalances, its awareness of tragedy and glory. Here is his wit; his irritability; his increased insistence on *compassione;* his effort (still) to teach us a bit of economics; his despair; his pride in his efforts; his sense—more profoundly conveyed now than ever—of the sacredness of a world in which he is "God's eye" and must not "surrender perception"; and most of all that mastery of technique that he said in 1918, is "the test of a man's sincerity." The poem containing history must end only because the poet can no longer write it, but history itself has not ended; the poem concludes by withdrawing from history and ascending into the joy that arises from a tragic sense:

         and to know beauty and death and despair
  and to think that what has been shall be,
      flowing, ever unstill.

Then a partridge-shaped cloud over dust storm.
The hells move in cycles,
            No man can see his own end.
The Gods have not returned. "They have never left us."
            They have not returned.
Cloud's processional and the air moves with their living.

In 1914, not yet thirty, Pound surveyed his development up to that time and found,

> In the "search for oneself," in the search for "sincere self-expres-
> sion," one gropes, one finds some seeming verity. One says "I am"
> this, that, or the other, and with the words scarcely uttered one
> ceases to be that thing.
>     I began this search for the real in a book called *Personae,* casting
> off, as it were, complete masks of the self in each poem.

In *Drafts and Fragments,* and in the suggestions of dissatisfaction with the enormous ideogram to which it places the final brush stroke, he continues the search and casts off the last mask.


◊   ◊


*from* CANTO 115


So I assumed a double part, and cried
And heard another's voice cry: 'What! are *you* here?'
                              T. S. Eliot, *Little Gidding*


THE OTHER PASSAGES MARKED *"from"* in *Selected Cantos* are indeed taken from complete cantos, but these lines form a fragment complete in itself; there is no more of Canto 115. As Timothy Materer says, they "may be read as a finished elegy for Wyndham Lewis rather than as a 'fragment.'"
Pound had been in correspondence with Lewis, his comrade-in-arms from the days of *Blast,* the Rebel Art Centre, and the Vortex, until shortly before Lewis's death in 1957. The two were leaders

of the "group" who, Pound announced in 1915, "are, if you like, 'arrogant' enough to dare to intend 'to wake the dead.' " In his essay "Vorticism" (1914), Pound wrote of Lewis and of the drawings he had made for an edition of *Timon of Athens:*

> I believe that Mr. Wyndham Lewis is a very great master of design; that he has brought into our art new units of design and new manners of organisation. I think that his series "Timon" is a great work. I think he is the most articulate expression of my own decade. If you ask me what his "Timon" means, I can reply by asking you what the old play means. For me his designs are a creation on the same *motif*. That *motif* is the fury of intelligence baffled and shut in by circumjacent stupidity.

The bravado of the words written as a manifesto were prophetic: Lewis continued in "the fury of his intelligence," elaborating the *motif* of *Timon* in books written over the next forty years.

Pound ended "Vorticism" with the words, "We worked separately, we found an underlying agreement, we decided to stand together," but the Vorticists did not stand together for long; the War and the same romantic individualism they protested against were more powerful than the Vortex. Pound was off to Paris and Rapallo; Lewis ◊ remained in London, expressing his contempt for the mediocrity he detected all around him and savaging "modernist" writing, including the *Cantos*. It was a work, he said in 1927, in which Pound "attitudinizes, frowns, struts, looks terribly knowing, 'breaks off', shows off, puffs himself out, and so obscures the really simple, charming creature that he is." By 1939, increasingly isolated by his own iconoclasm, Lewis decided to try his luck in America and spent the war years as an unwilling exile in Canada, living on the edge of obscurity and poverty. (Another exile, Ovid, is remembered in this fragment by "Sulmona.")

The war ended with the atomic explosion that left the scientists in terror. Lewis returned to London, but if the European mind stopped, his did not. Although he was forced to give up painting, he refused an operation to save his eyesight, for it entailed a risk, however slight, of impairing his mind. *Timon of Athens:*

    Trust not the physician;
  His antidotes are poison, and he slays

                (4.3)

"Pushed into an unlighted room," Lewis wrote, as he chose blindness (not, as an early version of the fragment reads, "accepted" it), "the door banged and locked forever, I shall then have to light a lamp of aggressive voltage in my mind to keep at bay the night." He continued to write in that darkness.

"Night under wind mid garofani" presents an image of Lewis's mind in those last years. (It is also an image of Pound's mind and spirit: For the rest of the elegy his own figure and Lewis's combine to form, like the figure in which Pound appears in *Little Gidding,* "a familiar compound ghost.") The *garofani* are flowers Lewis could no longer see in his windswept night but are also part of the natural universe that sustains Pound in the final pages of the poem. There may be a touch of irony, too, in these flowers, as Pound reminds us that he long ago rejected that part of Lewis's Vorticism that sought the separation of art from nature and exalted the machine and geometric forms. Would Lewis, had he been able, have stopped to observe the petals of the *garofani* left "almost" untouched by the apocalyptic wind? (The *garofano* is the pink or carnation, belonging to a genus classified by another figure in these lines, Linnaeus, who gave it its scientific name, *dianthus,* or the flower of the gods.)

The petals of the *garofani* are a transition from the night and the wind to the invocation, almost a prayer, of "Mozart, Linnaeus, Sulmona," representing the "persistent awareness" in the best tradition of the European mind. In Canto 113, Mozart and Linnaeus, joined by the latter's successor, Agassiz, are associated again with the petals of flowers and with resistance to the night:

Yet to walk with Mozart, Agassiz and Linnaeus
  'neath overhanging air under sun-beat
Here take thy mind's space
And to this garden, Marcella, ever seeking by petal, by leaf-vein
  out of dark, and toward half-light

The harmony of Mozart, Linnaeus, and Ovid (who may now be petals in the paradisal rose) contrasts with the "asperities" of Pound's own friends in the "green time" of his Vortex years. (No one was more given to asperity than Wyndham Lewis.) Pound now regrets the part of himself that delighted in conflicts, for in the late wisdom of *Drafts and Fragments* he sees (C.113) the "Error of chaos" and understands that "Justification is from kindness of heart."

The sudden movement from "my green time" to "A blown husk that is finished" is very fine, the metaphor suggesting an acceptance of the natural process of growth and death within the cycle of the seasons. While the "green time" was one of asperities, there is a quiet peace to the late autumnal landscape that surrounds the "blown husk." The personal pronoun ("*my* green time") gives way to the indefinite article ("*A* blown husk"), as the egoism of youth is exchanged for the humility of an old man who is already half absorbed into nature. We are reminded of the lesson learned in the cage at Pisa:

> The ant's a centaur in his dragon world.
> Pull down thy vanity, it is not man
> Made courage, or made order, or made grace,
>     Pull down thy vanity, I say pull down.
> Learn of the green world what can be thy place
>
> (C.81)

Though the husk is about to disappear, the natural landscape remains, governed by the eternal time of "tide's change" and showing a mysterious light against the dark sky. Though only a "pale flare," for Pound has not been able to reach the dazzling radiance attained by Dante's pilgrim, the singing light is a reminder of the music that so often accompanies light in the *Paradiso: "il canto di quei lumi"* [the singing of those lights].

In the lines about the "blown husk," Pound may seem to have shifted the elegy from Lewis to himself, but Lewis is still present. Pound could not have been unaware that in 1954 his friend had published a thinly disguised portrait of him as a "one-time poet" of which there remained "only a shadow, a shell." Yet the "disembodied instrument," Lewis continued, in an uncanny vision of the poet of *Drafts and Fragments,* "will still produce annually, perhaps, a slender volume with verses of the same matchless beauty." The husk/shell also suggests a memory of an image Lewis used, also in 1954, to describe the Lewis-like hero of his (wonderful) late novel, *Self Condemned:* As he takes a job at a provincial American college, "the Faculty had no idea that it was a glacial shell of a man who had come to live among them, mainly because they were themselves unfilled with anything more than a little academic stuffing."

In the two lines beginning "Time, space," Pound recognizes that neither of the subjects of his double elegy, one dead, one still alive, has found the answer and that the theories their younger selves developed about time and space were no answers either. Lewis's best-known book, *Time and Western Man* (1927), was an attack on what he saw as the predominant relativism and romanticism of the age, which he linked with "einsteinian physics" and "the great *time-philosophy* that overshadows all contemporary thought." Lewis saw Pound as one of those time-obsessed minds, "a revolutionary simpleton" and "in one word, a romantic." With characteristic asperity, he wrote, then, in 1927, Pound's epitaph:

> Pound is, I believe, only pretending to be alive for form's sake. His effective work seems finished.

Beneath the beautiful limpidity of *"from* Canto 115," the "blown husk" is recalling that premature epitaph and recognizing that it is time at last to accept it both for himself and for his old friend.

The *Heimat* (homeland) he had in mind, Cyril Connolly reports Pound as having told him, "roughly is Rapallo." *Very* roughly, I would think, for the cosmic elegy of these lines does not allow a reading as narrow as "Rapallo." The *Heimat* extends from Rapallo to Pound's America and to Lewis's (once Pound's) London—anywhere the dispersed members of the Vortex continued the effort "to wake the dead." Of Lewis, the most consistent Timon of his age, Pound wrote in 1935 that his "disordered and volcanic mind" was of great value, especially in a dead, and for the most part rotted, milieu. . . . A great energy like that of Lewis is beyond price in such a suffocated nation; something might come of disorder created by Lewis.

The *Heimat* is anywhere such a man expends the fury of his intelligence against the circumjacent stupidity and lack of energy of hollow men, "headpiece filled with straw." It includes the Athens of Shakespeare's *Timon* as well, for the final lines—

> where the dead walked
> and the living were made of cardboard

—recall the epitaph Timon wrote for himself:

> "Timon is dead, who hath outstretched his span.
> Some beast read this; there does not live a man."

◇  ◇

## CANTO 116

> What if I bade you leave
> The cavern of the mind?
> There's better exercise
> In the sunlight and wind.
>
> I never bade you go
> To Moscow or to Rome.
> Renounce that drudgery,
> Call the Muses home.
> W. B. Yeats, "Those Images"

In Canto 1, Tiresias predicted that Odysseus would "return through spiteful Neptune." The god who rules the sea of time and history pursues the voyager, smashing his fragile raft at the end of Canto 95, but "Leucothea had pity," and the drowning poet comes safely to shore. In Canto 116, we hear that he has been saved again, this time by "squirrels and bluejays." He appears to have made peace with Neptune, whose mind, like his own, is "leaping / like dolphins." The suggestion is that Pound/Odysseus has been able to catch, and to record as images, only glimpses of that flashing sea, or "Cosmos."

There is distinctly a *nostos* or homecoming in this canto, with a wry recognition that it is not the destination he had in mind when he began writing the poem. His "paradiso" is now enclosed in quotation marks, an earthly third heaven (*terzo cielo*) of human love, its geography mapped by Torcello/Venice, Tigullio/Rapallo. It is not a final resting place, however, for there is still "some climbing" toward the splendor of that light which makes the poem (perhaps poetry itself) inadequate. The relation of the visible, intelligible paradise—with its landscape of elms, squirrels and bluejays, the Venetian lagoon, and the sea at Rapallo—to the paradise beyond the poem, is somewhat like the elegy one of Pound's old friends, William Carlos Williams, wrote for another, "To Ford Madox Ford in Heaven":

> he has become
> a part of that of which you were the known
> part, Provençe, he loved so well.

Canto 116 is not a rejection of the long poem it is concluding but a redefinition, a careful definition, of the relation between the smaller cosmos of the poem (which does not cohere) and the Cosmos it takes for its subject, about the coherence of which there is no doubt. For a moment, Pound drops all attempts at ideogram and image, as if to say that what he has imagined (in the Coleridgean sense) is beyond his powers as a poet:

> i.e. it coheres all right

As Richard Pevear says, "The *Cantos* stand in relation to the coherence of their vision as an image stands to the insight it embodies." In *Drafts and Fragments,* the inadequacy of image to insight is recognized; the confessions of failure are a palinode not to the *Cantos* but to an impossible ambition.

The *Cantos,* we should observe, is no longer a poem at all; it is a "record," a "palimpsest," a "tangle of works," "my notes." Whatever it is, it is incomplete, for the palimpsest remains to be copied (but there is some doubt as to who, if anyone, will copy it), and the "great ball of crystal" remains to be lifted (but there is some doubt about who, if anyone, can do so; it seems beyond the strength of the "Unprepared young").

Standing among his "errors and wrecks," admitting the madness they contain or that brought them about, Pound still asserts the value of the effort and takes pride, after all, in his achievement. The distinction here between the vision and the possible is delicate and moving. The mood of the canto, for all its confessions of error, is not bleak or dark but warm and filled with light. It is not the light of the upper reaches of Dante's Paradise, but it is light nonetheless. That splendor is there, if not within these pages—

> "Something *there*,"
> sd/ Santayana
>
> (C.95)

—is without doubt, and the authority of the assertion seems unassailable after the severity of the self-criticism. The focal point of the canto is in the balance of:

> To confess wrong without losing rightness:

The colon leads to a balanced summation of the wrong and of the rightness, and to two final allusions to the figures who have guided Pound throughout the poem: Confucius and Dante. Yet the references are so light, so without demand for annotation, and what they refer to has become so thoroughly absorbed by the poet, that "allusion" is too strong; perhaps we should call them "reminders" or "memories."

Love and light have been associated, have been almost synonomous, throughout the poem, but especially in the later cantos:

> LOVE, gone as lightning,
> enduring 5000 years.
> Shall the comet cease moving
> or the great stars be tied in one place!
>
> (C.95)

The charity that poet and poem have had, but only "sometimes," is the paradisal light that is real, not a poetic conceit, but that he, an imperfect conductor of its energies, has been able to maintain only sporadically:

Le Paradis n'est pas artificiel
                    but is jagged,
For a flash,
            for an hour.
Then agony,
            then an hour,
                    then agony

                                                (C.92)

Pound associates this neoplatonic light with the Confucian vision of an organic universe. With the phrase "flow thru," he is remembering his own translation of *Analects* 15.2, where a disciple asks the Master how it is that he has learned so much, has committed so much to memory. Confucius denies that he "studies" anything, insisting that his knowledge comes from an awareness of the universe or "process." Pound finds the Chinese characters here so rich in suggestion, so hard to give in English, that he supplies three versions of Confucius's answer in a single paragraph:

Said: No, I one, through, string-together, sprout (*that is:* unite, flow through, connect, put forth leaf). For me there is one thing that flows through, holds things together, germinates.

The "one thing" that Confucius has learned to make flow through, and Pound has not, is the light Dante speaks of as he announces the subject of the *Paradiso* in its first canto, a light that pervades or impenetrates the universe (*penetra*) as it gives forth its splendor (*risplende*)—though Dante reminds us that it is a splendor showing "more in one place, less in another" [*in una parte più, e meno altrove*]. In the final lines of Canto 116, Pound admits (as Dante admits) that his poem shows only a little of that light yet asserts that it may "lead back" to the full splendor. He is remembering, from a few lines later in Canto 1 of the

*Paradiso,* Dante's faith that, although his poem can not embody what he has seen (and "the verb is 'see,' not 'walk on' "),

*Poca favilla gran fiamma seconda*

"A small spark kindles a great flame beyond."

The choice of "rushlight" is precise, suggesting a small, usually homemade, candle (originally a simple rush or reed dipped in oil) giving its dim light, "poco giorno," amid the encircling shadow, "gran cerchio d'ombra." Yet the word is obsolete enough to be fresh and to suggest that the full light may be about to "rush" at any moment into the darkness against which this small rushlight shines.

There is a final, more cryptic memory in Canto 116: "Ariadne." In its immediate context, it suggests that the beauty of the natural universe has saved the poet, brought him out of the maze. Yet in the later cantos, we have seen him recalling things his critics wrote about him long ago. In Canto 115, he remembers Lewis's premature announcement that his "effective work" was finished; and in Canto 99, he refers to Courtney's early review of *Personae.* Surely here Pound is remembering (and perhaps, as with Lewis's epitaph, finally accepting) the first substantial review ever given the *Cantos,* Glenway Wescott's notice of *A Draft of XVI Cantos* in the *Dial* for December 1925:

> The structure of the individual cantos is too subtle to be enjoyed; or perhaps there is no structure, perhaps this is a rag-bag like Sordello. Mr. Pound has never been a narrator; as a critic he was never able to give an orderly account of an idea; and if they are to multiply until they form an epic, it seems likely to be a labyrinth with a fine, half-materialized ghost for Ariadne.

The fine, half-materialized ghost who leads the hero from the labyrinthine epic and watches him prepare for the "take-off" is Pound himself, as *persona* of the final drafts and fragments of cantos.

*Page 117*

Cosmos / From the Greek verb "to order, arrange." Among the scientists in *Thrones* is Alexander von Humboldt, the great naturalist and explorer, whose culminating work is the five-volume *Kosmos* (1845–1862), an attempt to describe the whole of the physical universe and to correlate all branches of knowledge. In Canto 97, there is "A disc of light over von Humboldt."

Muss. / At Pisa, musing on his hero's downfall (C.80), Pound recognizes that the "strong man" pose of Mussolini was a flaw in that it left the Duce surrounded with inferior men:

> emphasis
> an error or excess of
> emphasis
> the problem after any revolution is what to do with
> your gunmen

This is followed by a line from Padraic Colum on the Irish Revolution, "Your gunmen tread on my dreams." "All of them," Pound says of Mussolini's circle (C.80), were "so far beneath him / half-baked and amateur / or mere scoundrels."

cuniculi / "Underground passages or canals." Mentioned in earlier cantos, the *cuniculi* derive from Pound's interest in the work of an Italian scholar who found near Rome a system of irrigation canals that appeared older than the accepted date for the birth of civilization in Italy.

An old "crank" / There is no need to identify the old "crank," though Pound, who was in direct and indirect contact with many "cranks" during the Saint Elizabeths years, surely has someone in mind. He is also glancing at himself.

mucchio di leggi / A "mass of laws," repeated from Canto 87, where it appears to be quoted from Mussolini and is translated as "a haystack of laws on paper." The point is that laws mean little without the proper men to interpret or enforce them.

Litterae nihil sanantes / "Writings that cure (or correct) nothing." From Adams to Jefferson, 28 June 1812:

> The various Ingenuity which has been displayed in Inventions of hypotheses to account for the original Population of America; and of the immensity of learning profusely expended to support them, have appeared to me, for a longer time than I can precisely recollect, what the Physicians call the Litterae nihil Sanantes. . . . questions of no moment to the present or future happiness of Man. Neither Agriculture, Commerce, Manufactures, Fisheries, Science, Litterature, Taste, Religion, Morals, nor any other good will be promoted, or any Evil averted, by any discoveries that can be made in answer to those questions.

Justinian / Among the lawgivers in Dante's and Pound's paradises, for his great codification of Roman law. Yet in Canto 87: "Justinian's codes inefficient."

## Page 118

I am not a demigod / The allusion here and in the line "i.e. it coheres all right" is to Pound's 1957 translation of Sophocles' *Women of Trachis.* The demigod-hero, Herakles, aware that he is about to die, remembers a prophecy given him by the oracle of Zeus (his father) at Dodona. He addresses his son, Hyllos:

> I am released from trouble.
> I thought it meant life in comfort.
> It doesn't. It means that I die.
> For amid the dead there is no work in service.
> Come at it that way, my boy, what
> SPLENDOUR,
> > IT ALL COHERES.

In a note, Pound adds, "this is the key phrase, for which the play exists." The stage direction after the speech says that Herakles "turns his face from the audience, then sits erect, facing them without the mask of agony; the revealed make-up is that of solar serenity."

"plus j'aime le chien" / Remark attributed to Frederick the Great: "The more I know of men, the more I love dogs."

Disney / Pound saw Walt Disney's nature films as in line with the work of Agassiz. "Take the serious side of Disney, the Confucian side of Disney. It's in having taken an ethos, as he does in *Perri,* that squirrel film, where you have the values of courage and tenderness asserted in a way that everyone can understand. You have got an absolute genius there."

Laforgue / Jules Laforgue (1860–1887), whose sophisticated ironies of diction and rhythm influenced the younger Eliot and Pound. Here Pound suggests that Laforgue had "deeps" of feeling for the universe, which his admirers missed in concentrating on his witty, disillusioned verse.

Spire / The French poet mentioned in Canto 81. He seems to have thanked Pound for pointing out the profundity of Laforgue.

Linnaeus / The Swedish naturalist (1707–1778) whose system of classification is the foundation of modern botany.

chi crescerà i nostri / As Dante enters the second heaven of Paradise, he is greeted by the radiant souls of thousands who led active, responsible lives. These "splendours" cry out, "Behold, one who will increase [make grow] our loves" [*Ecco chi crescerà li nostri amori*].

Venere / Pound remembers (through Dante) that Paradise is not a place to "walk on" but a state or vision. In the third (*terzo*) heaven, governed by Venus (*Venere*), Dante finds the souls of those whose earthly loves have been tempered to the love of God. Forms of *videre,* to see, are prominent in this section of the *Paradiso.*


*Page 119*

al poco giorno / The first line of a sestina by Dante. *Poco giorno* suggests both the quality and the duration of light on a winter's day. Rossetti's translation begins:

To the dim light and the large circle of shade
I have clomb, and to the whitening of the hills
There where we see no color in the grass.
Natheless my longing loses not its green.

Torcello / Island in the Venetian lagoon. Pound may have in mind the gold in the Byzantine mosaics there.

Vicolo d'oro / The Lane of Gold. A place in Rapallo formerly associated with lace making and weaving.

Tigullio / Rapallo is on the Bay of Tigullio.

◇

# Notes

◇

THE NOTES are keyed to catch phrases, page by page. All books and articles are by Pound unless otherwise identified. In titles of books and articles, Pound's name has usually been abbreviated to EP. The following short forms are used for works frequently referred to (all are New Directions editions and are included in the Selected Bibliography):

Confucius:   *Confucius: The Unwobbling Pivot, the Great Digest, The Analects*
G-B:   *Gaudier-Brzeska: A Memoir* (1960 ed.)
Kulchur:   *Guide to Kulchur*
LE:   *The Literary Essays of Ezra Pound*
Letters:   *The Letters of Ezra Pound (1907–1941)*
SP:   *Selected Prose (1909–1965)*

## Introduction

2   "Knowledge is NOT": *Kulchur*, 134.

2   Davie: *Ezra Pound*, 84–85.

3   redaction, made in 1965: The publishers' notes give the date erroneously as 1966. See Donald Gallup, *Paideuma* 1 (Spring-Summer 1972), 117–118.

5   Pound and Fenollosa: See Wai-lim Yip, *EP's Cathay* (Princeton, 1969); Andrew Welsh, *The Roots of Lyric* (Princeton, 1978); and Thomas Grieve, "Annotations to the Chinese in *Section: Rock-Drill*," *Paideuma* 4 (Fall-Winter 1975), 362–377.

6   "the total light process": *Confucius*, 20.

7   a sensible definition: *Kulchur*, 51.

8   medieval "tidiness": *SP*, 77.

8   to his father: *Letters*, 210.

8   "For forty years": *SP*, 167.

9   "durable," "eternal," "permanent": The distinction is made in "Religio, or, The Child's Guide to Knowledge" (1918), *SP*, 47.

274 ◊ *Guide to Ezra Pound's Selected Cantos*

9    religious element: See two important essays written during early stages of the poem's composition, "Religio," and "Axiomata," both reprinted in *SP*, 47–52.

## A Draft of XXX Cantos (1930)

10    "For forty years": *Introduzione alla Natura Economica degli S.U.A.* English tr., *SP*, 167.

10    "stale creampuffs": "Foreword (1964)" to the reissue of *A Lume Spento and Other Early Poems* (New York, 1965).

10    Pound's early career: See Thomas H. Jackson, *The Early Poetry of EP* (Cambridge, Mass., 1968); N. Christoph de Nagy, *The Poetry of EP: The Pre-Imagist Stage* (2nd ed. rev.; Bern, 1968); Herbert N. Schneidau, *EP: The Image and the Real* (Baton Rouge, 1969); John Espey, *EP's Mauberley* (Berkeley and Los Angeles, 1965; rev. ed. 1974); and J. P. Sullivan, *EP and Sextus Propertius* (Austin, Tex., 1964).

11    *Blast* and Vorticism: An excellent study is William C. Wees, *Vorticism and the English Avant-Garde* (Toronto, 1972). See also Timothy Materer, *Vortex: Pound, Eliot, and Lewis* (Ithaca, N.Y., 1979).

11    definition of the image: *Blast* (1914); reprinted in *G-B*, 86.

11    "The image is not an idea": "Vorticism" (1914); reprinted in *G-B*, 92.

12    Lewis's drawing for *Timon:* See Ronald Bush, *The Genesis of EP's Cantos*, 45–48.

12    "revolution in the arts": "Gaudier-Brzeska: A Postscript" (1934); reprinted in *G-B*, 141.

12    "austere, direct": "Prologomena" (1912); included in "A Retrospect," *LE*, 3–4.

12    "not limited by the conventional": *G-B*, 90.

12    Jackson: *Early Poetry of EP*, 119.

12    "crust of dead English" and "language to think in": *LE*, 193–194. See "A Language to Use and a Language to Think In," ch. 3 in Jackson's *Early Poetry of EP*.

13    "slides": *ABC of Reading*, 17.

14    Bush: *Genesis of EP's Cantos*, 230 ff. On problems presented by the early "Three Cantos," see also Hugh Kenner, *The Pound Era*, 356–360.

16 Letters of 1937 and 1939: *Letters*, 293, 322.
16 EP's answer to Hall: *Paris Review* 28 (Summer-Fall 1962), 49.

CANTO 1

18 syllogism . . . "knowledge to be verified by experience": *Kulchur*, 77–78.
18 "*older* than the rest": *Letters*, 274.
18 "high state of culture": *Kulchur*, 24.
18 "conspiracy of intelligence": *Kulchur*, 263.
19 *Patria Mia:* Reprinted in *SP*, 125–126.
19 "intelligence above brute force": 1952 addendum to *Kulchur*, 352.
19 "And as Zeus said": *Kulchur*, 146.
19 "departing in no way from speech": *Letters*, 48–49.
21 "cultural overlayering": Hugh Kenner, *The Poetry of EP*, 316.
22 "a second time": Pound finds the opportunity in Divus's *iterum*, a mistranslation of a rather vague "then" in Homer; he may be recalling, too, the repeated *bis* of *Aeneid* 6. 134.
22 Kenner: *Pound Era*, 536.
22 Read: "Pound, Joyce, and Flaubert: The Odysseans," in Eva Hesse, ed., *New Approaches to EP*, 127.
23 "I want a new civilization'": *Exile*, Spring 1928.
24 Persephone . . . as presiding goddess: See Guy Davenport, "Persephone's Ezra," in Eva Hesse, *New Approaches to EP*, 145–173.

CANTO 4

26 Catullus: Lines 66–75; Cornish's tr. in the Loeb Library.
27 "Psychology and Troubadours": *The Spirit of Romance*, 91–92.
28 an old man speaking: George Dekker believes the old man is Oedipus, "whose house has been cursed because of that crime." See Dekker's discussion of Canto 4, to which this note is an inadequate acknowledgment, in *The Cantos of EP*.
29 "In a Station of the Metro": *Poetry*, April 1913. The later, more familiar version uses a semicolon.
29 "irresponsible": "The homeric world, very human. . . . A world of irresponsible gods, a very high society without recognizable morals. . . ." *Kulchur*, 38.
29 Ovid tells us: *Met.* 6. 459–460.
30 the Furies: *Met.* 6. 428–434.
30 "A narrative is all right": *Kulchur*, 48.

32 Kwannon: "Three Cantos I," *Poetry*, June 1917, 119; reprinted in Bush, *Genesis of EP's Cantos*, 53–60.

32 Wilhelm: *The Cruelest Month* (New Haven, Conn., 1965), 262–263.

33 Vidal: Tr. Thomas G. Bergin, *Dante* (New York, 1965), 47.

33 Cavalcanti: EP's version, *The Translations of EP*, 95.

33 "Blasphemous intention": "Cavalcanti," in *LE*, 181.

35 Itys: *Met. 6.*

36 Actaeon: *Met. 3.* 138–259.

36 Poictiers: For EP's visits to his "sacred places" and how memories of them are woven into the *Cantos,* see Kenner, *Pound Era,* 320–348; and Donald Davie, "The Cantos: Towards a Pedestrian Reading," *Paideuma* 1 (Spring-Summer 1972), 55–62. Ronald Bush has suggested to me that Pound may be remembering the church of Notre Dame.

36 Vidal: The *vida* was probably elaborated from a conceit in one of his poems.

37 Pergusa: *Met. 5.* 385 ff. Gargaphia: *Met. 3.* 155 ff. Salmacis: *Met. 4.* 285 ff. Cygnus: *Met. 12.* 72 ff.

38 *Takasago:* Pound used Fenollosa's notes on the play. A translation is available in *The Noh Drama . . . Selected and Translated by the Special Noh Committee* (Rutland, Vt. and Tokyo, 1960).

38 Hsiang: Hugh Kenner (in a talk at Orono, Me., June 1975) says that the passage is based on a misreading of Fenollosa's handwriting. Yet with "Ran-ti" (as the name appeared in earlier editions) now corrected to "Hsiang," the passage corresponds well enough to the original *fu.*

39 Herodotus: *The Histories,* tr. Aubrey de Selincourt (New York, 1954), 54–55.

39 Sennin: *Letters,* 180.

39 Polhonac: Pound mentions the story in "Troubadours—Their Sorts and Conditions," *LE,* 94.

39 Herodotus: *Histories,* Selincourt, 16–17.

40 Cavalcanti, Sonnet 7: Pound's translation is from *New Age,* 14 December 1911. A later version, with the Italian text, is in *Translations,* 38–39.

CANTO 9

41 "We do NOT know the past": *Kulchur,* 60.

41 "conspiracy of intelligence": *Kulchur,* 263.

41 "picturesqueness": *Kulchur*, 259.

42 Pater: The first passage is from "Winckelmann"; the second, and that just below, from "Pico della Mirandola."

43 Burckhardt: *The Civilization of the Renaissance in Italy,* pt. 3, "The Revival of Antiquity" (1860), tr. S. G. C. Middlemore (Vienna, n.d.), 116–117.

43 "doggerel": *ABC of Reading,* 101. "Chaucer wrote while England was still a part of Europe. . . . He participated in the same culture with Froissart and Boccaccio, the great humane culture that went into Rimini, that spoke Franco-Veneto, that is in the roundels of Froissart and in the doggerel of the Maletesta."

44 "Am reading up historic background": EP to John Quinn, 10 August 1922, quoted in Daniel D. Pearlman, *The Barb of Time,* 302–303.

44 Kenner: "The Broken Mirrors and the Mirror of Memory," in Lewis Leary, ed., *Motive and Method in the Cantos of EP* (New York, 1954), 18.

44 Jefferson: *Jefferson and/or Mussolini,* 66.

44 "There is no mystery about the Cantos": *Kulchur,* 94 and frontispiece.

45 "The Tempio Maletestiano is both an apex": *Kulchur,* 159.

46 Hutton: Pound did not depend for material on Hutton's *Sigismundo Pandolfo Malatesta, Lord of Rimini;* he went back to Yriarte's *Un condottière au XV<sup>e</sup> siècle* (1882), the works of Pius II, Broglio's unpublished chronicle in the Rimini archives, and other sources.

47 Basinio and Pandone: John Hamilton Edwards and William W. Vasse, ed., *Annotated Index to the Cantos.* See also *ABC of Reading,* 48.

49 "The one history we have NOT": *Kulchur,* 115.

49 Foscari and Venice: An interesting account is Michael Mallet, "Venice and Its Condottiere, 1405–54," in J. R. Hale, ed., *Renaissance Venice* (London, 1973).

50 "receiver of all things": Pound described Leopold Bloom as *"polumetis* and a receiver of all things" in his 1922 essay *Ulysses, LE,* 404.

51 Istria: On the relation of the stone to the Tempio and to Venice in the *Cantos,* see the work by Pound's friend, Adrian Stokes, *Stones of Rimini* (London, 1934; reprinted New York, 1969). See also Stokes's *The Quattro Cento* (London, 1932; reprinted

New York, 1968) for a discussion of Malatesta and the Tempio; and Donald Davie's discussion of Stokes and the *Cantos* in *EP: Poet as Sculptor,* 127–131, 155–156.

54   "Past ruin'd Ilion": Included in *ABC of Reading,* 179.

CANTO 13

55   Pound . . . would prefer: "Immediate Need of Confucius" (1937), in *SP,* 75: "If my version of the *Ta Hio* is the most valuable work I have done in three decades I can only wait for the reader to see it."

55   "I believe the *Ta Hio": Make It New* (London, 1934), 18.

55   "a *mantram": SP,* 77: "specifically of the *first chapter* of the *Ta Hio;* which you may treat as a *mantram* reinforced, a mantram elaborated so that the meditation may gradually be concentrated into contemplation."

56   Creel: *Chinese Thought from Confucius to Mao Tse-Tung* (New York, 1953), 39.

56   "The men of old" and "When things had been classified": Passages from the *Ta Hio* in *Confucius,* 29–33.

58   "The concentration or emphasis on eternity": *Kulchur,* 38.

58   T'ang's bathtub: *Confucius,* 36.

58   "almost sacrilegious": Jean Seznec, *The Survival of the Pagan Gods,* tr. Barbara F. Sessions (New York, 1953; reprinted Princeton, 1972), 134. Seznec's view of the Tempio (132–137 and passim) forms an interesting contrast to Pound's.

59   A story in the *Analects:* I have quoted the version of *Analects* 14. 41 in Ch'u Chai and Winberg Chai, *The Humanist Way in Ancient China* (New York, 1963), 74.

59   "the sage keeps to the deed": Lao Tzu, *Tao Te Ching,* tr. D. C. Lau (New York, 1963), 58–59.

CANTO 14

61   "Metal is durable": *Gold and Work* (1944), in *SP,* 346.

62   *Ta hio: Confucius,* 79.

62   Spinoza: *LE,* 204.

62   Dante's "hell reeks with money": *LE,* 211.

62   "Dante MEANT *plutus": Letters,* 255.

62   no one but a "sap-head": *LE,* 86.

62   "grab-at-once state of mind": *Kulchur,* 41.

62   "the medieval discrimination": *LE,* 211.

64 "enters the rational spirit": Pound's tr. from Richard of Saint Victor, *SP*, 72.

64 *After Strange Gods:* When he was almost eighty, Pound made his family read it, saying, "I should have listened to the Possum" (Mary de Rachewiltz, *Discretions*. Boston, 1971, 306). Eliot's book "was not examined with sufficient care, nor did the present author chew on it sufficiently" (*SP*, 77).

65 Carne-Ross: In Peter Russell, ed., *An Examination of EP* (New York, 1950); reprinted in part in J. P. Sullivan, ed., *EP: A Critical Anthology* (New York, 1970), 214. Carne-Ross, in a letter to me of October 1975, writes that, although the views on which his 1950 article was based have changed, he still finds Cantos 14 and 15 "noisy and shallow."

65 "the idea of good government": *SP*, 6.

66 Langer: *Feeling and Form* (New York, 1953), 396.

66 "*not* worth recording as such": *Letters*, 293.

67 Calvin: *SP*, 70, 273.

67 St. Clement: Herbert Musurillo, S.J., *The Fathers of the Primitive Church* (New York, 1966), 188, 192.

CANTO 16

68 Kenner: *Pound Era*, 416.

68 modeled on the *Aeneid:* Pound's "aether" and "patet" echo the *aethera* and *patet* of *Aeneid* 6. 127, 130.

69 "much more impressive": Note added, probably in 1929, to *Spirit of Romance*, 48.

70 "For eighteen years": *G-B* (1960), 138, 140.

70 Fussell: New York, 1975, 64.

72 Erdman: *Blake: Prophet against Empire* (rev. ed.; New York, 1969), 227.

72 Peire Cardinal: *Spirit of Romance*, 48, 132.

72 Binyon: Pound reprinted sections of Binyon's essay three times, first in *Blast* (1915), then in *G-B* (1916) and in *Pavannes and Divigations* (1958).

73 Davie: *EP: Poet as Sculptor*, 129.

74 Hotspur: Pound often quotes from faulty memory or conflates passages that stand nearby in a text. In *I Henry IV* (5.2), a few lines before Hotspur's "O gentlemen, the time of life is short!" Vernon reports Prince Hal's challenge to Hotspur: "I never in my life / Did hear a challenge urged more moderately, / Unless

a brother should a brother dare / To gentle exercise and proof of arms."

75 passage in slangy French: Kenner, in liner notes for *Ezra Pound Reads His Cantos* (CMS 619), says that the speaker is Fernand Leger.

77 Steffens: The material Pound has drawn on is in Steffens's *Autobiography* (New York, 1931), pt. 4, chs. 13–14. The canto appeared in 1925, six years before Steffens published the autobiography, but Pound had read his journalism, and he knew Steffens intimately in Paris in the early 1920s.

## *Eleven New Cantos* (1934)

78 *Jefferson and/or Mussolini:* largely written in 1933; published 1935.

78 "blackness and mess": From an article on Joyce, published May 1933, reprinted in Forrest Read, ed., *Pound/Joyce* (New York, 1967), 251.

78 "Usury ruined the Republic": *The Economic History of the United States,* reprinted in *SP,* 174. This pamphlet gives Pound's most extended discussion of American history.

79 Memorial Edition . . . of Jefferson: Noel Stock, *The Life of EP,* 247.

79 "perhaps the last American": In a 1922 review of *Ulysses,* reprinted in *LE,* 408–409.

### CANTO 31

80 extraordinary correspondence: References to the Jefferson-Adams correspondence are from Lester J. Cappon's edition (Chapel Hill, N.C., 1959; reprinted New York, 1971). Other Jefferson letters are from the edition used by Pound, *The Writings of Thomas Jefferson,* ed. Andrew A. Lipscomb and Albert Ellery Bergh (Washington, 1903–1904). For a print-out of the immediate sources of the canto, see Robert M. Knight, "Thomas Jefferson in Canto XXXI," *Paideuma* 5 (Spring-Summer 1976), 79–93.

80 "ought to be in curricula": "The Jefferson-Adams Letters as a Shrine and a Monument" (1937–1938), in *SP,* 147.

80 Confucius . . . inspired: See H. G. Creel, *Confucius: The Man and the Myth* (New York, 1949), 276–301; and Hugh Kenner,

"EP and the Light of France," in his *Gnomon* (New York, 1958), 263–279.

80 "real man": *Confucius*, 57.

80 "research without thought": *Confucius*, 199.

81 "Johnson's verse": *Kulchur*, 181.

82 "time": Daniel D. Pearlman gives an extended discussion of "Attention to the Times and Seasons" in Canto 31, in *The Barb of Time*, 135–151.

83 *Analects: Confucius*, 207.

84 "experience . . . free government": Adams's note in a copy of Condorcet's *Esquisses*, in Zoltán Haraszti, *John Adams and the Prophets of Progress* (Cambridge, Mass., 1952; reprinted New York, 1964), 241.

84 "The political and literary world": Adams's note, written in 1813 on a flyleaf of his *Discourses on Davila*, in Haraszti, *John Adams*, 167.

84 Davie: *EP: Poet as Sculptor*, 135.

86 Ecclesiastes: As Kenner has pointed out, Ecclesiastes also stands behind the "Pull down thy vanity" passage in Canto 81.

88 Jefferson's range of interest: References to the flower and screw are in a letter to Dr. Styles, 17 July 1785. Mrs. Adams had brought the "curious" flower to Paris. A Parisian had invented a machine designed to move through air propelled by blades in the form of a giant screw. Jefferson thinks air too thin a medium; then he wonders if such a device might not work better in water; finally he remembers that David Bushnell had already made the experiment.

88 "When the nit-wits complained": *Jefferson and/or Mussolini*, 88–89.

88 Maison Quarrée: Jefferson to Madison, 20 September 1785.

89 Beaumarchais: For details see Georges Lemaitre, *Beaumarchais* (New York, 1949), chs. 7–9.

89 His tart pen: His marginalia are in Haraszti's excellent study, *John Adams*.

*from* Canto 38

92 Orage: See John L. Finlay, *Social Credit: The English Background* (Montreal and London, 1972). For Douglas's background, see ch. 3.

93 "a poem including history": *Social Credit: An Impact* (London, 1935; reprinted London, 1951), 5.

94 Kitson: EP cites him in Canto 77. See his *A Scientific Solution of the Money Question* (1894) and his *A Fraudulent Standard* (1917).

95 "nonexistent values": Douglas, *Economic Democracy* (London, 1920), 120.

95 *A + B:* Stephen Fender has shown that in Canto 38 Pound was working from a series of articles Douglas published in Orage's *New English Weekly* in 1932–1933. In the passage behind this excerpt in *Selected Cantos,* Douglas is paraphrasing his own *Credit Power and Democracy* (London, 1920). The text I have used is quoted by Gorham Munson in his valuable *Aladdin's Lamp* (New York, 1945), 143. Munson attempts to remove Social Credit from the antisemitic and right-wing causes with which it became identified after the Labour Party, which considered adopting it as policy, abandoned it in the early 1930s. There is no substantive connection between Social Credit and authoritarian politics, but in fact many of its proponents had authoritarian tendencies.

96 it follows for Pound: For important distinctions between Pound's moral-political and Douglas's technocratic versions of Social Credit, see Dennis Klinck, "Pound, Social Credit and the Critics," *Paideuma* 5 (Fall 1976).

96 rhetorical trinity: *Jefferson and/or Mussolini,* 105.

97 *ABC of Economics:* In *SP,* 239.

97 Griffith: *Kulchur,* 105.

97 appealed to those on the Left: Earle Davis, *Vision Fugitive: EP and Economics* (Lawrence, Kans., 1968), 7–76; and Christine Brooke-Rose, *A ZBC of Ezra Pound,* 232, discuss Marx and Douglas but don't clarify the distinction to my satisfaction. More lucid is Munson; see his entries under "Marx."

98 many intelligent people: For the involvement of intellectuals with social and economic theory during the period, see Finlay, *Social Credit* (Montreal and London, 1972); and Roger Kojecky, *The Social Criticism of T. S. Eliot* (New York, 1972).

98 *ABC of Economics: SP,* 238, 245–246.

99 "Doceat, moveat": *Polite Essays* (London, 1937), 49–50.

99 "a Don Quixote": *SP,* 210.

99 *E pur si muove:* C. H. Douglas, *The Alberta Experiment* (London, 1937), 66.

## The Fifth Decad of Cantos (1937)

100 "Blue china and slush boys": *Letters,* 279.

100 "It takes a while": Quoted in Charles Norman, *Ezra Pound* (New York, 1960), 444.

101 "Fair questions": *Letters,* 293–294.

101 "the clamping of words": Noel Stock, *The Life of EP,* 340.

101 Taoist quiet: Pound, disliking Taoism intensely, may not have been aware that the poems from which he fashioned Canto 49 had a Taoist element nor that even the Confucian books contain Taoist interpolations. See Hugh Kenner, *The Pound Era,* 454–457.

*from* CANTO 42

102 "built for beneficence": *SP,* 270.

102 Dekker: *The Cantos of EP,* 173–174.

102 Kenner: *Pound Era,* 427–429.

103 Davie: *EP: Poet as Sculptor,* 159.

105 Kenner: *Pound Era,* 427.

105 "Two kinds of banks have existed": *SP,* 270.

105 *Gold and Work: SP,* 339.

106 "moral and nominal": From the anonymous *Monte dei Paschi di Siena: Historical Notes,* published by the bank itself, Siena, 1955, pp. 45 and 43. I have drawn most of my information on the bank from this volume.

106 Jefferson: The quotation forms one of the four "chapters" in Pound's *Introductory Textbook,* first published in 1939, which he reprinted or included in other works at least thirteen times. See *Kulchur,* 353–356.

107 Dekker: *Cantos of EP,* 174.

109 *animo:* The documents are reprinted with commentary in Ben Kimpel and T. C. Duncan Eaves, "Sources of Cantos XVII and XVIII," *Paideuma* 6 (Winter 1977), 333–358.

109 joined mainstream banking: An account of how the bank broadened its scope and capital and (although it is proud of the fact that it remains public and distributes its profits to charity) essentially entered the mainstream of Italian banking during the

nineteenth century, is given in the anonymous *Monte dei Paschi: Historical Notes.*

111 MOUNTAIN: It would have been impossible for Pound not to have noticed that the bank's heraldic image bears three mounts. Why he has changed it to six is a puzzle. A reference to the six balls of the Medici?

## Canto 44

114 "beams and ropes of real history": *Kulchur,* 30.

114 "the traces of the Leopoldine reforms": *SP,* 177.

115 "Napoleonic flurry": *Kulchur,* 263. On Pound's attitude toward Napoleon, see "Napoleon: The Lesson of Meaningless Revolution," ch. 11 in James J. Wilhelm, *The Later Cantos of EP.*

117 *ben dell' intelletto:* On Pound and the *ben dell' intelletto* of the Enlightenment, see Hugh Kenner, "EP and the Light of France," *Gnomon* (New York, 1958), 263–279.

117 Pietro Leopoldo: Highly recommended for the period of Tuscan history that includes Leopold, Ferdinand, and Napoleonic invasion is Eric Cochrane, *Florence in the Forgotten Centuries: 1527–1800* (Chicago, 1973), ch. 6.

118 *Abbondanza:* See Cochrane, *Florence,* 198–200, 399–408.

118 "the first gentleman": See Cochrane, *Florence,* 503.

118 destruction of Arezzo: See Cochrane, *Florence,* 503.

## Canto 45

122 Calvin: He developed the argument in sermons and letters for two decades. The letter to Sachin is in *Opera* 10. 1., cols. 245–249, in *Corpus Reformatorum* 38. 1. Translation in Georgia Harkness, *John Calvin: The Man and His Ethics* (New York, 1911).

122 Nelson: 2nd ed., Chicago, 1969, 74.

123 Memling's "sparkling color": *McGraw-Hill Encyclopedia of Art* (1969) under "Memling."

123 *Behest, Cramoisie,* crimson, *Canker:* See the entries and related entries in *OED.*

123 Spenser: *Epithalamion,* 228.

123 "canker": Both as a variety of rose and as an insect that eats petals, it resonates in Blake's sick rose and invisible worm. In Blake's poem we also find *crimson*—a word that contains an invisible worm!

124 "very elliptical": *Letters,* 303.
124 "Light from Eleusis": *SP,* 53, 59.
125 Gonzaga: Authorities on Mantegna find no concubines in the mural. Pound may be following an older tradition or may have invented the detail for the canto.

## *Cantos LII–LXXI* (1940)

126 harshly treated by critics: Donald Davie, though he admires Canto 52, says of the Chinese cantos, "There is no alternative to writing off this whole section of Pound's poem as pathological and sterile," and of the Adams cantos, "Pound . . . makes a nonsensical hurly-burly of Adams's life" (*EP: Poet as Sculptor,* 161–163). Hugh Kenner finds in the Chinese cantos "a certain lack of resistance which enabled Pound to write these cantos quickly. . . . He wrote, in fact, too many pages for the ultimate good of the poem" (*The Pound Era,* 434). Clark Emery defends the Chinese cantos but has reservations on the Adams cantos (*Ideas into Action,* 168–179).

126 about thirty years: It is hard to be precise about the periods covered. A prelude to the Adams section traces the Adams family back to 1628. However, Pound's outline of the section, prefaced to Canto 52, begins with the Writs of Assistance and Adams's defense of Preston in 1770.

126 at exactly 1776: Kien Long, the last emperor mentioned in the Chinese cantos (he is the dutiful son in the passage quoted below), comes to the throne in 1736, and Pound manipulates history a bit in order to arrive at 1776, i.e., "wuz Emperor / fer at least 40 years."

127 nec lupo committere agnum: Adams to Brand-Hollis, 11 June 1790: "My fundamental maxim of government is never *to trust the lamb to the custody of the wolf.*"

128 what he thought would be the final section: See *Letters,* 328, 331, 334; Noel Stock, *The Life of EP,* 376.

*from* CANTO 52

129 Davie: *EP: Poet as Sculptor,* 156.
129 "Yueh Ling": See James Legge's translation and commentary in his *The Sacred Books of the East,* vol. 27 (Oxford, 1885); photographically reproduced in *Li Chi: Book of Rites,* ed. Ch'u Chai and Winberg Chai (New Hyde Park, N.Y., 1967).

129 "exaggerations of dogma": *Confucius,* 191. For Pound's attempt to disentangle Confucianism from legalisms, see "Mang Tsze" in *SP,* 88, 96.

129 "Odes: Risks": *Kulchur,* 232.

130 The Master said: Legge's translation of *Analects* 17. 11, which brings out the meaning better than does Pound's.

130 ideogram for *li:* See Legge, *Li Chi,* 9–10.

130 supplying ambiguities: From the poet who, as critic (*ABC of Reading,* 51), misses the point of Milton's "Him who disobeys me disobeys."

131 *Analects:* 3. 11, in *Confucius,* 203.

131 Diderot: From "Encyclopedia," in Stephen Gendzier's edition of Diderot, *The Encyclopedia: Selections* (New York, 1967), 92–95.

131 "Kung is modern": *Kulchur,* 272.

132 Lévi-Strauss: *The Scope of Anthropology,* tr. Sherry Paul and Robert A. Paul (London, 1967), 45–46.

133 *chih*(3): *Confucius,* 232.

CANTO 53

134 Canto 53: See Carroll F. Terrell, "The Chinese Dynastic Cantos," *Paideuma* 5 (Spring-Summer 1976), 95–121, which includes photographic reproductions of pages from de Mailla; and David Gordon's detailed examination of "The Sources of Canto LIII," in the same issue.

134 Aristotle: *Kulchur,* 319.

135 *"éclairé que le soleil":* De Mailla, vol. 1, 44.

135 "houses of twigs": De Mailla, vol. 1, 2.

136 Sullivan: "EP and the Classics," in Eva Hesse, ed., *New Approaches to EP,* 227.

137 *Ta Hio: Confucius,* 36.

140 *Shu Ching:* Clae Waltham, ed., *Shu Ching: Book of History: A Modernized Edition of the Translations of James Legge* (Chicago, 1971), 224 (pt. 4, document 25).

140 *Lin hing:* Waltham, *Shu Ching,* pt. 4, document 27.

141 He heard the wild geese: Pound is translating freely from *Odes* 2. 3. 9.

142 "a Douglasite assessment": *Kulchur,* 272.

142 C. T. Mao: *Kulchur,* 274.

143 "Rossoni": *SP,* 300.

144 Frobenius: See Kenner, *Pound Era*, 508; Guy Davenport, "Pound and Frobenius," in Lewis Leary, ed., *Motive and Method in the Cantos of EP* (New York, 1954); and Hesse in *New Approaches to EP*, 45–46.

144 Lacharme: See *Kulchur*, 204–205.

144 Aristotle: *Politics* 1. 9. Jowett's translation.

*from* CANTO 62

145 this section: The reader who wants to go carefully through Cantos 62–71 will find a print-out of the relevant passages from Adams in Frederick K. Saunders, *John Adams Speaking: EP's Sources for the Adams Cantos* (Orono, Maine, 1975).

147 the editor of his letters: Lester J. Cappon, in his edition of *The Adams-Jefferson Letters* (Chapel Hill, N.C., 1959; repr. New York, 1971), 244.

*The Pisan Cantos* (1948)

149 Washington courtroom: Julian Cornell, *The Trial of EP* (New York, 1966), 185.

150 now part of the poem: Hugh Kenner, *The Pound Era*, 469. Cantos 72 and 73, written in Italian, were published in an Italian newspaper in early 1945 and republished in 1973 in a small edition for copyright purposes. A thorough description is presented by Barbara Eastman, "The Gap in *The Cantos*: 72 and 73," *Paideuma* 8 (Winter 1979), 415–427.

150 Fasa: Leo Frobenius and Douglas C. Fox, *African Genesis* (London, 1938).

151 into the empyrean: Noel Stock, *The Life of EP*, 398; Kenner, *Pound Era*, 447–450.

151 political journalism: Invaluable for this phase of Pound's career is Niccolò Zapponi, *L'Italia di EP* (Rome, 1976).

151 broadcasts: The texts have been published as *Ezra Pound Speaking*, ed. Leonard Doob (New York, 1979). For a discussion of Pound's politics, see William M. Chace, *The Political Identities of EP and T. S. Eliot* (Stanford, Calif., 1973).

151 misuse of language: Mary de Rachewiltz discusses her father's non-Confucian language during the war years in her *Discretions* (Boston, 1971), 173–174.

156 *Time* magazine: Issues for May–October 1945 contain dozens of references that are directly reflected in the Pisan cantos. An irony that could not have escaped him is the large number of his own friends whom *Time* treats as cultural monuments.

156 time in the Pisan cantos: Daniel D. Pearlman, *The Barb of Time*, ch. 3, is excellent. See also Forrest Read, "The Pattern of the *Pisan Cantos*," *Sewanee Review* 75 (Summer 1957). Both discussions, different from mine in emphasis and terminology, lead essentially to the same point.

158 epic of judgment: The phrase is the subtitle of James J. Wilhelm's *Dante and Pound* (Orono, Maine, 1974).

158 Santayana: New York, 1926, 169.


CANTO 81

159 appearance of the eyes: A biographical interpretation quite different from mine is in Wendy Stallard Flory, "The *'Tre Donne'* of the Pisan Cantos," *Paideuma* 5 (Spring-Summer 1976), 45–52.

160 marked by iambic pentameter: Kenner, *Pound Era*, 488–493.

162 The libretto displays: See Donald Davie's brilliant essay "Rhythms in the *Cantos*," in his *Ezra Pound*, ch. 5.

163 "Vers Libre and Arnold Dolmetsch": *LE*, 437–440.

164 "grave" and "acute": See the entries in the *OED*.

164 *motz el son:* Excellent discussion in Kenner, *Pound Era*, 82–92, 369–374.

164 which Pound reviewed: "Vers Libre and Arnold Dolmetsch," *LE*, 437–440.

164 "was still part of Europe": *ABC of Reading*, 100–101.

165 Dante: *Purgatorio,* end of Canto 9: "As when a choir sings against instruments / And you can sometimes hear, and sometimes not, the words"; and *Paradiso*, 23. 31–32: "And through the living light intensely shone, / So clear, the gleaming Substance." Discussions of the hypostatic nature of Christ and of the relations between matter and spirit are in the *Divine Comedy*. In relation to a "shade beyond the other lights," see Dante's use of *ombra* in his attempt to convey an impression of the circling lights in *Paradiso, 13. 19.*

165 "subtlety": See the *OED* under "subtle" and "subtlety."

167 defines through particulars: See *ABC of Reading, 18–22.*

167 "Ballade of Good Counsel": Speare prints a modern version in which the line is "Subdue thyself, and others shall thee hear."

167  invention "of Chinese poetry": Eliot, introduction to Pound's *Selected Poems* (New York, 1926).

167  praised Blunt: "Status Rerum," *Poetry* 1 (January 1913), dated "December 10, 1912."

168  Dolores: Identification supplied me by David McKibbin, the authority on Sargent.

169  "cavero": The "caverò" in *Selected Cantos* is a misprint.

*from* CANTO 83

173  "two mystic states": *Kulchur*, 223–224.

174  neoplatonism . . . may lead in two directions: See R. Klibansky, *The Continuity of the Platonic Tradition during the Middle Ages* (London, 1952), 26.

174  Allen Upward: Pound on Upward, *SP*, 403–412. See also Davie, *Ezra Pound* (1975), 41–42 and passim; A. D. Moody, "Pound's Allen Upward," *Paideuma* 4 (Spring 1975); and Bryant Knox, "Allen Upward and EP," *Paideuma* 3 (Spring 1974).

175  "Mechanism, how it works": *Kulchur*, 119, 224.

175  "When you don't understand it": *Kulchur*, 127.

176  an Italian schoolbook: *Kulchur*, 141.

176  "The sage delighteth": *Analects* 6. 21. In *Kulchur* (p. 84), Pound quotes Upward's "The quality of the sage is like water," commenting that he doesn't know its source.

178  HUDOR: Kenner traces the word to Pindar's *Olympian 1:* "Water is the noblest of things." (*Pound Era*, 344–346).

178  Robert de Grosseteste: *LE*, 161. For the complex associations Pound makes among Grosseteste, Erigena, Cavalcanti, and Confucius, see Kenner, *Pound Era*, 450–453; and Walter B. Michaels, "EP and Erigena," *Paideuma* 1 (Spring-Summer 1972).

178  ignis est accidens: See Etienne Gilson's summary of Grosseteste on light in *LE*, 160.

178  Scotus: In addition to Kenner and to Michaels's article cited above, see references throughout *Kulchur* and *Letters*.

180  Plura diafana: See *LE*, 161.

CANTO 84

182  search for a leader: See Samuel Hynes, *The Auden Generation: Literature and Politics in England in the 1930s* (New York, 1977), chs. 2–5.

182  Mussolini, Jefferson, and Lenin: *Jefferson and/or Mussolini*, 70.

183 Farbenindustrie: See James Stewart Martin, *All Honorable Men* (Boston, 1950), 57–58. Martin's interesting account of his experiences in postwar Europe suggests that financial allegiances operating across the lines of battle may have been stronger than Pound suspected. His discussion of the wartime activities of the Dulles brothers is of interest.

183 Micah: 6: 9–10 and 4: 3–5.

183 Adams: To Benjamin Rush, 25 August 1811.

186 Beard: See *Letters,* 337.

186 Natalie: See Richard Sieburth, "EP: Letters to Natalie Barney," *Paideuma* 5 (Fall 1976), 284.

186 Wei, Chi and Pi-kan: See James Legge's note in his edition, in his *The Sacred Books of the East* (Oxford, 1885).

187 Henriot: See Francis J. Bosha, "Pound's Henriot," *Paideuma* 4 (Spring 1975).

187 ming²: *Confucius,* 20.

## Section: Rock-Drill (1955)

189 Frye: *The Stubborn Structure* (Ithaca, N.Y., 1970), 160–162.

189 de Gourmont: *SP,* 420. See Richard Sieburth, *Instigations: EP and Remy de Gourmont* (Cambridge, Mass., 1978).

189 Davie: "Cypress Versus Rock-Slide: An Appreciation of Canto 110," *Agenda* 8 (Autumn-Winter 1970), 19.

191 Davie: *Ezra Pound,* 69.

191 Lewis . . . his review: *New Statesman and Nation,* 7 April 1951.

191 Saint Elizabeths: See Harry Meacham, *The Caged Panther* (New York, 1967); and Carroll F. Terrell, "St. Elizabeths," *Paideuma* 3 (Winter 1974). The same issue of *Paideuma* contains a good account of Pound's first weeks in Washington by Charles Olson and other memoirs by visitors. See also Olson's notes in Catherine Seelye, ed., *Charles Olson and EP* (New York, 1975).

194 "Confucian universe": Interview, *Paris Review* 28 (Summer-Fall 1962), 23.

194 "In painting, the colour": *The Translations* (New York, 1953), 23.

195 *nomina sunt:* Pound attributes it to Aquinas and quotes it in relation to poetry as "equation"; *G-B,* 92.

195 Hesse: ed., *New Approaches to EP,* 14.

195 "cipher technique . . . pre-formed worlds": From an article by
Guenther Bloecker quoted on the dust jacket of the American
first edition of *Rock-Drill*, the copy for which clearly seems to
have been written or assembled by Pound.

195 "almost an ideogram": *Kulchur*, 307.

195 Davie: *EP: Poet as Sculptor*, 229.

*from* CANTO 85

198 three or four times in the *Shu:* I am not counting a few places
where *ling²* appears as part of a proper name.

199 what ministers and emperors say: It would be too elaborate here
to trace out all the tributaries of this "submerged river." My
statement is based on a study of each use of *ling²* in the *Shu* and
in the *Odes.*

199 "almost" an ideogram: *Kulchur*, 307.

199 "aperient": *Kulchur*, 307.

200 Frobenius: *Vom Kulturreich des Festlandes* (1923), quoted by
Eva Hesse, *New Approaches to EP,* 46. "Ygdrasil" appears in
Cantos 85 and 90.

200 The tree . . . is also a "gnomon": See Boris de Rachewiltz,
"Pagan and Magic Elements in EP's works," in Eva Hesse, *New
Approaches to EP,* 190–192.

200 "gnomic aorist": For this and all meanings of "gnomon," see the
*OED.*

201 de Santillana: *The Age of Adventure: The Renaissance Philosophers* (New York, 1956), 227.

201 he tells us: Sesto Prete, ed., *Galileo's Letter about the Liberation
of the Moon* (New York, 1965), 36.

201 Santayana: *Dominations and Powers* (New York, 1951), 38.

202 "top flights of the mind": Interview, *Paris Review* 28 (Summer-
Fall 1962), 47.

202 Galileo: *Dialogue on the Great World Systems* (First Day), tr.
Salusbury, rev. Giorgio de Santillana (Chicago, 1953), 68–69.

203 Jesuits: For this fascinating story, see Pasquale M. D'Elia, S.J.,
*Galileo in China* (Cambridge, Mass., 1960).

203 Wellington: Pound may be influenced here by suggestions made
in a right-wing book, Captain Russell Grenfell's *Unconditional
Hatred: German War Guilt and the Future of Europe* (New
York, 1953), 186–187, 177–179.

203  Queen Bess: See Leicester Bradner, *The Poems of Queen Eliza-beth I* (Providence, R.I., 1964).

*from* CANTO 88

204  Cantos 88 and 89: For a full discussion of Canto 88, and of Pound's use of Benton, see James J. Wilhelm, *The Later Cantos of EP*, 64–78. Wilhelm's enthusiastic work is an excellent study of the major themes and figures in *Rock-Drill* and *Thrones*.

204  Benton: The only biography, not entirely satisfactory, is William Nisbet Chambers, *Old Bullion Benton* (Boston, 1956). Benton's *Thirty Years' View* is available in several nineteenth-century editions: good reading, but ample of breath and small of print.

205  Bank of the United States: A good account of the Bank War is Arthur M. Schlesinger, Jr., *The Age of Jackson* (New York, 1945).

CANTO 95

208  "the major theme" and Richard of Saint Victor: Dust jacket of the American first edition of *Rock-Drill*. The "ergo" is Pound's thumbprint.

209  rewriting the poems of his youth: See N. Christoph de Nagy, *The Poetry of EP: The Pre-Imagist Stage* (Bern, 1968), 148; and Louis Martz's introduction to *Collected Early Poems*.

209  poem published in 1909: "In Durance," reprinted in *Personae* and *Collected Early Poems*.

209  Coleridge: The first passage is from "On the Principles of Genial Criticism" (1814), the others from "On Poesy or Art" (1818).

210  Plotinus: Coleridge quotes from Plotinus; the translation is by W. J. Bate.

211  de Gourmont: *Kulchur,* 302.

212  in Legge's words: Footnote to his translation of "The Doctrine of the Mean" (Pound's *Unwobbling Pivot*), in his *The Sacred Books of the East* (Oxford, 1885), 20. 8.

212  "Beddoesque": Reprinted in *Collected Early Poems*.

213  "The dry rot": Mandrake's speech is in act 1, scene 1, of *Death's Jest Book*.

213  "I am food": H. W. Donner, ed., *The Works of Thomas Lovell Beddoes* (Oxford, 1935), 638. See also Donner's *Thomas Lovell Beddoes: The Making of a Poet* (Oxford, 1935). Pound had a

lingering affection for the poet "who greatly moved me at eighteen," but whose archaic language could produce only "gold that is not quite 24 carat" ("Beddoes and Chronology," 1917, *SP,* 380).

213 "difficult to write a paradiso": Interview, *Paris Review* 28 (Summer-Fall 1962), 42.

213 Santayana: See *The Letters of George Santayana* (New York, 1953), 441–442, and references to Pound in the index. The passages below from *Dominations and Powers* are on pages 7 and 15.

215 Bede: The phrases are from works marked "doubtful and spurious" in vol. 90 of Migne's *Patrologia Lat.* Sources and some contexts in a note by John J. Espey, *Paideuma* 4 (Spring 1975), 181–182.

216 Van Buren: *Autobiography* (Washington, D.C., 1920), 457–460.

217 degli Uberti: Ricardo M. degli Uberti, "EP and Uberto degli Uberti: History of Friendship," *Italian Quarterly* 16 (1964).

218 two different nymphs: Anyone with a Loeb Library Ovid can see that they are distinct. However, the "Leucothea" on page 100 of *Selected Cantos* was "Leucothoe" in the first edition of *Rock-Drill,* in early printings of the complete *Cantos,* and in Faber editions until 1976. Leucothea is surely the correct reading, but Pound is playing with both stories. "Leucothoe in some writers is only another form of Leucothea," says Smith's *Dictionary of Greek and Roman Biography and Mythology* (1846), under "Leucothoe," citing Hyginus's *Fabularum liber* 125.

218 Fitzgerald: See *Memoirs of Desmond Fitzgerald* (London, 1968).

218 "Near to benevolence": *Confucius: Unwobbling Pivot* 20. 10.

219 Windsor: See Hugh Kenner in *Paideuma* 2 (Spring 1973), 41–42. The questions are discussed and documented (though some documents are not yet available) in Frances Donaldson, *Edward VIII* (London and Philadelphia, 1975).

219 Saint Bertrand: See Hugh Kenner, *The Pound Era,* 333–340, for the train of associations here.

219 Olson: *Charles Olson and EP* (New York, 1975), 40.

219 "de Nantes": For Pound's *Selection from the Collection Yvette Guilbert,* see Donald Gallup, *A Bibliography of EP,* B2. Poem to Fitzgerald: Gallup A7, B7. Von Freitag (or Freytag): Gallup C628a.

220 Pirandello: *SP,* 434.

221 "en l'Isle": Also a link with Calypso's island, which Odysseus is finally leaving on the raft.

221 Hilduin: *Areopagitica,* in Migne, *Pat. Lat.* 106.

222 Leucothea: Why her *kredemnon* becomes a bikini is the subject of Hugh Kenner, "Leucothea's Bikini," in Noel Stock, ed., *EP: Perspectives* (Chicago, 1965). On Leucothea and *Rock-Drill* in general, see also Kenner's "Under the Larches of Paradise," in his *Gnomon* (New York, 1958).


## *Thrones* (1959)

224 interview with Donald Hall: *Paris Review* 28 (Summer-Fall 1962). The interview was taped in 1960.


*from* CANTO 99

226 Creel: *Chinese Thought from Confucius to Mao Tse-Tung* (New York, 1953), 177.

227 note for . . . Canto 98: In Italian, dated July 1958, *L'illustrazione Italiana,* Milan, September 1958.

228 as any Confucian does: See L. S. Dembo's fine essay, *The Confucian Odes of EP* (Berkeley and Los Angeles, 1963) for the way Pound worked within the tradition of the Confucian masters. As Dembo says, in Confucianism "the root always takes precedence over the branch, the emotion over the act." Dembo does not entirely approve of Pound's Chinese translations; his criticism, however, is not with Pound's method but with his ability to put that method into practice.

229 "And after this": The translation by the sinologist David Gordon, who is translating here for an entirely different purpose, is in his "The *Sacred Edict:* Thought Built on Sagetrieb," *Paideuma* 3 (Fall 1974), 169–190, which offers detailed comment on Cantos 98 and 99. See also Carroll F. Terrell, "The *Sacred Edict* of K'ang-Hsi," *Paideuma* 2 (Spring 1973), which contains a photographic reproduction of two chapters from Baller.

230 Yao and Shun: Clae Waltham, ed., *Shu Ching: Book of History: A Modernized Edition of the Translations of James Legge* (Chicago, 1971), 6–7.

231 Courtney: Reprinted in Eric Homberger, ed., *EP: The Critical Heritage* (London and Boston, 1972), 44–45.

233 Michelet: Noel Stock, *Reading the Cantos* (New York, 1966), 106.
233 Ambrose: *New Times,* 13 July 1956. See also *SP,* 90.
233 anagogico: An extreme example of how Pound sometimes works in the later cantos. His mind becomes a magnetized field in which he is simultaneously interested in *x* number of things. When, sometimes by accident, a fact is drawn into that field, the mind surveys all possibilities; if it can be seen in relation to two or three or more of Pound's existing interests, it immediately gets locked in place somewhat in the manner in which a loose ion is attracted to a molecular structure.

If one goes to dictionaries, *anagogico* and its cognates are not given as "contemplation," but with meanings closer to "religious ecstasy" or "mysticism." Pound, however, is interested in "contemplation" because in the later cantos he is deeply interested in Richard of Saint Victor's formulation, *meditatio, cognitatio, contemplatio.* He is also interested in Saint Anselm, the Rémusat family, and, as we saw in Canto 95, anyone named Dionysius. It is inevitable that he reads Charles de Rémusat's *Saint Anselme de Cantorbéry* (Paris, 1853), where, on page 446, he finds a discussion of Anselm's use of *anagoge,* which Rémusat says Anselm uses in the sense of *contemplation.* He also sees there that in relation to *anagoge* Anselm cites "Denys," that is Saint Dionysius. By this time, the floating particle is well within the field of force of the *Cantos.* He finds an opportunity in Canto 99, where he has just been making another playful "mistranslation," to say that the kind of education and sensibility urged by the *Sacred Edict* may lead to *contemplatio,* as opposed to the forces in our civilization that make war on contemplation. As "anagogico," the particle finds a place in the structure.

*from* CANTO 105

238 Jaspers: *Anselm and Nicholas of Cusa* (New York, 1974), 3.
238 "Ugly? a bore": Migne, *Pat. Lat.* 158. 697. The long poem in Migne is rejected by scholars and bears no relation to Anselm's work.
238 *De grammatico:* Text, translation, and excellent analysis in Desmond Paul Henry, *Commentary on De Grammatico* (Dordrecht and Boston, 1974).
238 *Monologion:* Included with the *Proslogion* and *De grammatico* in the first volume of the great modern edition by Dom F. S.

Schmitt, S. *Anselmi Cantuariensis Archiepiscopi opera omnia,* 6 vols. (Edinburgh, 1946–1961).

238 through grammar: *Monologion,* Cap. 3, and for a direct treatment of the difficulty normal syntax encounters in discussing the Trinity, Caps. 78, 75.

238 William of Malmesbury: In Migne, *Pat. Lat.* 179, the edition Pound probably used. More helpful is Thomas Duffus Hardy's two-volume edition of *Gesta regum Anglorum* (London, 1840) and J. A. Giles's translation of Hardy's text, *William of Malmesbury's Chronicle of the Kings of England* (London, 1847).

241 Gerbert: To decide how to interpret the allusion to the astrolabe, we may have to recall Pound's only other mention of it in the essay on Cavalcanti (*LE,* 181). There he deplores Chaucer's "uselessly treating the Astrolabe."

241 Proslogion: An excellent survey of Anselm's life and works, together with text and translation, is M. J. Charlesworth, *St. Anselm's Proslogion* (New York, 1965).

*from* CANTO 108

242 *Tredecim Librorum Pater:* The inscription refers only to books published in his lifetime. There are thirteen *Reports,* four *Institutes,* and minor works. See Catherine Drinker Bowen, *The Lion and the Throne* (Boston, 1957), 535. Pound was an enthusiastic reader of Bowen's biography.

242 Bowen: *Lion and the Throne,* 504. See especially her discussion of the *Reports* and the *Institutes,* 504–524.

242 "The privileges of this House": December 1621. Quoted in Bowen, *Lion and the Throne,* 453.

243 Coke and the American Revolution: See Bernard Bailyn, *The Ideological Origins of the American Revolution* (Cambridge, Mass., 1967), 30.

243 October 1957: See Pound to W. M. Merchant, *Yale Literary Magazine,* December 1958.

243 Gordon: "Meeting E.P. and Then. . . ," *Paideuma* 3 (Winter 1974), 350–351.

243 a travesty of education: Harry Meacham, *The Caged Panther* (New York, 1967), 139, 69.

244 Bowen: *Lion and the Throne,* 511–512.

244 "the witness of times": Preface to the first *Report.*

244 Bowen: *Lion and the Throne,* 507, 520.

244 "to delight . . . the Reader": Second part of the *Institutes*, conclusion to *"Articuli super chartas,"* 579.

244 "Queen Elizabeth (Angliae amor)": Second part of the *Institutes*, *"Articuli super chartas,"* 578.

245 "The plenitude of law": On the jacket of the first American edition of *Thrones*.

245 Coke's second *Institute:* Canto 108 is drawn from the second *Institute*. There is no modern edition, nor standard edition. Many versions were published into the nineteenth century, adding to Coke's comments and proliferation of typefaces their own extensive notes. I have used the first edition, 1642, but readers who wish to inspect Coke's writings may have to use whatever edition is at hand. In editions I have seen, the pagination is the same, but that may not always be the case. The references below identify the sections in a way that can be used with any edition:

From "ELIZABETH" through "fundendam": Second part of the *Institutes, "Articuli super chartas,"* Ch. 20 (574–579); from "souls of the dead" through "Roma": *"Statutem de asportatis religiosorum"* (580–586); from "groisbois" through "penny": "The Exposition of 18 *Edw.* 3. Cap. 7. of Tithes" (633–643, 654); from "sale must be" through "no toll": "Statute of 31 *Eliz.* Cap. 12. concerning Sellers of Horses" (713–719); from "par cretance del ewe" through "reparando": "Statute of 22 H.8. Cap. 5. concerning the repairing of decayed Bridges, etc." (697 ff.); "For every new cottage": "Statute of 31 *Eliz.* Cap. 7. concerning Cottages and Inmates" (736 ff.).

248 nel Tirolo: Mary de Rachewiltz, *Discretions* (Boston, 1971), 58.

*from* CANTO 109

251 "personal signature": Hugh Kenner, *The Pound Era*, 485.

252 "Counterfeit stones": Coke, second *Institute, "Articuli super chartas"* Cap. 20. This passage and those quoted below are from pages 574 and 576.

253 reprinted in 1953: *Gists from Agassiz, or, Passages on the Intelligence Working in Nature* (New York: Square $ Series, 1953). The passages were nominally "selected by John Kasper," but in fact by Pound. "Phyllotaxis" is on pages 68–71.

254 wicket gate: A curious allusion, if it is one. The term is used three times within two pages in Bowen's life of Coke, *Lion and the Throne*, 131–132.

254 "of the beautiful ankles": The Homeric epithet is *kallisphuros*. Pound may have come across *kalliastragalos* in his reading and liked the sound of it.

254 belonged to his "line": Bernetta Quinn, *EP: An Introduction* (New York, 1972), 159.

## Drafts and Fragments of Cantos (1969)

255 Eliot: "For T. S. E.," *SP,* 464.

256 "difficult to write a paradiso": Interview, *Paris Review* 28 (Summer-Fall 1962), 47.

256 "head just doesn't WORK": Meacham, *The Caged Panther* (New York, 1967), 189.

256 "Five minutes a day": Richard Stern, "A Memory or Two of Mr. Pound," *Paideuma* 1 (Fall-Winter 1972), 216.

256 "error" and "bad intentions": Grazia Livi, "Interview with EP," *City Lights Journal,* no. 2 (1964), 42.

257 Reck: "A Conversation between EP and Allen Ginsberg," *Evergreen Review* 57 (June 1968), 29; reprinted in part in J. P. Sullivan, ed., *EP: A Critical Anthology* (New York, 1970).

257 Cory: "EP: A Memoir," *Encounter* 10 (May 1968); reprinted in Sullivan, *EP: A Critical Anthology.*

257 *Drafts and Fragments:* See Richard Pevear, "Notes on the *Cantos* of EP," *Hudson Review* 25 (Spring 1972), 31–70.

258 "test of a man's sincerity": *LE,* 9.

259 "search for oneself": *G-B,* 85.

## from CANTO 115

259 Materer: "A Reading of 'From Canto 115'," *Paideuma* 2 (Fall 1973), 205–207.

260 "to wake the dead": *G-B,* 117.

260 "Vorticism": *G-B,* 92–93.

260 Lewis . . . [on] the *Cantos: Time and Western Man* (London, 1927; reprinted Boston, 1957), 90.

261 "unlighted room": Lewis's farewell-to-art criticism in *The Listener,* May 1951.

261 not . . . "accepted": *Paris Review* 28 (Summer-Fall 1962), 13.

262 a thinly disguised portrait: "Doppelgänger," *Encounter,* January 1954. Reprinted in *Lucky for Pringle* (London, 1973), 221–222.

263  *Self Condemned:* The last chapter, which these words conclude, is called "Cemetery of Shells."
263  *Time and Western Man:* Pages 142 and 112. The phrases in the next sentence are from pages 38 and 27, and Pound's "epitaph" is from page 41.
263  Connolly: "A Short Commentary," *Agenda* 8 (Autumn-Winter 1970), 46.
263  "disordered and volcanic mind": *Kulchur,* 106.
264  *Timon:* 5. 3.

CANTO 116

265  Pevear: "Notes on the *Cantos* of EP," 52.
268  Wescott: Reprinted in Eric Homberger, ed., *EP: The Critical Heritage* (London and Boston, 1972), 216.
269  cuniculi: Noel Stock, *Reading the Cantos* (New York, 1966), 111.
271  Disney: *Paris Review* 28 (Summer-Fall 1962), 27.
271  Laforgue: Pound's interest in Laforgue was revived in the 1950s in conversations with Warren Ramsey, whose *Jules Laforgue and the Ironic Inheritance* (New York, 1953) contains an extended discussion of Laforgue and Pound.

◇

# Selected Bibliography

◇

I have used the fourth printing (1973) of the New Directions edition of the complete *Cantos*. Earlier editions by New Directions and Faber & Faber have minor textual variations; even the New Directions *Selected Cantos* does not correspond exactly to the text of the complete edition. A critical edition is badly needed. For the development of the text as it now stands, and for collation of textual variants, see Barbara Eastman, *EP's Cantos: The Story of the Text* (Orono, Maine, 1979). The indispensable guide to the publishing history of Pound's works is Donald Gallup's *A Bibliography of Ezra Pound* (London: Rupert Hart-Davis, 1963; second impression, corrected, 1969). The works listed below are those that seem likely to be of greatest help and interest to new readers of the *Cantos*.

BOOKS BY POUND

(Unless otherwise noted, the publisher is New Directions.)

*ABC of Reading.* 1934. Paperback edition, 1960.

*Collected Early Poems of Ezra Pound.* 1976. Edited by Michael John King. A critical edition of Pound's early work through *Ripostes* (1912), with previously unpublished and uncollected poems through 1917.

*Confucius: The Unwobbling Pivot, The Great Digest, The Analects.* 1951. Translations.

*Gaudier-Brzeska: A Memoir.* 1916. New edition with additional material, 1960.

*Guide to Kulchur.* 1938. New edition with additions, 1952.

*Jefferson and/or Mussolini.* 1935. Reissued New York: Norton, Liveright Paperbound Editions, 1970.

*The Letters of Ezra Pound (1907–1941).* New York: Harcourt Brace, 1950. Edited by D. D. Paige. Reissued 1971 by New Directions as *The Selected Letters of Ezra Pound.*

*The Literary Essays of Ezra Pound.* 1954. Edited, with an introduction, by T. S. Eliot.

*Personae: The Collected Poems of Ezra Pound.* 1926. New edition (with minor additions), 1949.

*Selected Prose (1909–1965).* 1973. Edited, with an introduction, by William Cookson.

*The Spirit of Romance.* 1910. New edition (with minor additions), 1953.

*The Translations of Ezra Pound.* 1953. Edited, with an introduction, by Hugh Kenner.


BOOKS ON THE *Cantos*

The University of California Press is projecting an ambitious dictionary of references in the *Cantos,* under the direction of Carroll F. Terrell. When it appears, it will replace the still useful, but not entirely reliable, *Annotated Index to the Cantos* (1–84), edited by John Hamilton Edwards and William W. Vasse (Berkeley and Los Angeles: University of California Press, 1957; second printing, with additions and corrections, 1959).

Brooke-Rose, Christine. *A ZBC of Ezra Pound.* Berkeley and Los Angeles: University of California Press, 1971.

Bush, Ronald. *The Genesis of Ezra Pound's Cantos.* Princeton: Princeton University Press, 1976.

Davie, Donald. *Ezra Pound.* Published as *Pound,* London: Collins, Fontana, 1975; as *Ezra Pound,* New York: Viking and Penguin, 1976.

Davie, Donald. *Ezra Pound: Poet as Sculptor.* New York: Oxford University Press, 1964.

Dekker, George. *The Cantos of Ezra Pound: A Critical Study.* New York: Barnes & Noble, 1963. Published as *Sailing after Knowledge,* London: Routledge & Kegan Paul, 1963.

Emery, Clark. *Ideas into Action: A Study of Pound's Cantos.* Coral Gables: University of Miami Press, 1958.

Flory, Wendy Stallard. *Ezra Pound and the Cantos: A Record of Struggle.* New Haven: Yale University Press, 1980.

Hesse, Eva, ed. *New Approaches to Ezra Pound.* Berkeley and Los Angeles: University of California Press, 1969.

Kenner, Hugh. *The Pound Era.* Berkeley and Los Angeles: University of California Press, 1971.

Pearlman, Daniel D. *The Barb of Time: On the Unity of Ezra Pound's Cantos.* New York: Oxford University Press, 1969.

Rosenthal, M. L. *Sailing Into the Unknown: Yeats, Pound, and Eliot.* New York: Oxford University Press, 1978.

Stock, Noel. *The Life of Ezra Pound.* New York: Pantheon, 1970.

Wilhelm, James J. *The Later Cantos of Ezra Pound.* New York: Walker, 1977.

# Index

◊